BIG SHIFTS AHEAD

BIG SHIFTS AHEAD

DEMOGRAPHIC CLARITY FOR BUSINESSES

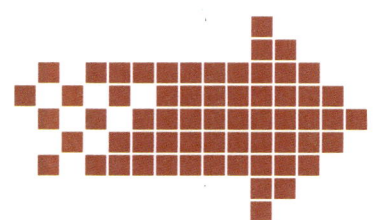

JOHN BURNS
CHRIS PORTER

Copyright © 2016 by John Burns Real Estate Consulting, LLC.

All rights reserved. No part of this book may be used or reproduced in any manner whatsoever without prior written consent of the author, except as provided by the United States of America copyright law.

Published by Advantage, Charleston, South Carolina.
Member of Advantage Media Group.

ADVANTAGE is a registered trademark, and the Advantage colophon is a trademark of Advantage Media Group, Inc.

Printed in the United States of America.

ISBN: 978-1-59932-722-8
LCCN: 2016948663

10 9 8 7 6 5 4 3

Cover design by George Stevens.

This publication is designed to provide accurate and authoritative information in regard to the subject matter covered. It is sold with the understanding that the publisher is not engaged in rendering legal, accounting, or other professional services. If legal advice or other expert assistance is required, the services of a competent professional person should be sought.

Advantage Media Group is proud to be a part of the Tree Neutral® program. Tree Neutral offsets the number of trees consumed in the production and printing of this book by taking proactive steps such as planting trees in direct proportion to the number of trees used to print books. To learn more about Tree Neutral, please visit **www.treeneutral.com**.

Advantage Media Group is a publisher of business, self-improvement, and professional development books. We help entrepreneurs, business leaders, and professionals share their Stories, Passion, and Knowledge to help others Learn & Grow. Do you have a manuscript or book idea that you would like us to consider for publishing? Please visit **advantagefamily.com** or call **1.866.775.1696**.

FROM JOHN

I dedicate this book to my parents, John and Mary Burns. My 1930s Savers parents raised four 1960s Equalers and one 1970s Balancer. They take so much pride in their six 1990s Connector and four 2000s Global grandchildren. Sadly, Mary Burns passed away during the editing stage of the book.

FROM CHRIS

I dedicate this book to my parents, Bob and Kathy Porter. My 1940s Achiever parents raised two 1970s Balancers and four 1980s Sharers. They love being with their twelve 2000s Global and 2010s post-Global grandchildren.

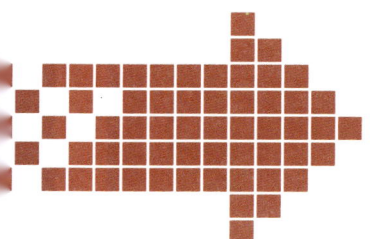

TABLE OF CONTENTS

INTRODUCTION 1

PART ONE: CONCLUSIONS AND NEW FRAMEWORKS

1: **CONCLUSIONS** 7
2: **GENERATIONS BY DECADE** 19
   THE 1930s SAVERS
   THE 1940s ACHIEVERS
   THE 1950s INNOVATORS
   THE 1960s EQUALERS
   THE 1970s BALANCERS
   THE 1980s SHARERS
   THE 1990s CONNECTORS
   THE 2000s GLOBALS
3: **THE 4 BIG INFLUENCERS** 71
   GOVERNMENT
   ECONOMY
   TECHNOLOGY
   SOCIETAL SHIFTS

PART TWO: THE BIGGEST DEMOGRAPHIC OPPORTUNITIES

4: **RISE OF THE WORKING WOMAN** 101
5: **A WAVE OF AFFLUENT IMMIGRANTS** 121
6: **RETIREE EXPLOSION UNDERWAY** 145

7:	FINALLY LEAVING THE NEST	159

PART THREE: LIFESTYLE SHIFTS

8:	RENTING IN THE SHARING ECONOMY	185
9:	HEADING SOUTH IN DROVES	209
10:	A NEW SURBAN™ WAY OF LIFE	221

APPENDIX 1: NEIGHBORHOOD CLASSIFICATIONS	237
APPENDIX 2: MORE FORECAST TABLES	245
ACKNOWLEDGMENTS	255
ABOUT THE AUTHORS	259
EXHIBIT LIST	263
INDEX	271

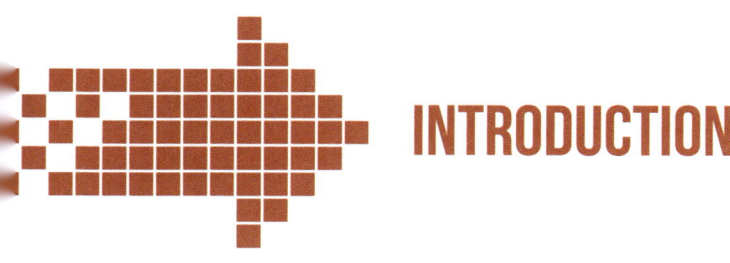

INTRODUCTION

The biggest demographic shifts since the Baby Boom continue to create opportunities and present challenges. America has more people in their early 20s and early 60s than ever before.

Opportunities abound. Women receive far more college degrees than men and increasingly earn more than their spouse. Immigration has shifted from impoverished refugees walking across the border or landing via boat, to affluent middle- and upper-class families fleeing the BRIC countries (Brazil, Russia, India, and China) after decades of amazing economic growth. An unprecedented surge in retirees drives a remodeling boom. Young adults—a term we use to refer to all or a portion of the population aged 18 to 34—should finally receive good raises, thanks in part to so many people retiring. Incredible new technologies create a sharing economy, helping Americans reduce expenses and stay more connected to each other than ever before.

Despite the advancements and increasing opportunities, daunting challenges need resolution. Retailers file bankruptcy. New technologies render knowledge-worker jobs obsolete. New home construction remains far below norm. Immigration from Mexico turns negative. Pension plans struggle with unprecedented withdrawals. More people than ever have college degrees, saddled with 500%

more student debt than in 2004, causing young adults to live longer at home than ever before. What shifts will occur next?

We wrote *Big Shifts Ahead* primarily for ourselves. As consultants to the construction and investment industries, we need to understand the demographic shifts transforming the country. We also need to communicate the trends to our clients in a way that makes the information digestible and usable for decision making. In this book, we pulled an overwhelming amount of information together for those who need to make decisions.

We redefined the generations by decade born, giving us much more clarity on the generational shifts occurring in America. The terms Baby Boomers, Gen X, and Millennials make sense when describing decades-long shifts in birth rates. However, a 31-year-old Millennial father and a 16-year-old Millennial high school student share little in common. Retired 70-year-old Baby Boomer grandparents collecting Social Security and 53-year-old Baby Boomers struggling to save enough money to put their high schoolers through college also have little in common. We all identify much more with people our own age and in the same stage of life.

A good friend, who also happens to be a best-selling author, kept encouraging us to *tell a story*—a story that would communicate the shifts we are facing in a personable, relatable way. For example, documenting exactly how many older Americans increasingly work past age 65 quantifies an important trend. But hearing 63-year-old executive Steve Burch describe his passion for work and his plans to keep putting in the hours as long as he can drives the point home. Charts demonstrating exactly how much those born in the 1980s and 1990s delay forming households offer helpful intelligence. But hearing 29-year-old Kyle Zierer relate his experiences living at home makes the trend more understandable. Huge shifts in college education have transformed society, and 49-year-old single mom Lisa Jackson's story brings it all together.

We presented our preliminary findings more than two dozen times to more than 1,000 people and learned a lot from their feedback. We could see the light bulbs go off as people now understood why their friends and family behaved so differently from them and why their businesses needed to change to keep up with the shifts. The three new frameworks we developed to pull the information together proved so educational that we decided to include several forecasts. We forecasted the number of households that will be created by 2025, where they will be located, and the percentage who will live urban versus suburban. We chose to forecast to 2025, which was ten years out from the most recent data we had available, and ten years seemed like a reasonable amount of time to make for meaningful estimates. We will keep these forecasts up to date on www.bigshiftsahead.com and www.realestateconsulting.com as we get new information that leads us to change our views of the future.

In part 1, we identified 4 Big Influencers that shape generational shifts. These influencers—government, economy, technology and societal shifts—will change the future, just like they changed the past. The influencers provide a great framework to summarize and analyze the shifts occurring today, with an eye to what will happen in the future.

Seven shifts are impacting society so dramatically that we devoted a chapter to each. In part 2, we discuss the four biggest shifts impacting society. Shifts led by college-educated women, new sources of immigration, workaholic retirees, and young adults born after 1980 will dominate the next decade. In part 3, we discuss the three shifts impacting where and how Americans will live. Americans will migrate south, increasingly living in a more affordable urban-like environment we call surban™ and increasingly choose renting over owning.

Making the information usable required us to translate "demographer-speak" into plain English. We sweated over arcane data definitions, long formulas, and standard deviations. We stressed over multiple data sources that occasionally disagreed. While maintaining data integrity, we simplified the language. For example, we use the term "working-age population" to define those aged 20–64. We know that many 20-year-olds attend college rather than work and many 67-year-olds have not yet retired. We labeled those born in the 1970s "Balancers," fully aware that some of them have had little balance in life. Decision makers require simplification backed by supportable facts. *Big Shifts Ahead* offers both.

NOTE:

MANY OF THE FIGURES IN THE TEXT ARE BASED ON JOHN BURNS REAL ESTATE CONSULTING CALCULATIONS OF DATA FROM THE US CENSUS BUREAU AND PUBLIC-DOMAIN GOVERNMENT RECORDS. MANY CALCULATIONS AND MORE DETAIL CAN BE FOUND ON THE BOOK'S WEBSITE, BIGSHIFTSAHEAD.COM

PART ONE

CONCLUSIONS AND NEW FRAMEWORKS

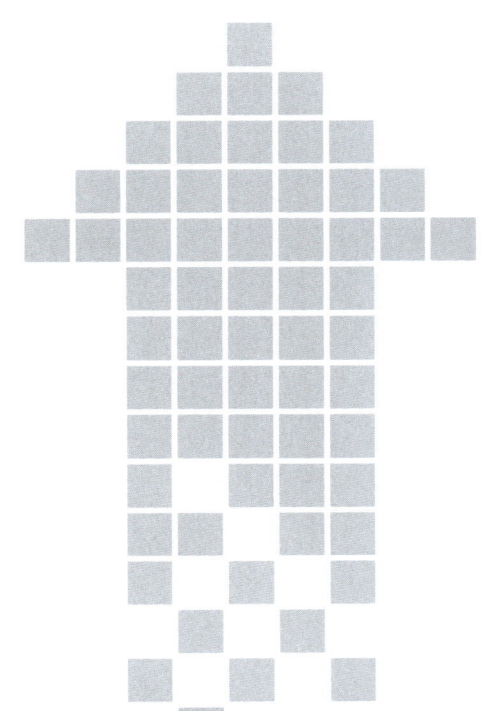

1: CONCLUSIONS

Sweeping demographic and generational shifts are quickly transforming America. Every individual and business feels the impact of government policies, the sharing economy, new technologies, and rapidly changing societal norms. Many of the shifts make life better for some and worse for others. The game has changed dramatically. Those who understand and plan for the big shifts ahead better than others will win.

We developed three new frameworks to make trends easier to identify and analyze. Each framework brings clarity to the overwhelming volume of data and anecdotes that leave so many confused.

We also identified the four biggest demographic opportunities, as well as the three biggest shifts related to how and where people will live. We support our findings with 100+ color charts in this book and far more available for free online.

THREE NEW FRAMEWORKS
Framework 1: Generations by Decade Born

To prepare for the big shifts, we need to change the conversation. We redefined the generations by decade born, resulting in much easier analysis of groups with a lot in common. Figure 1.1 shows the population by decade, the portion of the population born in another country, their age in 2015, and the total population in that generation. Forty to forty-four million American residents were born every decade from the 1950s through the 2000s—many of whom were born overseas.

BIG SHIFTS AHEAD

321 MILLION AMERICANS IDENTIFY WELL WITH PEOPLE THEIR OWN AGE.

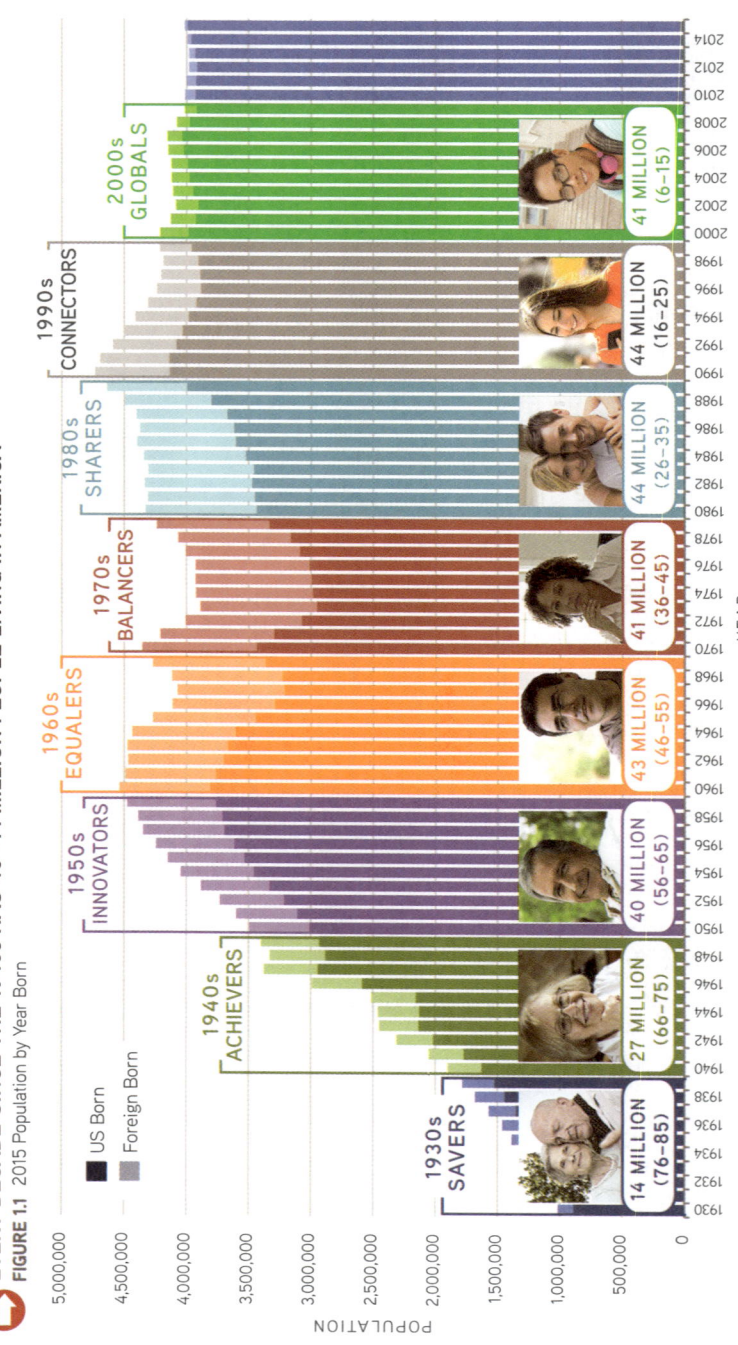

FIGURE 1.1 2015 Population by Year Born

EVERY DECADE SINCE THE 1940s HAS 40–44 MILLION PEOPLE LIVING IN AMERICA

Source: John Burns Real Estate Consulting, LLC calculations of US Census Bureau 2014 National Projections

8

We gave each generation a name associated with a shift they led in society. Those born in the

- 1930s led a shift to saving;
- 1940s led a shift to achieving;
- 1950s led a shift to innovating;
- 1960s led a shift toward more equal opportunities for women;
- 1970s led a shift toward more work and family balance;
- 1980s led a shift toward the sharing economy;
- 1990s led a shift toward staying connected; and
- 2000s will likely lead a shift toward more global awareness and interaction.

The following generational names by decade more accurately describe each generation.

GENERATIONAL CLARITY

1930s SAVERS	Shaped by forced frugality in childhood and booming economies during their working years. Drove the shift from cities to suburbs and started a surge in divorces. Ranging from 76 to 85 in 2015, they are spending on medical and remodeling, and struggling with how to live longer than anticipated in a low-interest-rate environment.
1940s ACHIEVERS	Driven to succeed financially, they began the surge in dual-income households and lower expenses (fewer kids), empowered by approval of the birth-control pill in 1960. Continuing to achieve financially today—19% of 65–69 year-olds still work full time, nearly double the Savers' rate at that age.
1950s INNOVATORS	Started new companies at rates not equaled since, boosting productivity and longevity with their inventions. Acquired possessions such as big houses at unprecedented levels, aided by credit cards, mortgages, and 30+ years of falling interest rates. Maintaining active lifestyles as they begin drawing on Social Security and spending their unprecedented net worths.
1960s EQUALERS	With both sexes pushing for more equal opportunities in the world, the Equaler women were the first beneficiaries of Title IX, and the first black US president came from this generation. For the first time, more than 60% of women worked. Dads more than doubled their involvement in childcare. They will retire less affluent than prior generations.

1970s BALANCERS	Raised by more dual-income and divorced parents than ever before, Balancer teens embraced TV and video games. Reacting against their oft-divorced parents' workaholic lifestyles, they divorce less, stay home with kids more, and have children later in life. Disproportionately hurt by the housing crash, they own fewer homes and have much lower net worths. Twenty-three percent are foreign-born.
1980s SHARERS	Invented the sharing economy out of necessity, taking advantage of new technologies. The most-educated cohort ever, they are racked with student debt, underemployed, and a full 20% live below the poverty line. They share locations, likes, photos, cars, etc. to connect with friends and live in urban areas where there is more to do and mass transit.
1990s CONNECTORS	With many still in school, many of their shifts have yet to emerge. They grew up with Internet access and know little privacy. More were raised by a single parent than previously, and early Connectors continue the growing trend of having children out of wedlock. Highly educated, underemployed, and wary of credit.
2000s GLOBALS	The Globals are growing up with multicultural friends and value diversity. They will bear the burden of prior generations' underfunded retirement obligations. With technology a big part of their education to date, we expect big shifts from the Globals.

Framework 2: The 4 Big Influencers

We found four reasons that generations change over time. Government policy, economic cycles, new technologies, and shifts in societal acceptability cause most of the generational shifts. Paying close attention to these 4 Big Influencers will allow you to more accurately project what will shift next. Here are a few examples of how the 4 Big Influencers have shifted society in the past:

1. **Government** – Government laws, programs, and investments at the federal, state, and local levels changed society more than we initially realized. Via the GI Bill and massive highway investments, the federal government boosted homeownership 18% in the 1940s and 1950s. Low state government income-tax policies have shifted population growth south. Local government redevelopment investments have revitalized urban areas.

2. **Economy** – Economic growth in childhood and early adulthood determines lifetime spending attitudes. Falling interest rates over time have boosted home and investment values, determining wealth in retirement. Those born in the 1950s are retiring as the most affluent generation ever. Those born in the 1970s have far lower net worth and homeownership at their age than any group in the last 40 years. The Great Recession of the late 2000s shifted society dramatically, exacerbating a number of trends, like delaying childbirth, and reversing others, like rising net worths.

3. **Technology** – Mass-produced cars created suburban living. The birth-control pill enabled a 20% decline in births. The smartphone destroyed privacy while allowing

the sharing economy to develop. Technology wiped out manufacturing jobs and now threatens knowledge workers. New technologies will determine which jobs get replaced and which people become unemployable thanks to inexpensive background checks.

4. **Societal Shifts** – Divorces tripled from the 1950s to the 1980s, encouraging the children of those divorced couples to become financially independent by getting educated, which they did. Societal pressure on a 25-year-old to marry has completely reversed, from "when are you going to marry?" to "why don't you hold off for a while?" Women are now more likely to have a child before they get married than after. Society's acceptance of these changes has reduced divorces and delayed both marriage and childbirth. Many of the biggest societal shifts we found trace back to 2001, the year of the tragic 9/11 terrorist attacks.

Future government policies, economic cycles, technological revolutions, and societal shifts will continue to change America.

Framework 3: The 4-5-6 Rule

The 4 Big Influencers impact each generation differently. We analyzed the lives of each generation, grouping them into 5 Main Life Stages: childhood, early career, family formation, late career, and retirement. By studying the 4 Big Influencers and their impact on each life stage, we learned a great deal about each generation. This framework allowed us to answer the 6 Key Consumer Questions most executives ask:

1. How much money will consumers have?

2. What will they choose to purchase?

3. When will they make these purchases?
4. Where will they live/spend?
5. Who will they live with (spend money on and share expenses with)?
6. Why will they buy certain products and not others?

We call this the 4–5–6 Rule, as shown in figure 1.2.

THE 4-5-6 RULE FOR DEMOGRAPHIC PREDICTIONS
FIGURE 1.2

The 4 Big Influencers
1. Government
2. Economy
3. Technology
4. Societal Shifts

During People's 5 Main Life Stages
1. Childhood
2. Early Career
3. Family Formation
4. Late Career
5. Retirement

Help Answer the 6 Key Consumer Questions
1. How many will there be and how much money will they have?
2. What will they purchase?
3. When will they purchase?
4. Where will they live/spend?
5. Who will buy and who will they live with (spend money on and share expenses with)?
6. Why will they buy certain products and not others?

4 BIGGEST DEMOGRAPHIC OPPORTUNITIES

While we identified plenty of opportunities, four huge transformations reshaping America stand out the most:

- **Women.** Women now earn 58% of all of the college degrees in the country. They earn more than their spouses 38% of the time. Women continue to have children later and alone. Both men and women stay at home more to raise the kids, a trend that started around 9/11. By 2025, we expect 78 million working women to play an even greater role in the workforce—8 million more than in 2015.

- **Immigrants.** America's foreign-born population doubled from 1990 to 2010, resulting in 44 million immigrants living in the US in 2015. At the current pace, the foreign-born population will grow to 52 million by 2025—more than one of every seven residents. The background of the immigrant has changed dramatically too. Far more immigrants now arrive via airplane and with money to spend, and far fewer sneak across the border in search of a low-paying manual-labor job.

- **Retirees.** By 2025, 18 million more people will be 65 or older than in 2015, a whopping 38% increase from 48 million in 2015 to 66 million in 2025. In 2016, 3.5 million people turned 65 compared to just 2.2 million turning 65 in 2006, and the numbers will trend higher. Companies that accurately tailor their products to 66 million Americans over the age of 65 in 2025 will profit.

- **Young Adults.** Those born from 1989 to 1993 constitute the largest five-year age group in the country. These 23- to 27-year-olds live at home or crowd into urban apartments more than any generation before them. For several reasons, their incomes will grow faster than most believe. They will lead the addition of 12.5 million more households from 2015 to 2025—86% more households than created in the prior ten years. Builders will construct 13.7 million new homes and apartments to meet the demand.

Cynthia Laguna provides a great example of three of these transformations. Cynthia, a 1980s Sharer, migrated legally from Mexico at the age of three, sharing a house with 26 others. Encouraged by her hard-working parents, Cynthia graduated from college. She then lived at home for six years, saving a down payment, and eventually purchasing a house. As the breadwinner, she qualified for the mortgage without any assistance from her husband.

3 BIG SHIFTS IN LIVING PREFERENCES

Readers of this book will find all sorts of applications to their lives and their businesses. Since so many people and companies care about the future of housing, we highlighted 3 Big Shifts in living preferences.

- **Rentals.** Owning has clearly declined in importance. People rent, borrow, and share more than in the past. The homeownership rate has already declined to the lowest level in more than 40 years. Homeownership should decline further—to less than 61% by 2025. The housing crisis in the late 2000s highlighted the risks of homeownership to a younger population now in adulthood. They know the risks. They lack enough confidence in their job to take on a 30-year mortgage commitment. Both the number of homeowners and renters will increase. By 2025, we expect

5.2 million more owner households and 7.3 million more renter households.

- **South.** Growth will continue to flow south toward the affordable sunshine states. California, the Northeast, and the Midwest will continue to grow more slowly. The southern regions where 42% of Americans currently live will welcome 62% of US household growth. State tax and growth policies determine where America lives.

- **Surban**™. A new supply of smaller homes with little or no yards in high-population areas will meet the demand to commute less and live closer to restaurants and entertainment. We coined the word "surban™" for these developments—bringing the best of urban living to a more affordable suburban environment.

Those who understand these seismic demographic shifts will develop a competitive advantage. These trends can accelerate or even reverse, driven by unpredictable events. As we will show, a significant number of trends completely reversed themselves after the unpredictable tragedy on 9/11. Let's get started.

2: GENERATIONS BY DECADE

How can decision makers group the high school classes of 2002 and 2018 into the same Millennial generation? Many 2002 graduates have bounced around from job to job in search of a better income to pay off student loans and drive for Uber at night while the kids sleep. Many members of the high school class of 2018 study hard in school while constantly texting friends and taking Netflix study breaks. These two Millennial groups share very few interests.

What do those born in 1946 have in common with those born in 1963? Most septuagenarian Baby Boomers retired years ago. They receive Social Security checks, have no mortgage or rent payment, and dote on their grandkids. Many of those born in 1963 will work for at least ten more years and have kids in college or living at home. Some run half marathons on the weekend, refusing to admit their real age and, far more than would like to admit it, live paycheck to paycheck.

We redefined the generations by decade born. This new definition makes demographic trends far easier to analyze. Figure 2.1 shows the traditional definitions across the top, our new definitions by decade born in the middle, and a distribution by life stage along the bottom. For most of us, life stage matters more than anything else. Are we single or living with a partner? Do we have kids or grandkids, and how old are they? Do we have a good job?

BIG SHIFTS AHEAD

FIGURE 2.1 Generational Clarity

DEFINING GENERATIONS BY DECADE BORN GROUPS PEOPLE INTO SIMILAR LIFE STAGES, MAKING ANALYSIS FAR MORE RELEVANT.

GENERATIONAL CLARITY — usable definitions

Traditional Definitions: 19+/- years in length

New Definitions by decade born

Generation	Sub	Decade	Label	Descriptor	Ages
SILENT	EARLY				
SILENT	LATE	1930s	SAVERS		
BABY BOOMERS	EARLY	1940s	ACHIEVERS	Retired	Ages: 61–70
BABY BOOMERS	LATE	1950s	INNOVATORS	Still working	Ages: 52–60
GENERATION X	EARLY	1960s	EQUALERS	Have plenty of home equity	Ages: 42–51
GENERATION X	LATE	1970s	BALANCERS	Have no/little home equity	Ages: 33–41
MILLENNIALS	EARLY	1980s	SHARERS	No Internet in grade school	Ages: 23–32
MILLENNIALS	LATE	1990s	CONNECTORS	Always had Internet	Ages: 14–22

LIFE STAGES

Life Stage	1930s	1940s	1950s	1960s	1970s	1980s	1990s	Total
Young Singles (≤ 45)		1%	5%	4%	22%	38%	67%	100%
Young Childless Couples (≤ 45)		13%		25%	9%	13%	8%	100%
Young Families (Oldest Kid ≤ 9)					21%	35%	25%	100%
Mature Families (Oldest Kid 10–18)				71%	39%	14%		100%
Mature Couples and Singles*		86%	95%		9%			100%
Retirement Age	100%							100%

*Household head is either 46–65 or has an adult child living with them. 2014 data rolled forward to 2015. Note: percentages less than 1% have been left out, and rounding adjustments were made to total to 100%

20

These decennial definitions offer more logical groupings and easier comparisons for great analysis. Every group now spans ten years and includes roughly the same number of people.

We always include figure 2.2 in our demographic discussions. The graphic includes the current population totals, number of American and foreign-born, and the major societal shifts led by each generation. You can download this chart free at www.bigshiftsahead.com.

People associate Gen X with the big decline in births in the late 1960s and 1970s. Indeed, 8 million more people were born in the US in the 1950s than the 1970s.

Significant immigration, however, filled in the 1970s void in births. Every decade from people born in the 1950s to the present includes 40 million to 44 million people today. These uniform decennial populations make for easy math. Anyone tracking some trend, for instance, knows that a shift of 1% represents around 400,000 people in that decade.

Let's look at Gen X as another great example of why grouping generations by decades makes more sense. Born from 1965 to 1983, Gen-Xers were 32 to 50 years old in 2015. The early members of Gen X purchased their first homes in the booming economy of the '90s. The late Gen-Xers bought their first home in the mid-2000s, just before the great housing market crash. Consider how widely these home-buying environments and the financial experiences of these two groups within Gen X differed. Early Gen-Xers enjoy plenty of home equity while late Gen-Xers suffered through more foreclosures than any other group.

Also, many individuals don't identify with their generational label, but most people can identify with others their age. We suggest fine-tuning all talk of Gen X, Millennials, or Boomers—too broad to provide insight—with our new decennial generations.

BIG SHIFTS AHEAD

EACH DECADE LED A SIGNIFICANT SHIFT IN SOCIETY.

FIGURE 2.2 2015 US Population by Place of Birth

Source: John Burns Real Estate Consulting, LLC calculations of US Census Bureau 2014 National Projections

22

2: GENERATIONS BY DECADE

BIRTHS SURGED IN THE 1950s AND 1980s.

FIGURE 2.3 2.3 US Births per Year

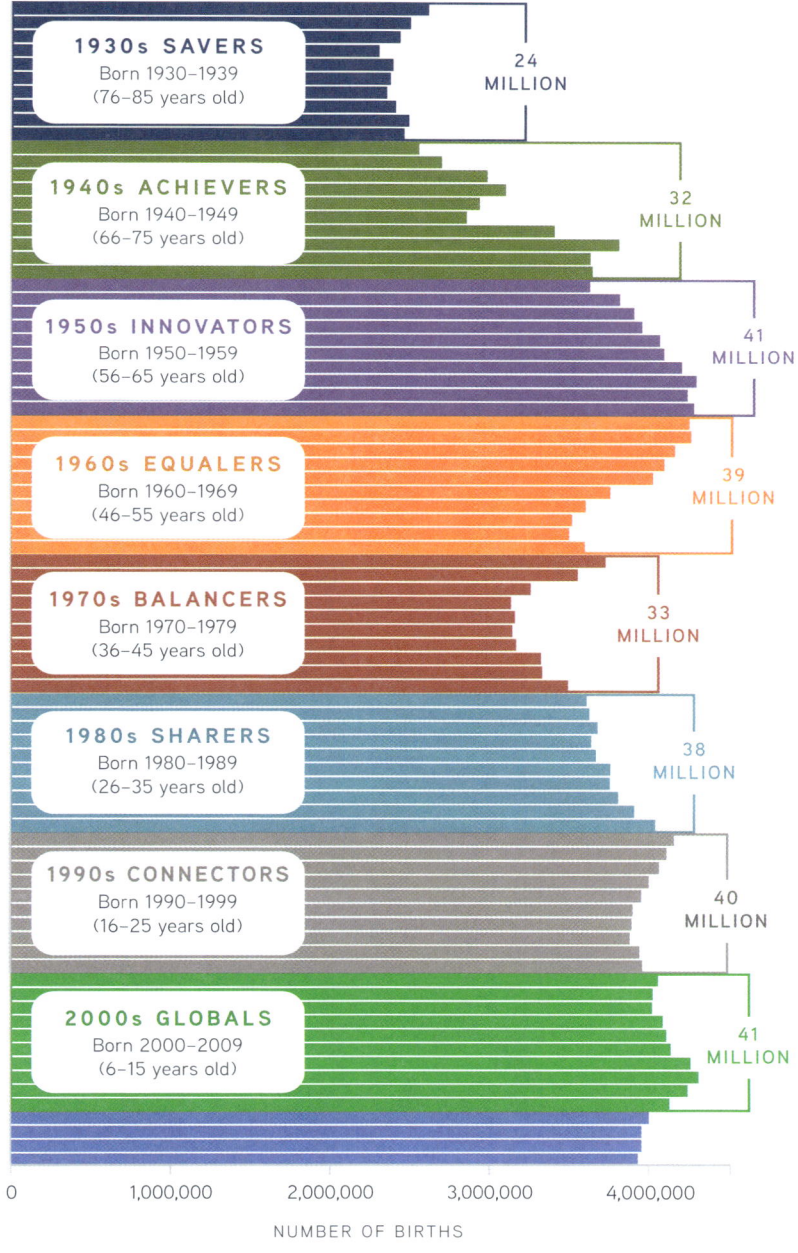

Source: Department of Health and Human Services, National Center for Health Statistics and CDC

We gave each generation a nickname drawn from a major contribution it made to a societal shift. We call the 1930s generation "Savers." Saving became a hallmark of those born into the frugality of the Great Depression and World War II. We call the 1980s generation "Sharers." Children born in the 1980s pioneered what we now call the sharing economy. They share the details of their lives on social media and save money by sharing goods from dresses to bikes to apartments. We consistently color-coded the generations throughout the book. This will allow you to easily track each generation. Charts show information associated with the

- 1930s Savers in dark blue;
- 1940s Achievers in olive green;
- 1950 Innovators in purple;
- 1960s Equalers in orange;
- 1970s Balancers in red;
- 1980s Sharers in turquoise;
- 1990s Connectors in gray; and
- 2000s Globals in light green.

The catchy labels describe something that makes each generation great and unique. Each generation should be proud of the shifts they led. We found it helpful to think of the high school classmates of notable people and celebrities born in each decade, such as

2: GENERATIONS BY DECADE

Warren Buffett and Mary Tyler Moore for the 1930s Savers;

Dolly Parton and Arnold Schwarzenegger for the 1940s Achievers;

Steve Jobs and Oprah Winfrey for the 1950s Innovators;

Sarah Jessica Parker and Tom Cruise for the 1960s Equalers;

Leonardo DiCaprio and Jennifer Garner for the 1970s Balancers;

Mark Zuckerberg and Beyoncé Knowles for the 1980s Sharers; and

Selena Gomez and Justin Bieber for the 1990s Connectors.

THE 1930s SAVERS

"The biggest mistake is not learning the habits of saving properly."

—Warren Buffett[1]

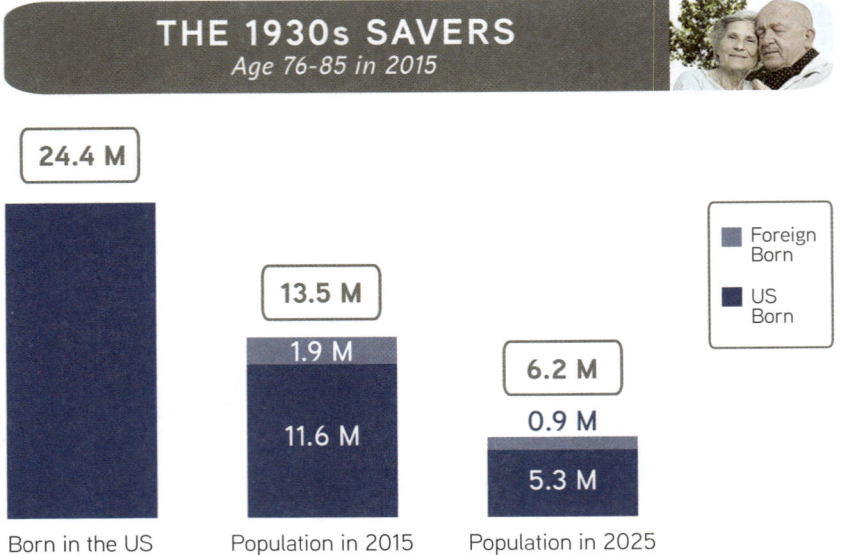

Source: John Burns Real Estate Consulting, LLC calculations of US Census Bureau data

Think of the 13.5 million 1930s Savers as the classmates of Warren Buffett, Mary Tyler Moore, Elizabeth Taylor, and John McCain. Their ages ranged from 76–85 in 2015. The oldest of them reached the official retirement age of 65 in 1995. About half of the original 24.4 million Savers remain alive today, and only 6.2 million will be alive in 2025, including 900,000 born elsewhere.

The 1930s Savers changed society dramatically. We find it important to understand this decade to project the future. The Savers' early life experiences have similarities with those born in the

---

[1] Warren Buffett, Interview, "The Dan Patrick Show," January 22, 2014, https://www.youtube.com/watch?v=muh8lL6s5ow.

2000s. However, their midlife experiences were very different from those born in the 1970s. Understanding the experiences and actions of the 1930s Savers provides great context for forecasting the future actions of younger generations.

Born into the Great Depression and food rationing during World War II, they learned how to save. As adults, they built up their savings accounts and borrowed only when necessary. Solid employer pension plans helped them save for retirement.

The government helped the 1930s generation save. In the 1930s, newly elected President Roosevelt created unemployment insurance and Social Security. The 1930s Savers became the first generation to contribute to those programs their entire working lives.

New technologies impacted this generation just like they impacted later generations. The radio became the prime piece of furniture in living rooms during this Golden Age. Families gathered around this magical new technology to hear soap operas, news reports, and the president's "fireside chats." As kids, the Savers loved their new radio technology in ways that the 1980s Sharers loved dial-up modems and AOL subscriptions.

Wartime experiences made them less accepting of the foreign-born. Atomic bombs, communist expansion, and the Holocaust impacted them deeply. Some Savers transitioned from high school directly into the Korean War. They grew up patriotic and desired stability and tradition.

The TV shows *Father Knows Best, Leave It to Beaver,* and *The Honeymooners* capture the era well. Breadwinner fathers went off to work for employers they might remain with for decades. TV mothers kept house and watched the kids. Domestic roles would never again appear so clearly defined. Young Savers explored a new kind of music led by artists such as Elvis Presley, Buddy Holly, and Chuck Berry.

While they valued traditional family structures, Savers also watched their mothers go off to work during the war years. More 1930s Saver women joined the labor force than ever before, despite limited opportunities. 1930-born Sandra Day O'Connor, the future Supreme Court Justice, graduated near the top of her Stanford law school class. After 40 law firms turned her down for an interview, she began her career as a deputy county attorney after offering to work for no salary.[2] Today, women earn 47% of all law degrees and more than 100,000 women belong to the American Bar Association.[3]

The Savers purchased more homes than any prior generation. Homeownership rose 18% from 1940 to 1960. Highway infrastructure investments opened up the suburbs. The GI Bill and new government mortgage agencies called FHA and Fannie Mae insured and purchased mortgages to grow homeownership. Saver fathers drove to their jobs from the nation's first suburbs. Nearly 80% own homes today.

---

[2] "'Out Of Order' At The Court: O'Connor On Being The First Female Justice," *Fresh Air*, National Public Radio, March 5, 2013, http://www.npr.org/2013/03/05/172982275/out-of-order-at-the-court-oconnor-on-being-the-first-female-justice.

[3] "A Current Glance at Women in the Law," American Bar Association - Commission on Women in the Profession, July 2014, https://www.americanbar.org/content/dam/aba/marketing/women/current_glance_statistics_july2014.authcheckdam.pdf.

THE GI BILL SPURRED AN 18% HOMEOWNERSHIP BOOST FROM 1940 TO 1960.

➡ **GI BILL CAUSED HOMEOWNERSHIP SURGE**
FIGURE 2.4 US Homeownership Rates (1900–2015)

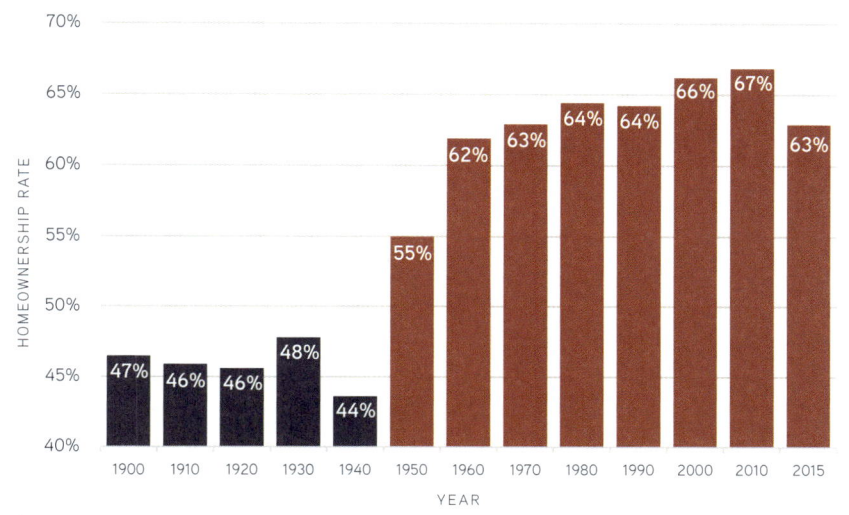

Year	Homeownership Rate
1900	47%
1910	46%
1920	46%
1930	48%
1940	44%
1950	55%
1960	62%
1970	63%
1980	64%
1990	64%
2000	66%
2010	67%
2015	63%

Sources: US Census Bureau, Decennial Census and Housing Vacancies and Homeownership Survey, John Burns Real Estate Consulting, LLC

The mass-produced automobile—another transformative technology—spurred the massive postwar growth of suburbs such as Levittown (outside New York City) and Park Forest (on Chicago's fringe). Construction of the Interstate Highway System in the 1950s complemented the rise of the car and furthered suburban development. Auto travel increased 775% from the time the first 1930s Savers turned 16 in 1946 until the last one turned 65 in 2004.

1950s HIGHWAY CONSTRUCTION ENABLED SUBURBAN LIFE, RESULTING IN A 775% INCREASE IN AUTOMOBILE TRAVEL FROM THE 1930s SAVERS' YOUTH UNTIL RETIREMENT.

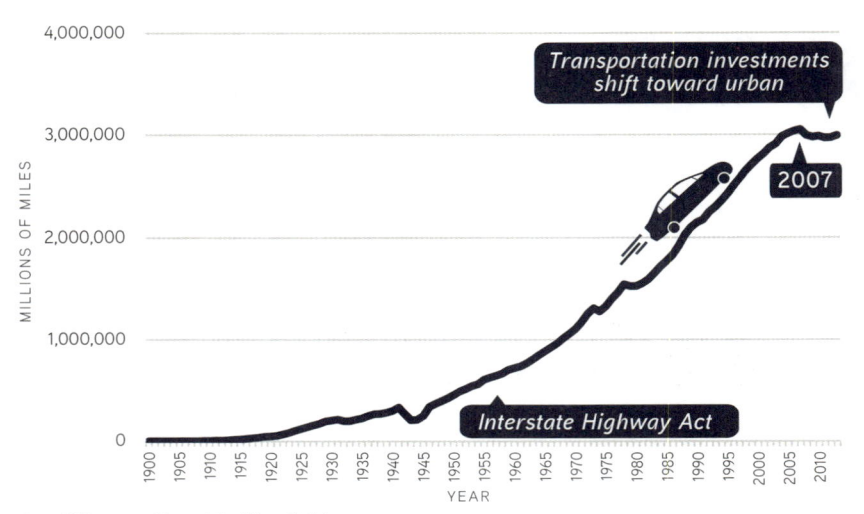

THE RISE AND PLATEAU OF DRIVING
FIGURE 2.5 Vehicle Miles of Travel

Transportation investments shift toward urban

2007

Interstate Highway Act

Source: US Department of Transportation, Highway Statistics

Despite the idyllic family life portrayed on TV, the Savers divorced like no generation before them. 1930s Saver Elizabeth Taylor, an extreme example, divorced seven times. In 1961, this generation began a 193% spike in divorces that plateaued 20 years later. Their children witnessed the terrible pains of divorce, causing them to marry later in life and more cautiously.

2 : GENERATIONS BY DECADE

THE 1930s SAVERS LED AN ALMOST 200% SPIKE IN DIVORCES.

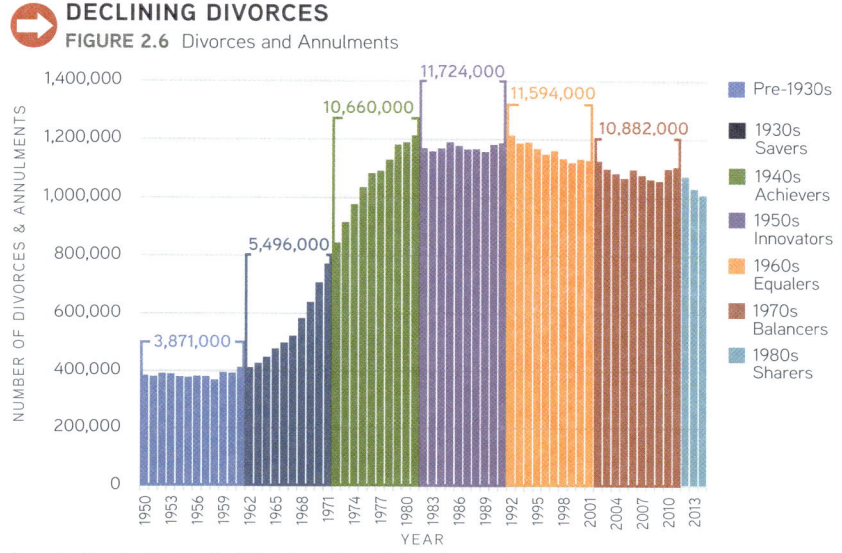

DECLINING DIVORCES
FIGURE 2.6 Divorces and Annulments

Key data points shown on chart:
- 3,871,000 (Pre-1930s)
- 5,496,000 (1930s Savers)
- 10,660,000 (1940s Achievers)
- 11,724,000 (1950s Innovators)
- 11,594,000 (1960s Equalers)
- 10,882,000 (1970s Balancers)

Legend:
- Pre-1930s
- 1930s Savers
- 1940s Achievers
- 1950s Innovators
- 1960s Equalers
- 1970s Balancers
- 1980s Sharers

Source: John Burns Real Estate Consulting, LLC calculations of Centers for Disease Control and Prevention data;
* Color coded based on 32 years old as the median age of first divorce. Note: For states that do not collect this data (varies by year), we estimated the number based on the number of people in that state. Annulments included above.

The fiscally conservative Savers had enough savings to weather stagflation in the 1970s, high interest rates in the early '80s, and three stock market crashes. At age 63, the typical Saver retired wealthy and as a homeowner with no mortgage. Though affluent, today's Savers receive much lower interest earnings than anticipated and know they will live longer than planned.

Savers benefit greatly from Social Security and Medicare. Sixty-two percent head their own household compared to just 45% of their grandparents at the same age. Government entitlements enabled millions of households to live independently, creating huge demand for housing and aging-in-place services. For their next move, they will consider assisted-living facilities or remodeling to stay in place. Health remains their greatest concern.

GOVERNMENT ASSISTANCE PROGRAMS AIDED A SURGE IN THE RATE OF OLDER PEOPLE LIVING ON THEIR OWN—FROM 45% TO 62%.

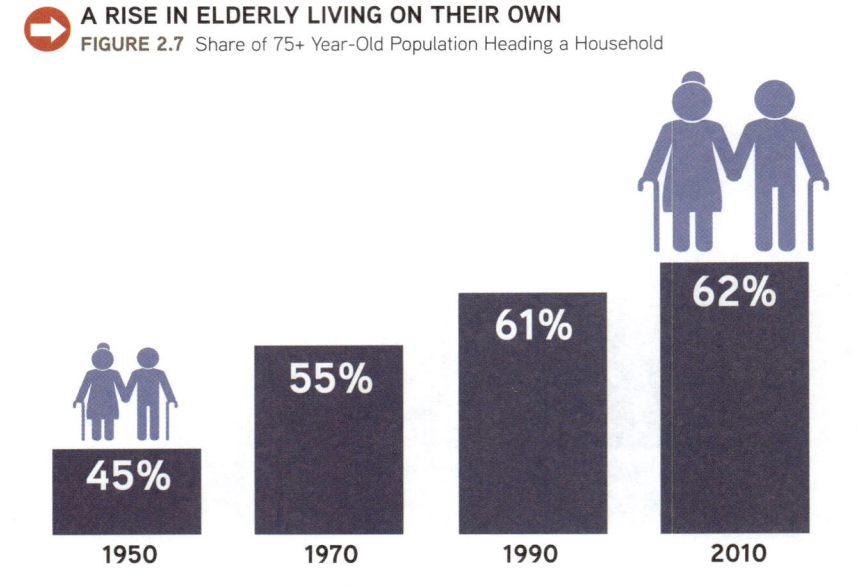

A RISE IN ELDERLY LIVING ON THEIR OWN

FIGURE 2.7 Share of 75+ Year-Old Population Heading a Household

1950	1970	1990	2010
45%	55%	61%	62%

Source: John Burns Real Estate Consulting, LLC based on US Census Bureau data

THE 1940s ACHIEVERS

"My songs are the door to every dream I've ever had and every success I've ever achieved."

—Dolly Parton[4]

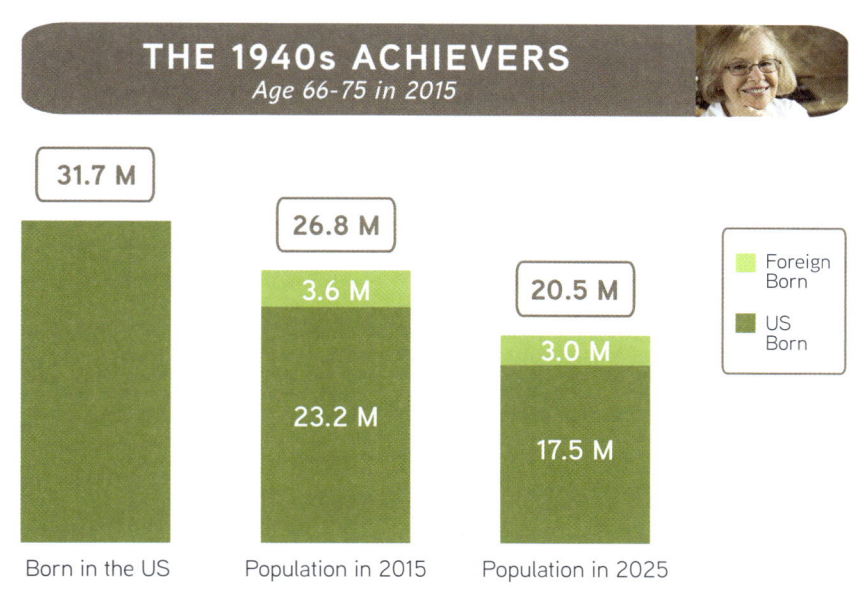

THE 1940s ACHIEVERS
Age 66-75 in 2015

	Born in the US	Population in 2015	Population in 2025
Total	31.7 M	26.8 M	20.5 M
Foreign Born		3.6 M	3.0 M
US Born		23.2 M	17.5 M

Source: John Burns Real Estate Consulting, LLC calculations of US Census Bureau data

Think of the 27 million 1940s Achievers as the classmates of Martha Stewart, Bill Clinton, Dolly Parton, and Austrian-born Arnold Schwarzenegger. Achievers ranged in age from 66 to 75 in 2015. Twenty-three million of the original 32 million Achievers remain alive today. Thanks to immigration, the totals have swelled to 27 million. We expect 21 million Americans aged 76–85 in 2025.

As the first generation raised in the suburbs, the '40s children took full advantage of the opportunity. They graduated from college in record numbers. Achiever women joined the workforce and began

---

4   Dolly Parton, "Hungry Again," 1998, album liner notes.

to close the large male–female income gap. Couples had far fewer children in the process.

The Achievers grew up with musical icons such as Elvis and Buddy Holly, and later the Beatles and the Rolling Stones. Their musical heroes—oft-censored rock stars—contrasted with the wholesome middle class shows they watched on television.

They lived their teens or 20s in the tumultuous 1960s, affected by massive social change and world events. Their 20s included the Cold War, Vietnam, the assassinations of President Kennedy and Martin Luther King, Jr., and the civil rights movement. Young people questioned the establishment as never before, as well as the rigid social roles of their parents.

Disposable income surged. The number of dual-income families increased by 20%. Fewer kids meant less expenses. Achievers borrowed heavily to buy the things they wanted, starting the surge in credit-card debt in the 1960s. They purchased new 1960s and 1970s homes, with mismatched color schemes, floral designs, and colored appliances.

RISING DEBT HAS BOTH INCREASED AFFLUENCE AND MADE EACH GENERATION MORE SUSCEPTIBLE TO FINANCIAL DIFFICULTIES IN TOUGH ECONOMIC TIMES.

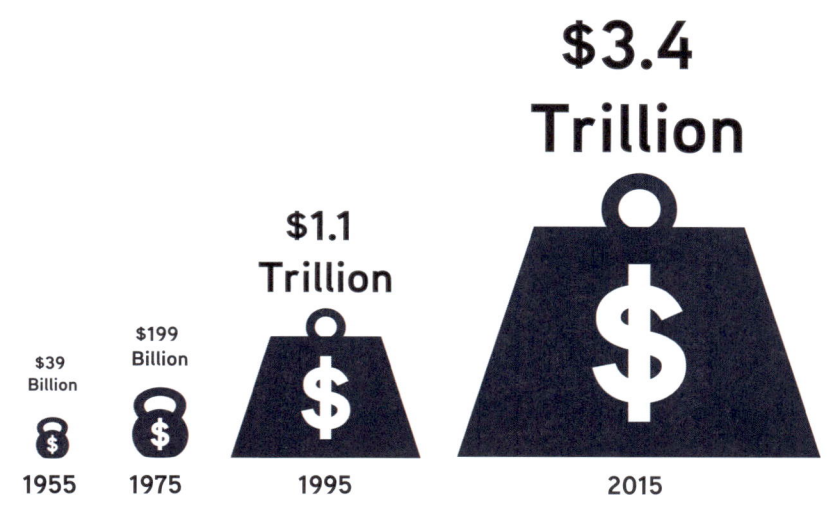

TOO MUCH DEBT TO REPAY
FIGURE 2.8 Total Consumer Credit Owned and Securitized

$39 Billion — 1955
$199 Billion — 1975
$1.1 Trillion — 1995
$3.4 Trillion — 2015

Source: Board of Governors of the Federal Reserve System, St. Louis Fed

The Achievers also fought for civil rights and women's rights. They began the substantial rise in a sense of fairness that manifested in the 1960s Equalers. New technologies complemented women's struggles, as the birth-control pill empowered women to work longer and rise higher in their careers. Birth-control legalization in 1960 and abortion legalization in 1973 contributed to fewer children. While the Saver mothers birthed 3.1 kids on average, Achiever mothers lowered that number to 2.3. The birth rate eventually fell to 1.9, before rebounding recently.

MAJOR EVENTS AND TECHNOLOGIES LED TO A BABY BOOM OF 3.1 KIDS PER WOMAN AND A BABY BUST OF 1.9 KIDS PER WOMAN ONLY 25 YEARS LATER.

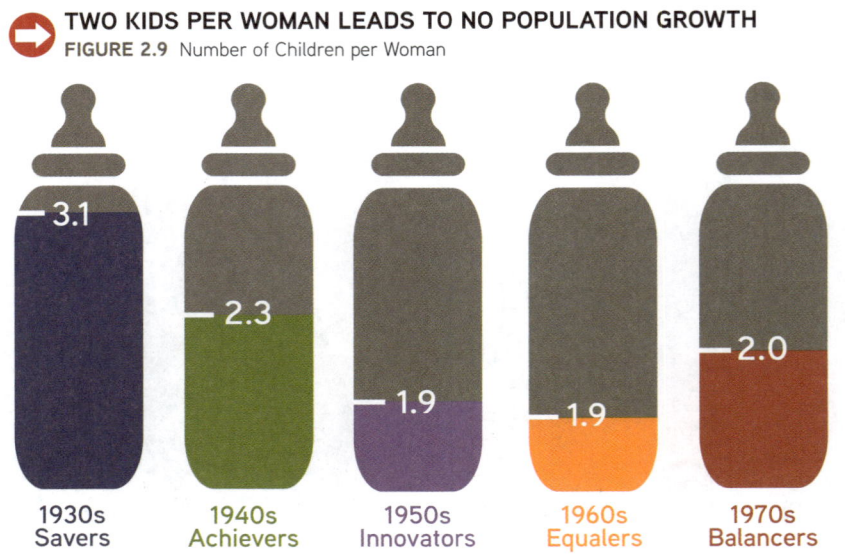

TWO KIDS PER WOMAN LEADS TO NO POPULATION GROWTH
FIGURE 2.9 Number of Children per Woman

1930s Savers	1940s Achievers	1950s Innovators	1960s Equalers	1970s Balancers
3.1	2.3	1.9	1.9	2.0

Source: US Census Bureau, Current Population Survey
Note: the data has been mostly biannual since 1988, so we averaged the years before and after to show the trends
*Based on a survey of women aged 40–44 at the time of the survey

Female 1940s Achievers led a dramatic increase in young women's incomes off a very low base. Young women's incomes rose an inflation-adjusted 143% from 1962 to 2007. Recent declines in income for both men and women mask the tremendous progress women made for decades.

YOUNG WOMEN INCOMES INCREASED 143% FROM 1962 TO 2007.

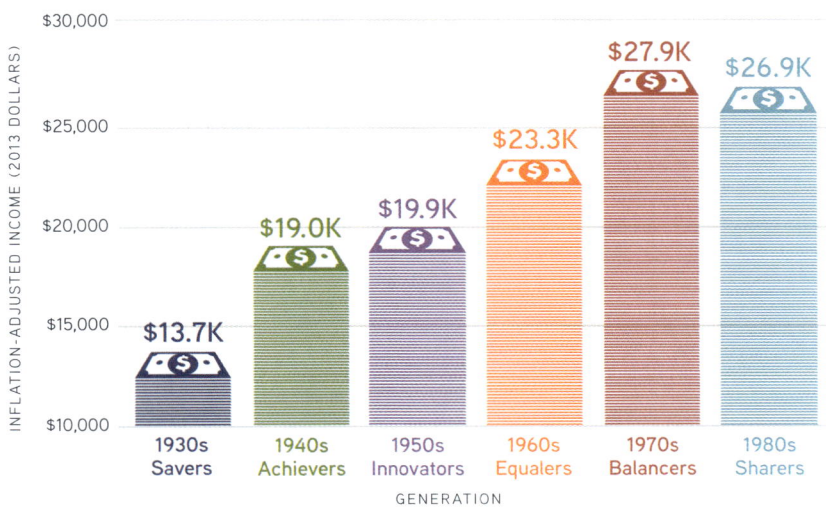

RISING YOUNG FEMALE INCOMES ENDED IN THE 2000s
FIGURE 2.10 Female Median Real Income, Women Aged 25–34 (2013 Dollars)

Generation	Income
1930s Savers	$13.7K
1940s Achievers	$19.0K
1950s Innovators	$19.9K
1960s Equalers	$23.3K
1970s Balancers	$27.9K
1980s Sharers	$26.9K

Source: US Census Bureau, Current Population Survey, Annual Social and Economic Supplements; averaged over 5 years for 1980s Sharers

Shifting gender roles, increased female economic independence, and the strain of dual-income households produced the highest divorce rate ever. More than 1.2 million couples filed for divorce every year during the 1980s. The divorces heavily impacted their '60s and '70s kids. The girls took note of the devastating impact on their less-educated mothers. Many promised themselves they would become financially independent.

Dual-income households created distinct financial advantages for the Achievers. They earned 18% more money late in their careers than the Savers. They amassed greater net worth than any group before them too. Far fewer of them live in poverty, and they rely less on Social Security and pensions than prior generations.

THE 1940s ACHIEVERS EARNED THE MOST MONEY IN THEIR PRERETIREMENT YEARS OF 55–64.

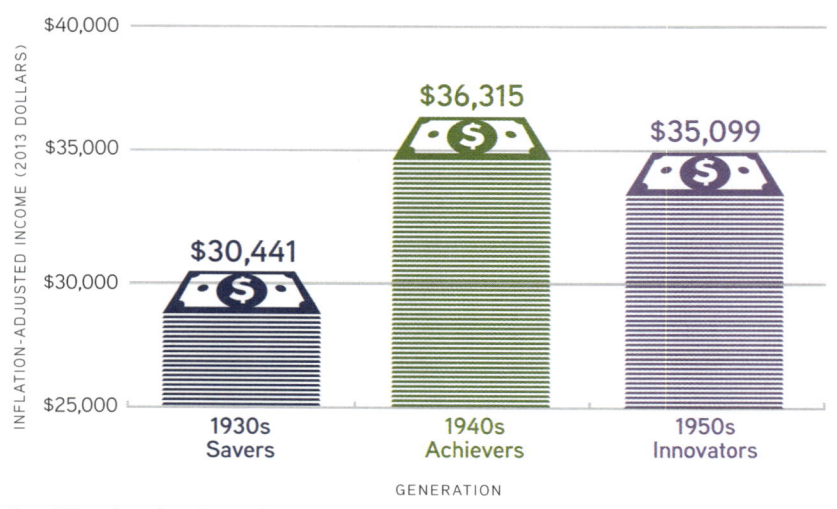

THE ACHIEVERS MADE THE MOST MONEY PRERETIREMENT
FIGURE 2.11 Real Median Income of People 55 to 64 (1947–2013)

- 1930s Savers: $30,441
- 1940s Achievers: $36,315
- 1950s Innovators: $35,099

INFLATION-ADJUSTED INCOME (2013 DOLLARS)

GENERATION

Source: US Census Bureau, Current Population Survey, Annual Social and Economic Supplements; averaged over 5 years for 1950s Innovators

While all of those born in the 1940s have reached the official retirement age, the Achievers keep achieving. Around 20% continue to work past the age of 65, twice the percentage as those born 20 years earlier. Many continue to work simply because they're healthy and want to work. They also realize they could live another 30 years and one day might need the additional savings.

Many Achievers prefer higher-density living with plenty of entertainment within a short walk. They buy or rent both in the big cities as well as newly redeveloped areas in small cities, which we call surban™ living. Surban™ living has become such an important trend that we devoted an entire chapter to it.

THE 1950s INNOVATORS

"Innovation distinguishes between a leader and a follower."
—Steve Jobs[5]

THE 1950s INNOVATORS
Age 56-65 in 2015

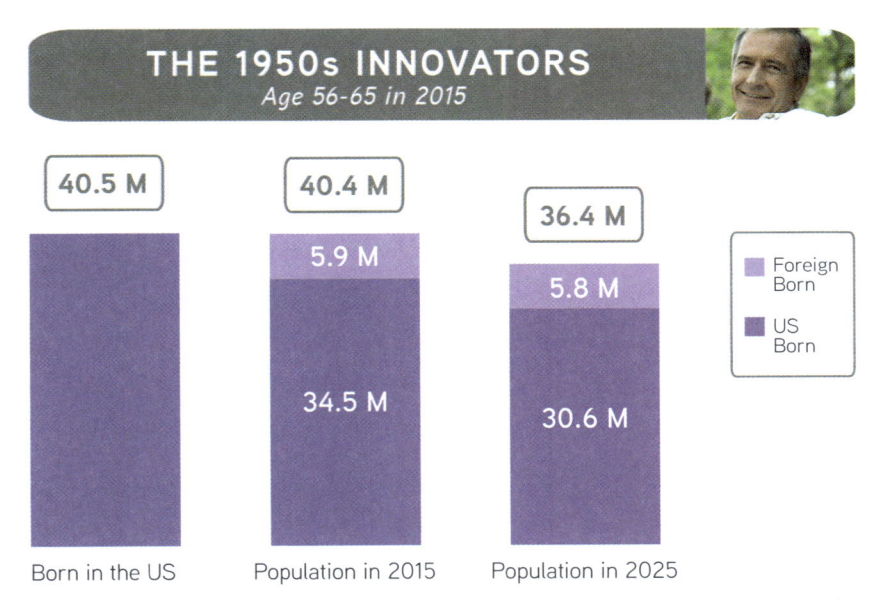

	Born in the US	Population in 2015	Population in 2025
Total	40.5 M	40.4 M	36.4 M
Foreign Born		5.9 M	5.8 M
US Born		34.5 M	30.6 M

Source: John Burns Real Estate Consulting, LLC calculations of US Census Bureau data

Think of the 40 million 1950s Innovators as the classmates of Steve Jobs and Bill Gates, as well as Oprah Winfrey and Ellen DeGeneres. The Innovators led major technological innovations and broke down old societal barriers. Maternity wards boomed in the 1950s, sending 41 million babies out into the world. In 2025, we expect 36.4 million of them aged 66 to 75 years old, including almost 6 million born elsewhere.

The Innovators entered an America unprepared for the 70% population surge compared to only two decades prior. Schools grew crowded and students struggled to stand out. Many studied with

---

5   Carmine Gallo, *The Innovation Secrets of Steve Jobs: Insanely Different Principles for Breakthrough Success* (McGraw-Hill Professional Publishing, 2010).

the intention of becoming astronauts. Neil Armstrong's first steps on the moon turned droves of kids into would-be scientists and space explorers. As young adults, they drove huge computer and biotechnology advancements. Steve Jobs and Steve Wozniak founded Apple Computer. Bill Gates and Paul Allen founded Microsoft. The Innovators revolutionized the ways we live and do business.

Their TV shows reflected the large youth population and the counter-culture that emerged during the 1960s. Shows such as *I Dream of Jeannie*, *Star Trek*, *The Partridge Family*, and *The Monkees* offered a decidedly fantastical spin. Musical styles ranged from folk and hard rock to disco and punk.

Many Innovators spent their childhood years in staid suburban communities. They represented the largest group of children to grow up in new suburban terrain, where '60s homes featured vivacious, quirky décor with wild color schemes, floral designs, and colored appliances.

The Innovators achieved even higher levels of education, partially due to government loans from the likes of lender Sallie Mae, a government agency founded in 1972 that formally ended its government ties in 2004. Innovators left home as soon as they could, forming households earlier and in greater numbers than any generation before or since. We nicknamed this trend the "Meathead effect" after Rob Reiner's character on the hit TV series *All in the Family*. Nobody of that generation wanted to be the "Meathead" living with their parents or in-laws.

Young Innovators left home at unprecedented rates. Many analysts incorrectly assumed today's young adults would do the same. At the Innovators' ten-year high school reunion in 1980, 49% headed a household, by far the largest percentage ever. Their household formation rate at age 28 exceeded the Achievers before them by 3%, and the Equalers after them by 5%. With most of today's reporters and business executives born in the 1950s and 1960s, the common conversation revolves around "what is wrong" with today's young adults who live at home. In reality, a better conversation might revolve around what differed so much when the Innovators came of age in the 1970s and 1980s.

The Innovators benefited from decades of sustained economic growth. Government deficit spending fueled some of that growth. They bought homes with government help. Thirty years of falling interest rates boosted the values of their homes, as well as their stock and bond portfolios. Innovators borrowed heavily and started their own companies. They changed the way we live, inventing personal computers, smartphones, and a host of biotech products. The innovating spirit the Innovators started has since dwindled. Entrepreneurship has fallen in half since they hit their stride in the 1970s.

ENTREPRENEURSHIP HAS PLUMMETED SINCE THE 1950s INNOVATORS FOUNDED MICROSOFT AND APPLE IN THE LATE 1970s, FROM 16% OF ALL BUSINESSES TO 8%.

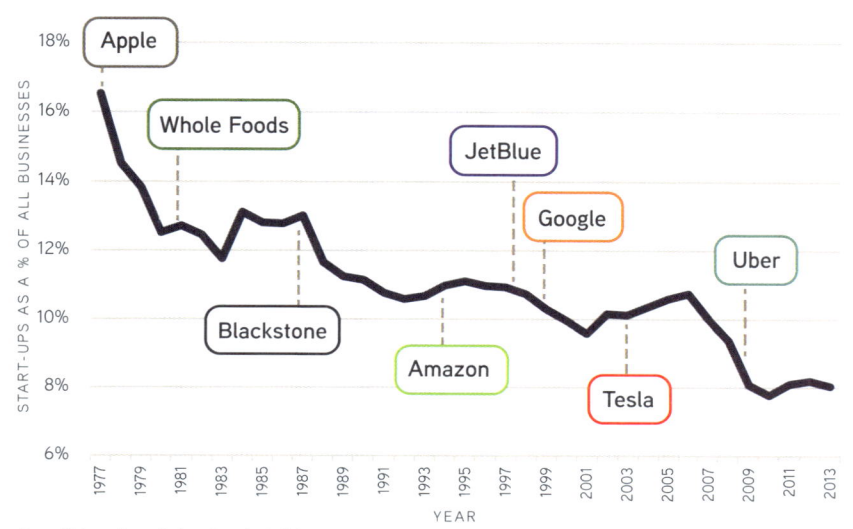

PLUMMETING ENTREPRENEURSHIP
FIGURE 2.12 New Start-Ups as a Percent of All Businesses

Source: US Census Bureau Business Dynamics Statistics

Innovators, of course, bought innovative entry-level houses. The 1970s Eichler designs featured environmentally friendly products, bright walls, plenty of natural light, carpeting, colored appliances, and microwaves. Their affluence allowed them to quickly buy larger homes, known as McMansions, in the 1980s. These large homes on small lots included big rooms, lavish architecture and décor, and muted appliance colors. The average new home size grew 57% over 40 years, with explosive growth in the 1980s. As a result, the new-home industry largely abandoned low-priced, entry-level homes, where the bulk of demand exists.

THE 1950s INNOVATORS EARNED THE MOST MONEY IN THEIR PEAK EARNING YEARS OF 45–54.

THE INNOVATORS MADE THE MOST MONEY IN THEIR PEAK EARNING YEARS

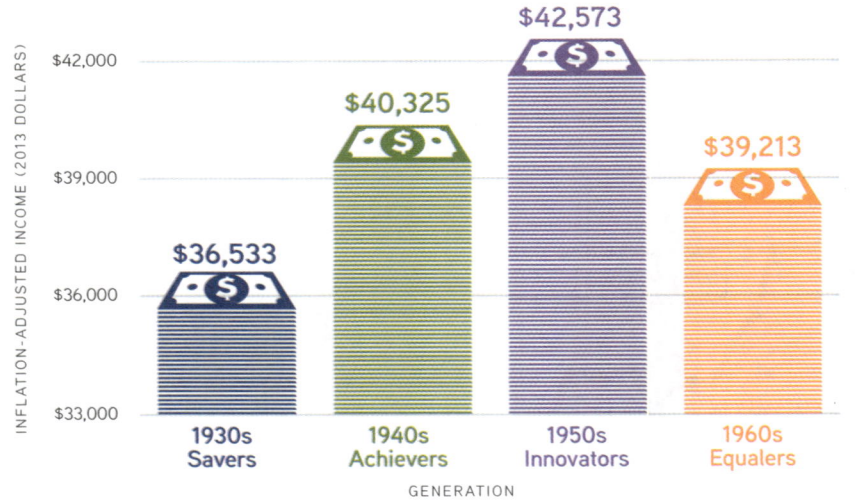

FIGURE 2.13 Real Median Income of People 45 to 54 (1947–2013)

Generation	Income
1930s Savers	$36,533
1940s Achievers	$40,325
1950s Innovators	$42,573
1960s Equalers	$39,213

Source: US Census Bureau, Current Population Survey, Annual Social and Economic Supplements; averaged over 5 years for 1960s Equalers

Ironically, smaller families lived in those larger houses. Even more ironically, most parents spent all day at work. As the first generation able to plan their pregnancies, Innovators chose to parent fewer children. They purchased birth-control pills in unprecedented numbers and grew the number of abortions dramatically.

The Innovators remain very attached to their planned children. Sixty-three percent say they want their adult children to continue living with them.[6] The very Innovators who couldn't leave their parents' homes fast enough are the ones encouraging their adult children to live at home.

Innovator parents remain deeply involved in their children's lives, inspiring the term "helicopter parents." For example, one survey found that parents submitted the résumés of their 1985-born children 31% of the time.[7] Mom and Dad's willingness to help their kids into adulthood has certainly contributed to the young adult's desire to stay at home.

The Innovators enjoy unprecedented wealth. They earned more money (adjusted for inflation) in their peak earning years of 45–54 than did any generation before or after them, breaking the record set by the Achievers. Heading into their retirement years, they have amassed a cumulative $18 trillion dollar net worth.

---

[6] "What Parents Tell Us About Their Adult Children Living At Home," Fannie Mae National Housing Survey, July 2014, http://www.fanniemae.com/resources/file/research/housingsurvey/pdf/nhsjuly2014presentation.pdf.

[7] Michigan State University, Collegiate Employment Research Institute, "Parent Involvement in the College Recruiting Process: To What Extent?", 2007, http://ceri.msu.edu/publications/pdf/ceri2-07.pdf.

THE 1950s INNOVATORS HEAD INTO RETIREMENT WITH $18 TRILLION, THE MOST OF ANY GENERATION.

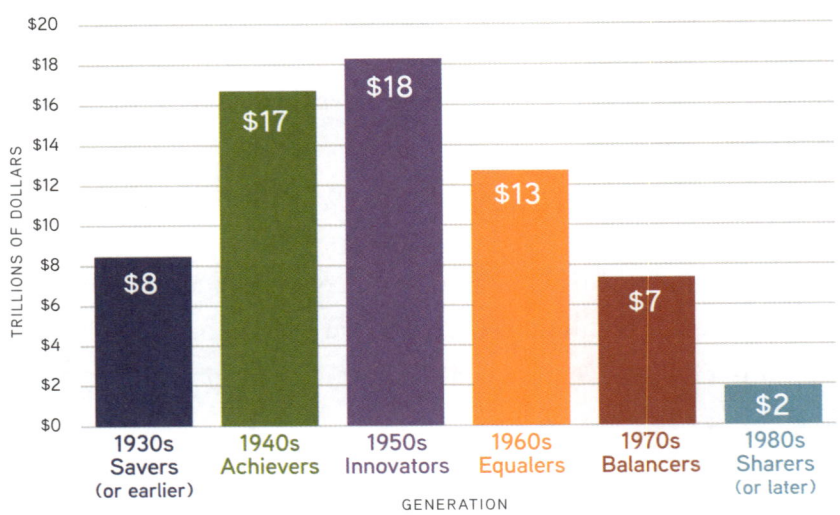

THE INNOVATORS HAVE $18 TRILLION IN NET WORTH
FIGURE 2.14 Net Worth by Generation

Generation	Net Worth (Trillions)
1930s Savers (or earlier)	$8
1940s Achievers	$17
1950s Innovators	$18
1960s Equalers	$13
1970s Balancers	$7
1980s Sharers (or later)	$2

Source: John Burns Real Estate Consulting, LLC calculations of Board of Governors of Federal Reserve System 2013 Survey of Consumer Finances

The workaholic Innovators will keep working past 65 like no generation before them. At 55–64, 5% more of them work than the Achievers did at the same age, and 11% more work than the Savers when they were aged 55 to 64. Employers will need the help, as the coming surge in retirement will create a huge labor shortage—a topic covered in detail later.

For Steve Burch, an Innovator born in 1953, 65 represents nothing more than a number. An executive, Burch has worked for major corporations such as Chrysler and Pulte Homes. Burch not only eschews retirement plans, but he has not even considered what might nudge him in that direction.

"I think the thing I need to do, and I haven't really sat down and thought it through carefully enough, is to start to develop markers:

when these kinds of things start happening, I'll need to disengage," Burch says. "But I haven't really set those up yet. I definitely haven't thrown an age number [for retirement] up there."

Nearing the official retirement age, Burch shows no signs of slowing down. He spent most of his career in corporate offices but now works from his home in Las Vegas for an employer based in California. He misses the morning office routine—coffee, workout, shower, and drive—so he does his best to recreate it. He starts work at 6:00 a.m. in his home office and even on slow days finds something to keep him busy until 5:00 or 5:30 p.m. Friends in his age group tend to share similar attitudes about work and retirement, Burch said.

"I have a lot of friends in academia because I spent a long time there, and those guys, one in particular, are just like, 'Why would I retire? I love teaching. I love taking care of the kids. I still write. I'm still really important in the field, and my opinion matters,'" Burch said. "Another guy I still talk to from those days is a real estate broker. He's an avid diver and likes to go to Cabo San Lucas and all these other exotic places to dive. It's expensive. He's going to keep working, mostly to enjoy his hobbies."

THE 1960s EQUALERS

*"We learned about honesty and integrity—
that the truth matters...and success doesn't
count unless you earn it fair and square."*

—Michelle Obama[8]

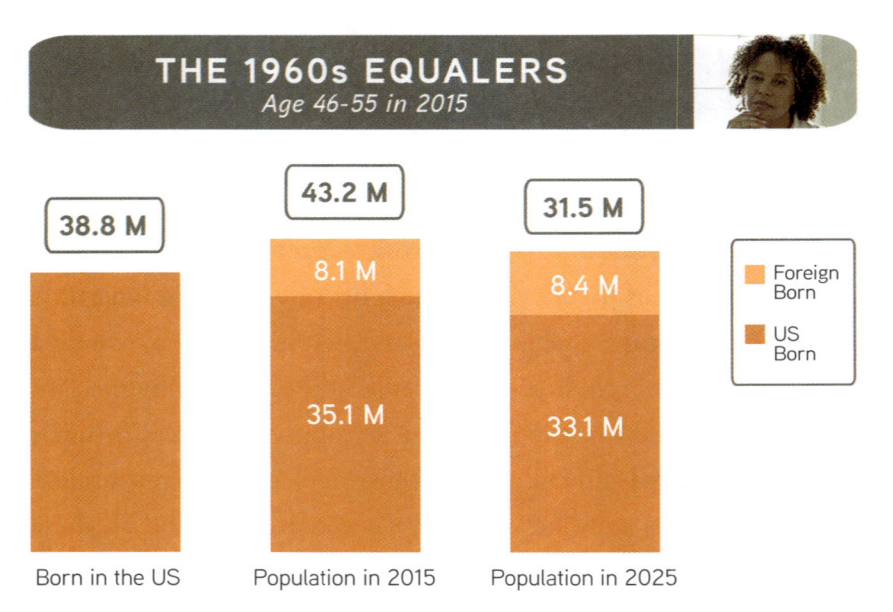

THE 1960s EQUALERS
Age 46-55 in 2015

	Foreign Born	US Born	Total
Born in the US		38.8 M	38.8 M
Population in 2015	8.1 M	35.1 M	43.2 M
Population in 2025	8.4 M	33.1 M	31.5 M

Source: John Burns Real Estate Consulting, LLC calculations of US Census Bureau data

Think of the 43 million 1960s Equalers as the classmates of Tom Cruise, Michelle Obama, Sarah Jessica Parker, and Robert Downey Jr. Their ages in 2015 ranged from 46 to 55.

This generation tore down barriers. For the first time, more women graduated from college than men. More women became financially independent. More than two-thirds of working-age women worked.

---

8   Michelle Obama, "Speech to Democratic National Convention," September 4, 2012.

In their childhoods, immigration increased and civil rights legislation worked its way into society. The Supreme Court handed down the *Brown v. Board of Education* decision integrating public schools in 1954. Many school districts delayed taking concrete steps toward desegregation until the '70s and even '80s, when young Equalers attended classes. Martin Luther King Jr. would likely be quite pleased to know that Barack Obama, a six-year-old Equaler at the time of King's assassination, would become President of the United States 40 years later.

The social shift toward greater equality manifested itself in TV shows with stronger female leads—*The Mary Tyler Moore Show, Charlie's Angels, Laverne and Shirley, The Bionic Woman.* People of color appeared on television more frequently, too, on shows that evolved from the likes of *Sanford and Son* (about a junkyard owner) to *The Cosby Show* (about a doctor). The Equalers' music included everything from hard rock to disco—Van Halen, Bruce Springsteen, the Bee Gees, and Lionel Ritchie.

Girls identified with an increasing number of role models. Tennis great Billie Jean King defeated aging male champion Bobby Riggs in 1973. Astronaut Sally Ride became the first woman in space in 1983.

Title IX legislation passed in 1972. The new law revolutionized girls' access to higher education, as we'll see in our chapter on the rise of the working woman.

1960s Equaler and coauthor John Burns experienced the rising role of women early in his career. After graduating in 1985, he joined a CPA firm and worked on audits mostly managed by women. While the partners were primarily men, he worked equally under male and female supervisors. Equality at the junior level prevailed.

The rise in dual-income households inspired an efficiency boom on the part of Equalers struggling to do it all. First came the Day-Timer and then the Franklin Planner. Laptops, tablets, and takeout food made life easier.

Despite rising efficiency and dual incomes, the 1960s Equalers struggle with the lowest net worth in generations. The typical 1960s Equaler net worth totaled $105,000 in 2013, much lower than the three previous generations. The Equalers have experienced much slower economic growth during their working years than prior generations. Many entered the workforce during the early-'80s recession. The economy rebounded later in that decade, but two bigger recessions hit Equalers hard during the 2000s. The US economy during the 2000s grew only slightly faster than during the 1930s and far more slowly than any decade in between.

THE 1960s EQUALERS HAVE LOWER NET WORTH THAN PRIOR GENERATIONS.

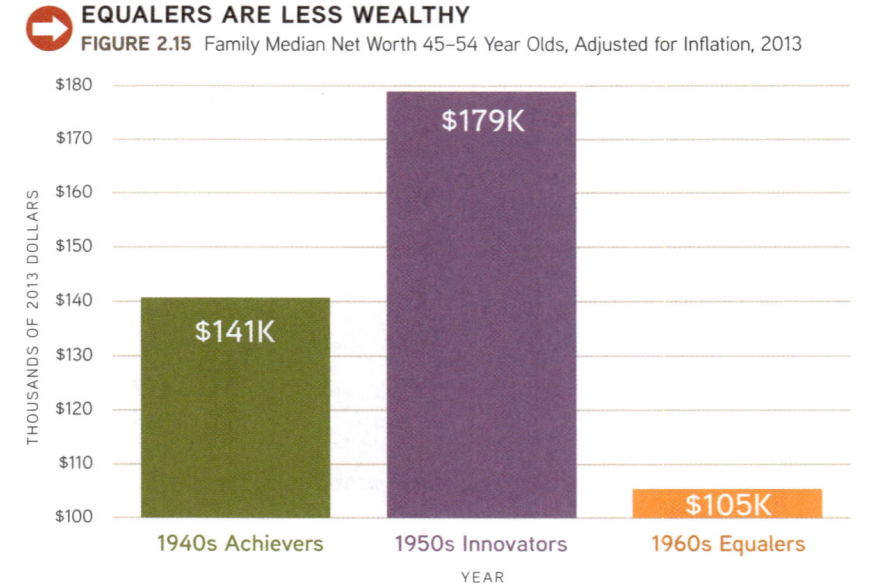

EQUALERS ARE LESS WEALTHY
FIGURE 2.15 Family Median Net Worth 45–54 Year Olds, Adjusted for Inflation, 2013

- 1940s Achievers: $141K
- 1950s Innovators: $179K
- 1960s Equalers: $105K

Source: 2013 Survey of Consumer Finances, colors based on the majority of 45–54-year-olds in the survey year

The children of the 1960s grew up to buy their first homes at the start of the government-engineered early 1990s homeownership push. They purchased spacious houses with skylights, vaulted ceilings, and two-story foyers. These homes catered to dual-income households with large kitchen islands (handy for takeout or a quick meal) and personal sanctuaries for those with hectic schedules. New homes included large master suites, luxurious baths, and walk-in closets. Equalers struggled through the Great Recession in the late 2000s at ages when people typically purchase houses. The second-home markets struggled. Many of them also bought large move-up homes right before the housing market crashed—and suffered for that timing.

True to the name we've given their generation, Equaler men take on a much bigger share of childcare and housework than their fathers did. In 2004, nearly 21% of nonworking Equaler males, aged 35 to 44 at the time, cited childcare as the reason they didn't work. Contrast that with only 3% of 1940s Achievers men at the same age. While many mothers will attest this doesn't mean men participate equally in childcare, it does show a shift toward more equal participation. More fathers stay at home as well, while Mom works.

1960s EQUALER DADS INCREASINGLY STAY AT HOME TO RAISE THE KIDS.

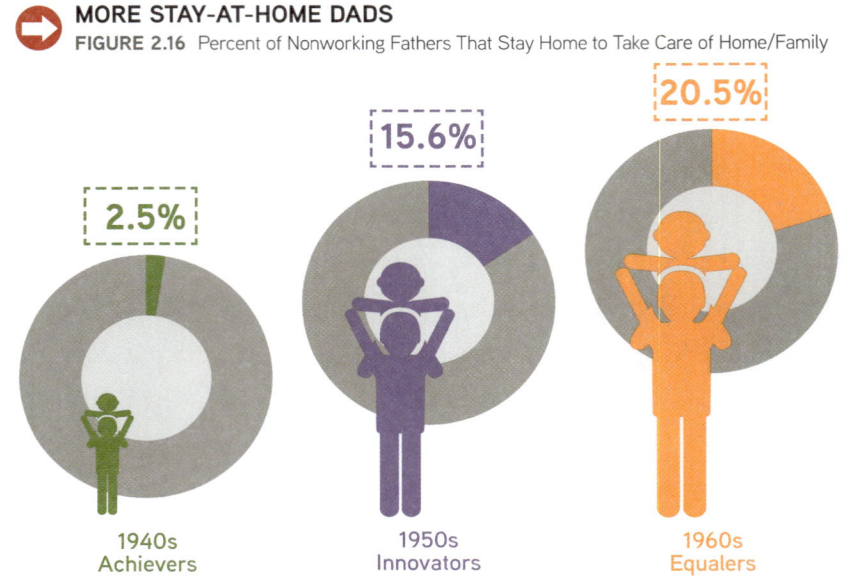

MORE STAY-AT-HOME DADS
FIGURE 2.16 Percent of Nonworking Fathers That Stay Home to Take Care of Home/Family

2.5% — 1940s Achievers
15.6% — 1950s Innovators
20.5% — 1960s Equalers

Source: John Burns Real Estate Consulting, LLC calculations of US Census Bureau, Current Population Survey, Annual Social and Economic Supplements

Equalers will retire less affluent. They will rely heavily on their 401(k) savings rather than pension plans. Their share of Social Security will likely diminish too. Many Equalers intend to live with their kids in retirement to save money. Living together helps everyone financially.

THE 1970s BALANCERS

"[It's about] getting the kids up and fed, getting one to school, getting the other down for a nap, going to the grocery store, picking one up from school, getting the other one down for another nap, cooking dinner ...I live my life at these two extremes. I'm either a full-time stay-at-home mom or a full-time actress."

—Jennifer Garner[9]

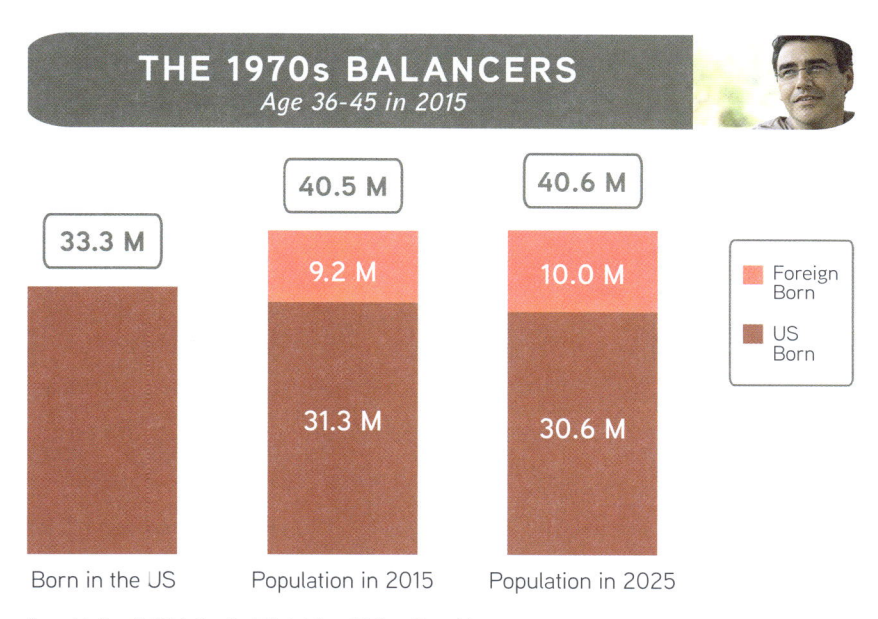

THE 1970s BALANCERS
Age 36-45 in 2015

Born in the US	Population in 2015	Population in 2025
33.3 M	40.5 M (9.2 M Foreign Born + 31.3 M US Born)	40.6 M (10.0 M Foreign Born + 30.6 M US Born)

Source: John Burns Real Estate Consulting, LLC calculations of US Census Bureau data

Think of the 41 million 1970s Balancers as the classmates of Leonardo DiCaprio, Jennifer Garner, Reese Witherspoon, and Kobe Bryant. Their ages ranged from 36 to 45 in 2015. They comprise the most diverse group of all generations, with 23% of them born in another country.

---

9   Jenny Comita, "Jennifer Garner: School drop-offs, diaper changes, and the occasional love scene—all the while being stalked by the paparazzi. Jennifer Garner masters the art of motherhood, Hollywood-style," *W Magazine*, January 2010, http://www.wmagazine.com/culture/film-and-tv/2010/01/jennifer_garner.

Aged 22 to 31 years old on the tragic day of 9/11, the 1970s Balancers best exemplify some of the societal shifts that occurred that day. On 9/11, Americans looked themselves in their mirror and asked, "What matters most to me in life?" As you will see in many of the charts in this book, numerous trends reversed themselves that day.

The 1970s Balancer childhood years were more isolated than prior generations. For most, both parents worked, leaving the kids home alone in the afternoon. TV shows and video games such as Donkey Kong and Pac-Man provided company. The number of TV sets per house rose 25% during the 1980s. Personal computers became widely accessible. The Balancers didn't join extracurricular clubs, athletic teams, or student government as much as earlier generations. They shared the house with fewer siblings too. They relied on fast food more than ever before, doubling the rate of childhood obesity in the process.

The Balancers wanted their MTV, and they got it. Professional music videos exploded in the '80s, long before YouTube's offerings. Those videos featured increasingly provocative dance numbers and eventually grunge and rap. They listened to Madonna, Michael Jackson, Prince, Pearl Jam, Nirvana, Dr. Dre, and Snoop Dogg. TV shows depicted less-conventional families such as in *Full House* or *Friends*. They came to define friends as family.

Once again, television producers identified an early societal shift. In 1992, Candice Bergen's television character Murphy Brown chose to give birth as a single mother. The nation took notice when Vice President Dan Quayle criticized her decision. The 13–22-year-old Balancer women also took notice. Parenting alone surged.

Balancer careers started well. They competed less for jobs since there were fewer of them. The '90s Internet revolution sparked a strong economy. At the height of the tech boom, the highly educated 1970s Balancers' incomes neared an all-time high for 25–34-year-olds.

After the 9/11 tragedy, Balancers led a pronounced societal shift toward more focus on family. Both men and women began staying at home more. This shift reversed a trend that had lasted more than 50 years.

BY 2000, 73% OF WORKING-AGE WOMEN WORKED.

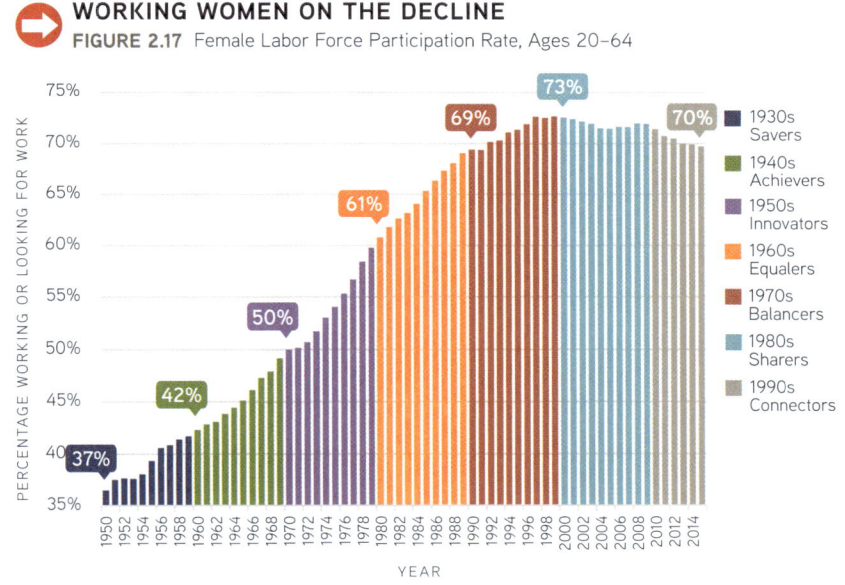

WORKING WOMEN ON THE DECLINE

FIGURE 2.17 Female Labor Force Participation Rate, Ages 20–64

Source: John Burns Real Estate Consulting, LLC calculations of Bureau of Labor Statistics data; color-coded based on the year a generation turns 20

The percentage of dual-income households completely reversed course, dropping from 57% of married couples in 2000 to 51% in 2014. The decline in workers per household has contributed to less income than prior generations too. Income alone does not define success for Balancers, unlike prior generations. A happy personal life is just as important.

53

1970s Balancer and coauthor Chris Porter experiences the shift to have more family and work balance every day. His wife, Jess, left her job as a school principal when their first child was born. While work takes up a huge chunk of each day, Chris devotes as much time as possible to his family. Technology helps, as he can return emails one-handed while holding a child or access the company network from his laptop at naptime on the weekend.

1970s BALANCER COUPLES LED THE WAY FOR MORE WORK/FAMILY BALANCE, WITH ONLY 51% OF HOUSEHOLDS NOW HAVING 2+ WORKERS.

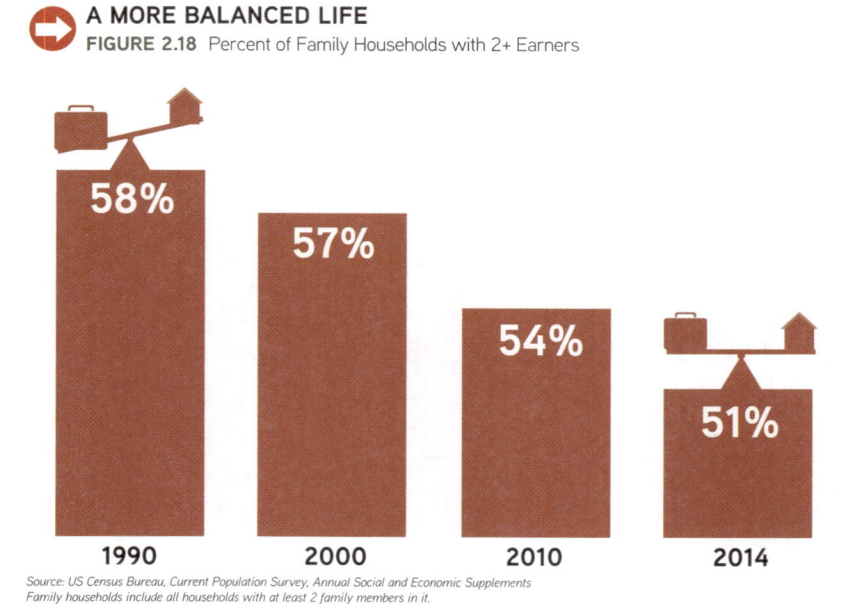

A MORE BALANCED LIFE
FIGURE 2.18 Percent of Family Households with 2+ Earners

1990	2000	2010	2014
58%	57%	54%	51%

Source: US Census Bureau, Current Population Survey, Annual Social and Economic Supplements
Family households include all households with at least 2 family members in it.

Balancer women start their families later in life. They further their educations and careers before having kids. Enabled by technologies like in vitro fertilization (IVF), their biological clock does not tick as loud in their early 30s as it did for prior generations of women.

2: GENERATIONS BY DECADE

1970s Balancers also led a shift to stay at home with the kids. In that pivotal year of 2001, stay-at-home moms increased after decades of decline. Six percent more mothers stay at home now than in 2000. Far more women now work from home, too, enabled by Internet access.

STAY-AT-HOME MOMS PLUMMETED FROM 44% IN 1975 TO 23% IN 2000. THE BALANCERS LED A REVERSAL TO 29% SINCE.

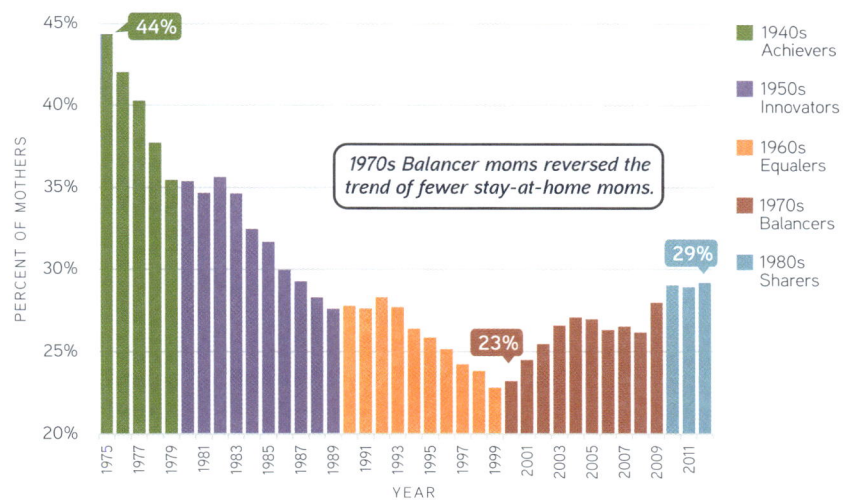

MORE MOMS ARE NOW STAYING HOME
FIGURE 2.19 Share of Moms Who Stay at Home Full Time

1970s Balancer moms reversed the trend of fewer stay-at-home moms.

Source: John Burns Real Estate Consulting, LLC calculations of US Census Bureau, Current Population Survey, Annual Social and Economic Supplements via IPUMS-CPS; colors based on a 30-year-old mother

1970s Balancer fathers spend more time with family. They have tripled the hours per week spent on childcare in comparison to their dads. Men and women born in the '70s share more domestic duties, including housework and childcare. As a variety of blogs, TV shows, and events attest, plenty of men have embraced the shift in gender roles. A rising number of men also stay at home.

When the housing bubble burst in the late 2000s, millions of Americans lost their jobs. Home values fell. Foreclosures hit the 1970s

Balancers harder than any other generation. Balancers had purchased starter homes for their young families in the early 2000s, often borrowing the entire purchase price. Unable to make the mortgage payment, Balancers fell from having the highest homeownership rate ever for their age group to the lowest homeownership rate for their age group.

Balancer families turned to renting single-family homes. Almost 12% of all households in the country now rent a home. In 2013, young families rented twice as many single-family homes as apartments. Large, publicly traded companies emerged to satisfy the demand, purchasing and maintaining these homes for families to rent.

Many Balancers who escaped foreclosure don't have much equity in their home today. Home purchases have slowed as a result.

The housing crash of the late 2000s and the decision to work less have left the Balancers far worse off financially than prior generations. The Balancers' net worth amounts to only $47,000 per household today—about half the net worth of the previous generation at the same age. They will almost certainly buy fewer homes than previous generations and live more frequently with their parents later in adulthood.

2: GENERATIONS BY DECADE

AT $47K, 1970s BALANCERS HAVE THE LOWEST NET WORTH IN GENERATIONS.

THE BALANCERS HAVE LOW NET WORTH
FIGURE 2.20 Median Net Worth 35–44 Year-Olds, Adjusted for Inflation

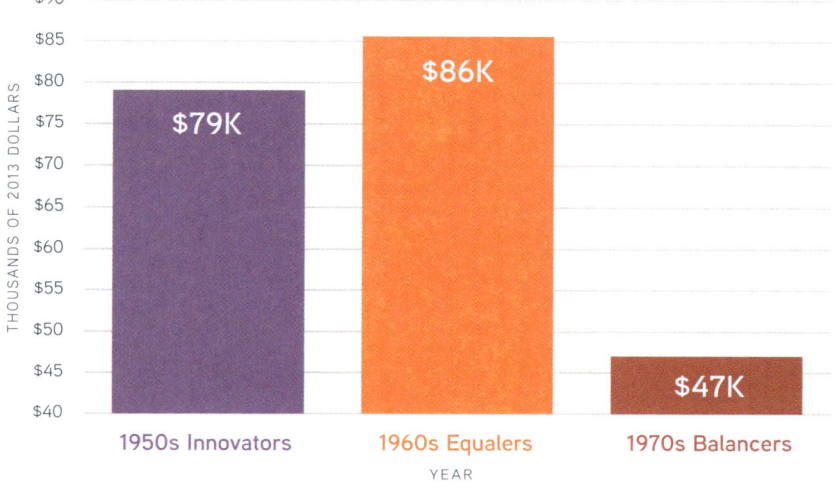

Generation	Median Net Worth
1950s Innovators	$79K
1960s Equalers	$86K
1970s Balancers	$47K

THOUSANDS OF 2013 DOLLARS
YEAR

Source: 2013 Survey of Consumer Finances, colors based on the majority of 45–54-year-olds in the survey year

THE 1980s SHARERS

"Facebook was not originally created to be a company. It was built to accomplish a social mission—to make the world more open and connected."

—Mark Zuckerberg[10]

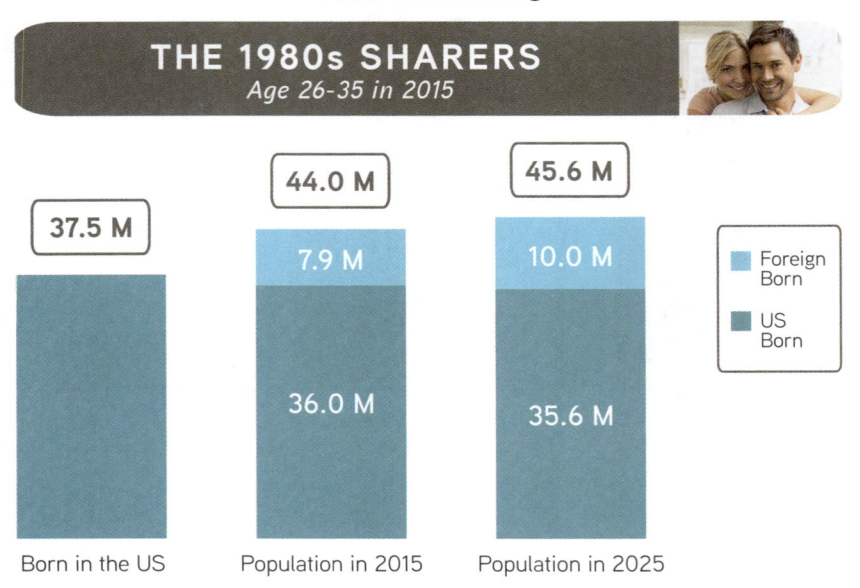

THE 1980s SHARERS
Age 26-35 in 2015

	Born in the US	Population in 2015	Population in 2025
Total	37.5 M	44.0 M	45.6 M
Foreign Born		7.9 M	10.0 M
US Born	37.5 M	36.0 M	35.6 M

Source: John Burns Real Estate Consulting, LLC calculations of US Census Bureau data

Think of the 44 million 1980s Sharers as the classmates of Beyoncé Knowles, LeBron James, Mark Zuckerberg, and Taylor Swift—people who share all things personal via social media. Their less-affluent peers also share possessions and see value in renting rather than owning. Due to continued immigration, we expect their numbers to grow to 45.6 million by 2025, including 10 million immigrants.

Those born in the 1980s created the sharing economy. Using their smartphone, they share photos on Instagram, opinions on

---

10   United States Securities and Exchange Commission, "Facebook, Inc. Form S-1 Registration Statement," February 1, 2012, https://www.sec.gov/Archives/edgar/data/1326801/000119312512034517/d287954ds1.htm.

Twitter, and recommendations on Yelp. They rent rooms on Airbnb, and hitch rides on Uber and Zipcar. Tough economic times and onerous student debt contribute to their need to share.

The Innovators doled out participation trophies and other accolades to the 1980s Sharers, making them less competitive. They also micromanaged their two kids in unprecedented ways.

The pop culture they consumed included a preponderance of teen pop (the Backstreet Boys, Britney Spears, the Spice Girls), rock (Coldplay) and rap (Eminem). Their TV shows portrayed society's relaxing moral standards. The ironically named *Family Guy* became popular, as well as shows with overt sexual content such as *Sex and the City*, *Baywatch*, *Friends*, and *Melrose Place*.

Many 1980s Sharers get along exceptionally well with their folks. Around 63% of their parents prefer their adult children living at home to living elsewhere. Thirty percent of Sharers cite debt as the reason they postpone buying a house.[11] Debt—primarily student debt—prevents many Sharers from buying cars, getting married, and having kids.

---

11   Janna Herron, "Survey: Student loan debt forces many to put life on hold," Bankrate Money Pulse survey, July 9–12, 2015, http://www.bankrate.com/finance/consumer-index/money-pulse-0815.aspx.

STUDENT DEBT DELAYS MARRIAGE, KIDS, AND HOME BUYING FOR UP TO 30% OF YOUNG ADULTS.

STUDENT DEBT DELAYS YOUNG ADULT MILESTONES
FIGURE 2.21 Percent of People Aged 18–40 with Student Loan Debt Who Delayed These Milestones because of That Debt

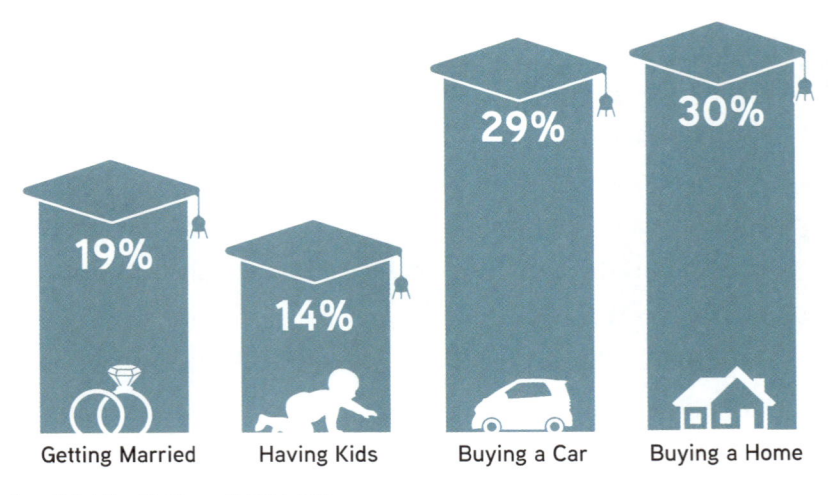

Getting Married	Having Kids	Buying a Car	Buying a Home
19%	14%	29%	30%

Source: Bankrate Money Pulse Survey, published August 2015

In comparison to their grandparents, 1980s Sharers delay marriage by five years and childbirth by three years. More than half of Sharers remained single and childless in 2013, up a whopping 10% from just seven years prior. At age 30, people used to call single women "old maids." Societal pressures to marry and have children have eased.

1980s SHARERS SIGNIFICANTLY DELAYED MARRIAGE AND CHILDREN, WITH MORE THAN HALF NOW SINGLE AND CHILDLESS IN THEIR LATE 20s.

SINGLE AND CHILDLESS FOR LONGER
FIGURE 2.22 Percent of 25–29 Year-Olds Single and without Children

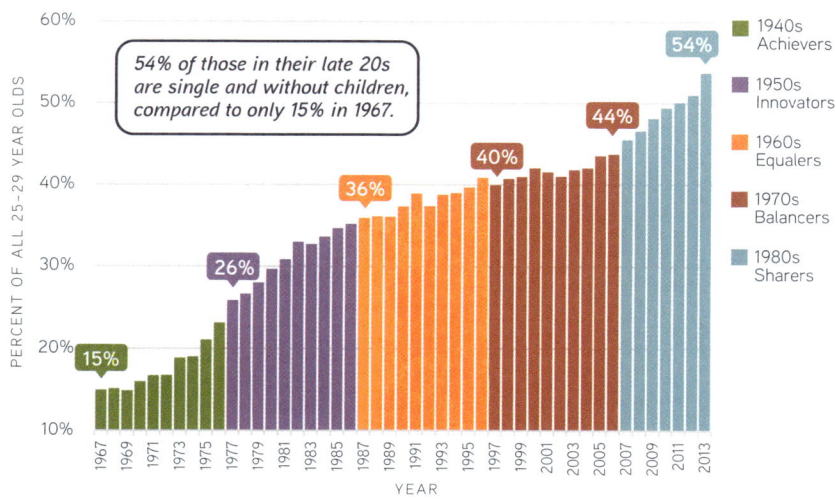

54% of those in their late 20s are single and without children, compared to only 15% in 1967.

Legend:
- 1940s Achievers
- 1950s Innovators
- 1960s Equalers
- 1970s Balancers
- 1980s Sharers

Source: John Burns Real Estate Consulting, LLC calculations of US Census Bureau, Current Population Survey, Annual Social and Economic Supplements via IPUMS-CPS

The thrifty 1980s Sharers earned more college degrees than any generation before them. Thirty-five percent of Sharers graduated from college—the highest percentage of any generation. Student debt hit an all-time record with the Sharers, ballooning from $260 billion in 2004 to $874 billion in 2011, when the youngest Sharers turned 22. Student-loan debt for all ages now tops $1.2 trillion, or more than $30,000 per student.

STUDENT-LOAN DEBT INCREASED NEARLY FIVE-FOLD FROM 2004 TO 2015 AND NOW TOTALS MORE THAN $1.2 TRILLION.

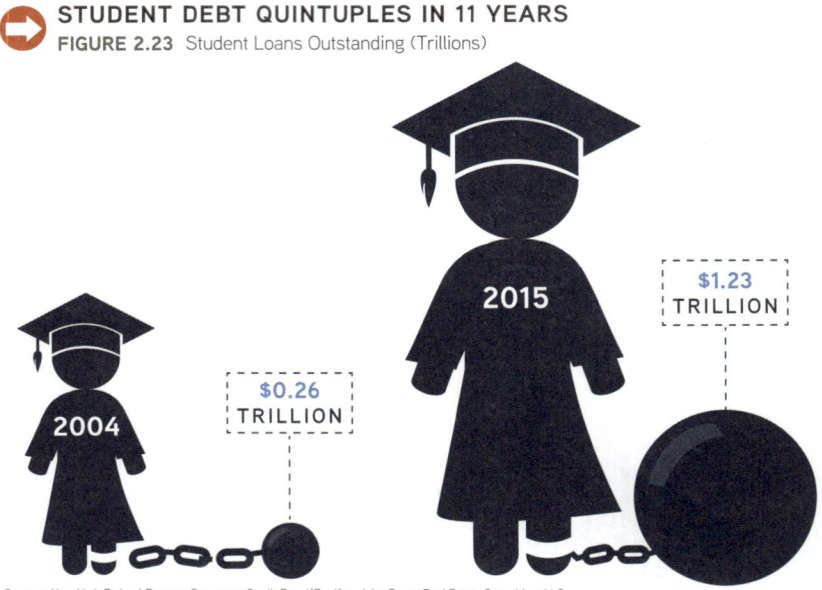

STUDENT DEBT QUINTUPLES IN 11 YEARS
FIGURE 2.23 Student Loans Outstanding (Trillions)

2004 — $0.26 TRILLION
2015 — $1.23 TRILLION

Sources: New York Federal Reserve Consumer Credit Panel/Equifax; John Burns Real Estate Consulting, LLC

1980s Sharers have dealt with tough financial obstacles, since the Great Recession occurred just as they entered the job market. Those challenges haven't sapped their zest for life, though. Adults under the age of 35 were 63% more likely to agree with the statement, "The share economy allows me to take more risks" than older adults.[12] The 1999 Columbine shooting by one of their own and the 9/11 terrorist attacks served as stark reminders to enjoy life day by day. YOLO (you only live once) has become a Sharer rallying cry.

The Sharers take pride in dealing creatively with fewer resources. They pool resources through endeavors such as Kickstarter and other

---

12 Ford Motor Company, *Looking Forward with Ford: 2015 Trends*, 44–46, https://www.at.ford.com/content/dam/atford/archive/2014_NA/Dec/Ford-2015-TrendReportBook.pdf.

crowdfunding sites. They care about their impact on the environment and see urban life as both efficient and cool. That view, plus insurance expenses, has made driver's licenses less necessary. Only 81% of the Sharers held a driver's license at age 20–24, compared to 87% of the 1970s Balancers at the same age.

The Sharers have had lower incomes than the Balancers. During the Sharer's careers, young-adult incomes declined about 1% per year for 13 consecutive years. That is not all bad news, as the decline was from an all-time high for the Balancers early in their careers. Adjusting for inflation, Sharer incomes resemble the Innovators' and Equalers' at the same age. The 1980s Sharers, however, struggle with far more student debt.

YOUNG ADULT INCOMES FELL ABOUT 1% PER YEAR SINCE 2000, DESPITE RISING EDUCATION LEVELS.

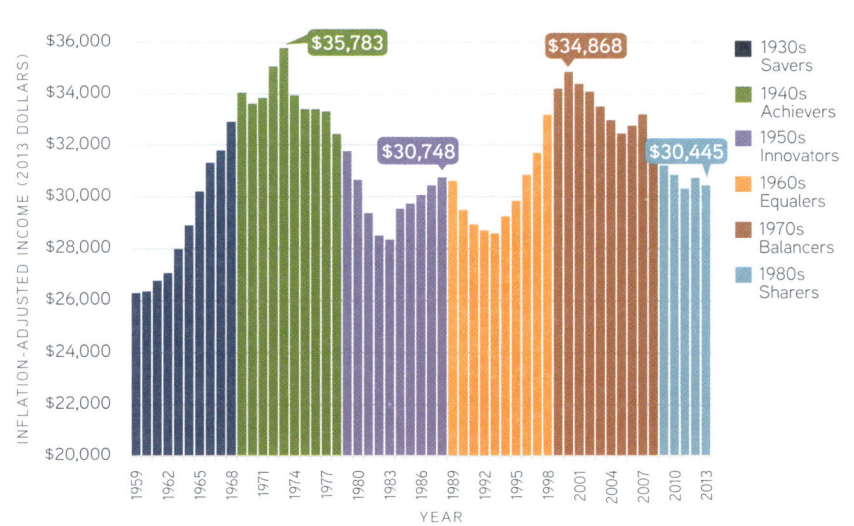

YOUNG ADULTS INCOMES PLUNGING 1% PER YEAR SINCE 2000

FIGURE 2.24 Real Median Income, People Aged 25–34 (2013 Dollars)

- 1930s Savers
- 1940s Achievers: $35,783
- 1950s Innovators: $30,748
- 1960s Equalers
- 1970s Balancers: $34,868
- 1980s Sharers: $30,445

Source: US Census Bureau, Current Population Survey, Annual Social and Economic Supplements

In some ways, Sharers resemble the Innovator generation of Bill Gates and Steve Jobs. In late 2015, Forbes reported that 29 Sharer entrepreneurs each built a $400+ million personal net worth.[13] Most founded tech companies such as Facebook, WhatsApp, Airbnb, Snapchat, and Pinterest.

The Sharers who left home frequently live in urban locales. Since they don't have kids, they can live urban. Cities that invested in improving their downtowns, reducing crime and adding entertainment, captured much of the growth. For financial and family reasons, most will eventually move to the suburbs or to the South for affordability and schools.

---

13   Luisa Kroll, "America's Richest Entrepreneurs Under 40," *Forbes*, November 18, 2015, http://www.forbes.com/sites/luisakroll/2015/11/18/americas-richest-entrepreneurs-under-40/.

THE 1990s CONNECTORS

"Success is nothing if you don't have the right people to share it with; you're just gonna end up lonely."

—Selena Gomez[14]

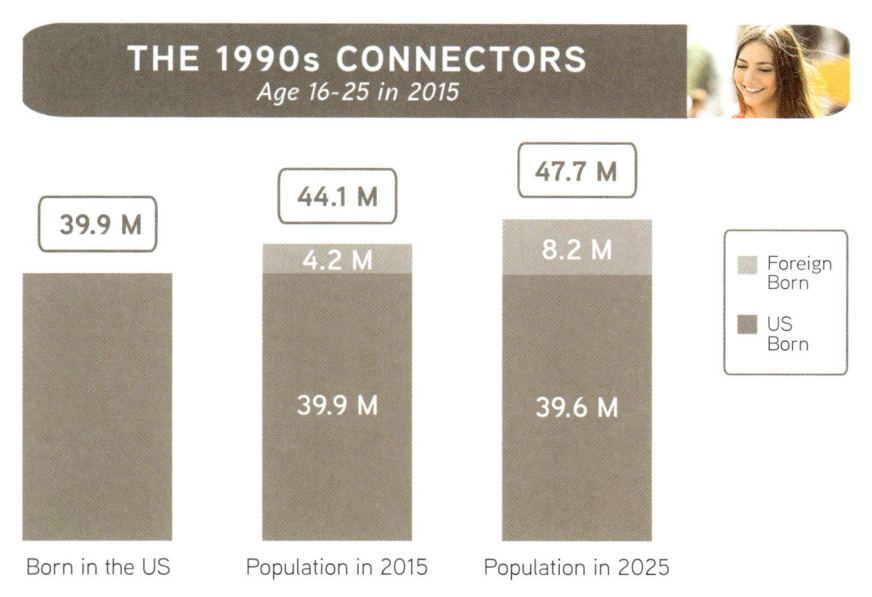

THE 1990s CONNECTORS
Age 16-25 in 2015

	Born in the US	Population in 2015	Population in 2025
Total	39.9 M	44.1 M	47.7 M
Foreign Born		4.2 M	8.2 M
US Born	39.9 M	39.9 M	39.6 M

Source: John Burns Real Estate Consulting, LLC calculations of US Census Bureau data

Think of the 44 million 1990s Connectors as the classmates of Jennifer Lawrence, Selena Gomez, Malia Obama, and Canadian-born Justin Bieber. Their childhoods coincided with rising diversity tied to an immigration surge. They stay connected 24/7 to their global friends and the world. Their numbers should swell to 47.7 million by 2025, including 8.2 million born elsewhere.

Births surged from 1989 to 1993, resulting in a greater number of 23- to 27-year-olds living in the US in 2016 than at any time in history. The Connectors will be by far the largest generation in 2025.

---

14 Selena Gomez, "Ryan Seacrest with Selena Gomez," interview, E! Network, July 21, 2013, https://www.youtube.com/watch?v=w9VmyzGc8QY.

The lives of those born in the 1990s revolve around connecting with friends and family. They connect to and depend on their parents. They connect wirelessly with each other from a young age.

The Connectors faced tough social and economic challenges growing up. These outside forces continue to shape their generation. They watched their parents struggle with the Great Recession in the late 2000s. Their families broke along the way. Only 46% of children born between 1996 and 2012 lived in the same household as both biological parents in 2013. Such factors might explain in part the value they place on friends, whom they consider tantamount to family. In 2014, 76% of adults agreed with this statement: "My definition of family includes good friends who aren't blood relatives."[15]

The Connectors embrace diversity. Many of their parents immigrated here. Many of them can only remember Barack Obama as president. They don't remember the military adopting its "Don't ask, don't tell" policy in 1993. By the time the oldest turned 11, the military had already repealed the policy. As the oldest turned 26, same-sex marriage became legal, and "gender identity" became a national issue.

Perhaps it shouldn't surprise anyone that the Connectors' music celebrates uniqueness. They stream Beyoncé, Katy Perry, Lady Gaga, Maroon 5, Taylor Swift, Justin Bieber, and Miley Cyrus songs on their smartphones. Their TV shows emphasize diverse families, as well as friends with the status of family: *The Big Bang Theory*, *Gossip Girl*, *Modern Family*, and *How I Met Your Mother*. They stream content from YouTube (where an agent discovered Justin Bieber). Netflix plays commercial-free TV.

---

15   Ford Motor Company, *Looking Forward with Ford: 2015 Trends*, 44–46, https://www.at.ford.com/content/dam/atford/archive/2014_NA/Dec/Ford-2015-TrendReportBook.pdf.

Connectors get news from their friends' posts online. They follow social trends online as well. Many show no hesitation about posting intimate details and desires, opinions, and photos online. Snapchat has evolved as the preferred communication vehicle, since posts are not stored online.

Connectors know little privacy. In 2014, 73% of American adults agreed with the statement, "As a society, we have given up on the concept of privacy." The same survey noted that 56% of those under age 35 would share their location to get a discount coupon, compared to 42% of those over 35.[16]

Almost 20% of 1990s Connectors register as officially obese—two to three times higher than their parents. The long-term impact of childhood obesity needs more study.

---

16   Ford Motor Company, *Looking Forward with Ford: 2015 Trends*, 44–46, https://www.at.ford.com/content/dam/atford/archive/2014_NA/Dec/Ford-2015-TrendReportBook.pdf.

20% OF 1990s CONNECTORS QUALIFY AS OBESE—MORE THAN DOUBLE THE RATE OF THEIR PARENTS.

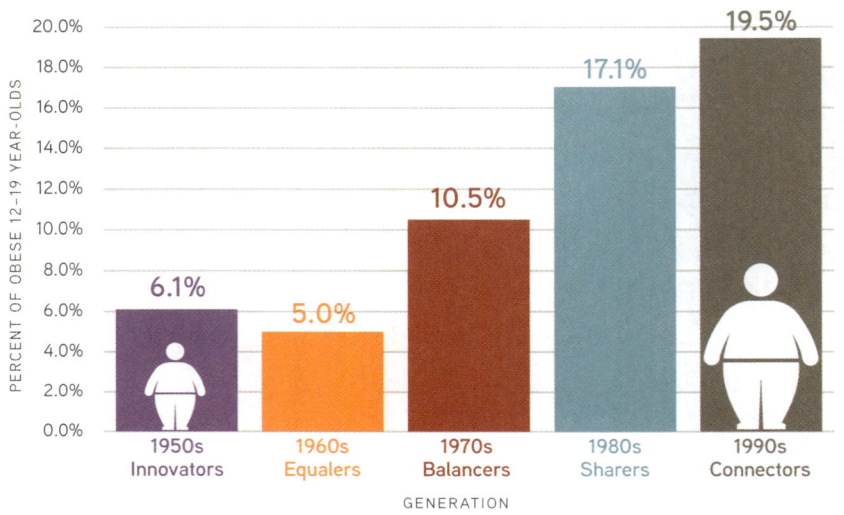

A QUADRUPLING OF CHILDHOOD OBESITY
FIGURE 2.25 Percentage of Obese 12–19 Year-Olds

Generation	Percent
1950s Innovators	6.1%
1960s Equalers	5.0%
1970s Balancers	10.5%
1980s Sharers	17.1%
1990s Connectors	19.5%

Source: Centers for Disease Control and Prevention

The Great Recession left more than 40% of Connector high school grads underemployed. They live with their helicopter parents and rely on them to an excessive degree. Only 52% of 16–19-year-olds have drivers' licenses, down sharply from 70% in 1979.

42% OF YOUNG ADULTS WORK IN JOBS BELOW THEIR QUALIFICATION LEVEL.

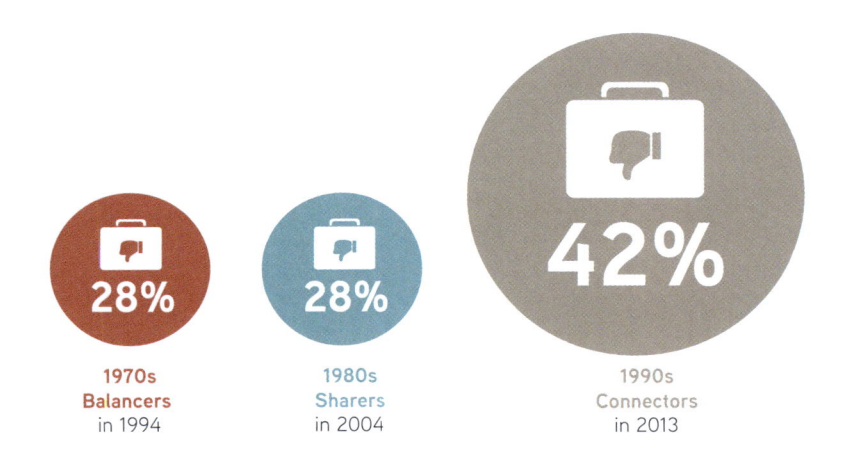

YOUNG ADULTS REALLY STRUGGLING
FIGURE 2.26 Underemployment Rate of Recent High School Graduates

28%
1970s
Balancers
in 1994

28%
1980s
Sharers
in 2004

42%
1990s
Connectors
in 2013

Source: US Census Bureau, Current Population Survey; Economic Policy Institute

The Connectors not only face difficulty finding good jobs, they struggle to pay hefty college loans. The slow economy and mounting college debt will certainly delay household formations and homeownership.

In sharp contrast to their parents, the Connectors spend more cautiously. They take on less credit-card debt, increasingly paying with cash or debit cards. In a 2014 survey, 63% of people aged 18 to 29 owned no credit cards.[17] Less debt will mean less spending, despite their enormous numbers. In some ways, they remind us of the 1930s Savers, who learned to be thrifty during the tough economic times in their childhood.

---

17 Jeanine Skowronski, "More millennials say 'no' to credit cards," Bankrate, August 2014, http://www.bankrate.com/finance/credit-cards/more-millennials-say-no-to-credit-cards-1.aspx.

THE 2000s GLOBALS

THE 2000s GLOBALS
Age 6-15 in 2015

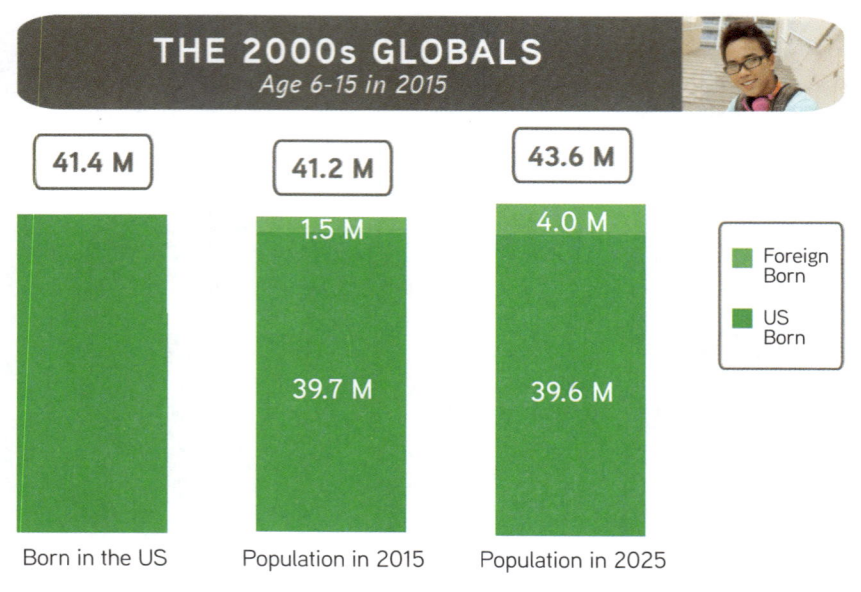

41.4 M	41.2 M	43.6 M
	1.5 M	4.0 M
	39.7 M	39.6 M
Born in the US	Population in 2015	Population in 2025

Legend: Foreign Born / US Born

Source: John Burns Real Estate Consulting, LLC calculations of US Census Bureau data

The 41 million children born in the 2000s haven't reached adulthood yet. Their numbers should swell to 43.6 million by 2025 due to immigration.

We call them the Globals because they are growing up in such a globally aware world. We don't know much about them yet since they are so young. Worldwide news spreads instantaneously now, thanks to smartphones. Many of their friends' parents come from all over the world. The emphasis on STEM (science, technology, engineering, and mathematics) education today should set them up to continue making big changes to society. On a more sobering note, they will inherit the government indebtedness and underfunded retirement programs their parents and grandparents created, making financial success difficult to achieve.

3: THE 4 BIG INFLUENCERS

Four categories of external influence have shifted demographics over time. These 4 Big Influencers are government, the economy, technology, and societal shifts. Societal shifts include changes in society's acceptance of norms, ranging from interracial and same-sex marriage to attitudes toward single parenting.

We developed the 4–5–6 Rule to provide a framework for connecting the 4 Big Influencers to the decisions people make. The **4** Big Influencers during people's **5** Main Life Stages help answer the **6** Key Consumer Questions most people want to know about generational shifts. In chapter 2, we summarized how the 4 Big Influencers (government, economy, technology, and societal shifts) impacted the 1930s Savers through the 1990s Connectors. The same events impacted the generations differently, based upon their life stage at the time. We identified five main life stages: childhood, early career, family formation, late career, and retirement. For example, the Great Recession delayed household formation for the 1980s Sharers, forced many 1970s Balancers through foreclosure, and delayed retirement for 1940s Achievers. The Great Recession's impact changed the answers to all 6 Key Consumer Questions most decision makers must ask about each generation.

These six questions are:

1. **HOW** many consumers will there be, and how much money will they have?

2. **WHAT** will they purchase?

3. **WHEN** will they purchase?

4. **WHERE** will they live/spend?

5. **WHO** will buy, and with whom will they live (spend money on and share expenses with)?

6. **WHY** will they buy certain products and not others?

Grouping data and discussion into these four categories of influence makes it easier to study and debate the big demographic shifts we see occurring in America. Future government policies, changes in economic conditions, new technologies, and changes in societal acceptance will alter each generation even more in the future.

Consider the contrasting impacts of these 4 Big Influencers on the generations:

1. **Government** – Contrast the 1992 GSE Act that started the boom in homeownership with the 2010 Dodd-Frank Act that makes homeownership very difficult for many today.

2. **Economy** – Contrast the strong economy in the 1960s and 1970s that gave the Achievers the early career boost they needed to borrow and spend their way to success with the anemic economy from 2001 through 2015 that has sent shockwaves of caution through today's fiscally conservative young adults.

THE 4 → 5 → 6 RULE

FOR DEMOGRAPHIC PREDICTIONS

FIGURE 3.1

4 — *The 4 Big Influencers*
1. Government
2. Economy
3. Technology
4. Societal Shifts

5 — *During People's 5 Main Life Stages*
1. Childhood
2. Early Career
3. Family Formation
4. Late Career
5. Retirement

6 — *Help Answer the 6 Key Consumer Questions*
1. How many will there be and how much money will they have?
2. What will they purchase?
3. When will they purchase?
4. Where will they live/spend?
5. Who will buy and who will they live with (spend money on and share expenses with)?
6. Why will they buy certain products and not others?

3. **Technology** – Contrast how birth control caused a 20% decline in births in the 1960s and 1970s with in vitro fertilization and egg-freezing technology that has resulted in rising births to women over the age of 40 today.

4. **Societal Shifts** – Contrast the decades-long rise in women's participation in the workforce through the year 2000, with the decline that started right around 9/11.

Government, economic, technological, and societal shifts influence generations differently, depending on their age and life stage at the time of the shift. The 5 Main Life Stages we analyzed for each generation are:

1. **Childhood** (ages 5 to 18–22): Parents, peers, school, the economy, and major news events influence people heavily during these impressionable years. As illustrated in the prior chapter, TV shows over the years have depicted these changes well.

2. **Early Career** (ages 18–22 to 35): The health of the economy, education levels, and debt levels largely guide decisions to rent a place, take a job, and start a family at this time of greater independence.

3. **Family Formation** (ages 20s to 30s): Declines in social pressures to marry young, the rise in the acceptability of divorce, and the adoption of birth control and fertility technologies changed US demographics forever.

4. **Late Career** (ages 40s to 50s): The economy, mortgage rates, and income growth during these years set the stage for important decisions, such as home buying and funding children's educations. These external influences, as well as work ethic and education levels, determine each

generation's ability to spend during their prime spending years of 36 to 55. The 4 Big Influencers set them up either favorably or unfavorably for their golden years.

5. **Retirement** (ages 55+): The 4 Big Influencers shape decisions about when to retire and where to live. Asset (home, savings, pensions, etc.) appreciation over time determines the level of discretionary spending. Interest rates determine retirement income as well. Government programs (Social Security, Medicare, etc.) provide a safety net for the necessities. State and local tax policies often cause retirees to relocate to lower-tax areas.

We found that some facets of even obvious changes contradict the conventional thinking. The Internet appears to increase mobility, theoretically allowing more workers to find the job they want and live wherever they want. In actuality, US residents have steadily moved less often over the last three decades. Other well-documented trends—income inequality or America's growing immigrant population—often get misinterpreted, their causes and implications distorted. For example, rarely do you hear about the rise in both spouses having a college education as a contributor to income inequality.

Nearly every discussion about how one young adult differs from his/her parents or grandparents fits into one of these four categories: government, economy, technology, and societal shifts. What were mortgage rates when you bought a home?

> **NEARLY EVERY DISCUSSION ABOUT HOW ONE YOUNG ADULT DIFFERS FROM HIS/HER PARENTS OR GRANDPARENTS FITS INTO ONE OF THESE FOUR CATEGORIES: GOVERNMENT, ECONOMY, TECHNOLOGY, AND SOCIETAL SHIFTS.**

Did you enter the workforce before or after the Internet arrived? Had laws banning discrimination in housing, employment, or education passed before you came of age? Did you face expectations to stay home and raise kids full time? Mapping how these key influencers affected various generations and national trends in the past allows decision makers to anticipate how the 4 Big Influencers will shape future spending patterns.

GOVERNMENT

Government policies, programs, and legal rulings create dramatic demographic shifts. We summarize some of the biggest impacts in this section. By understanding the past, this section should help you plan for shifts caused by future government actions. Please do not construe anything in this section as a policy endorsement. We are not qualified to opine on policy—just to report the impacts.

The enormous impact of government policy on demographic trends appears clearly in where people live and how people spend. Government policy plays a huge role in homeownership, which in turn affects countless industries—homebuilding, moving, furnishings, appliances, and utilities, just to name a few. Federal government highway investments in the 1950s created the suburbs. More recently, local government urban revitalization investments contributed to an urban population resurgence.

Throughout the early 1900s, about 45% of households owned their home. Since 1960, homeownership has registered north of 60%. In large part, the spike was due to massive government influence wielded through government agencies and laws such as the FHA (Federal Housing Administration), Fannie Mae, the Fed, and the GI Bill. The FHA has insured more than 34 million properties since 1934. It allows purchases with just a 3.5% down payment, putting homeownership within reach for millions (FHA-insured loans accounted for one in four new home-financings during 2009 and 2010). The government created Fannie Mae in 1938 to boost homeownership by expanding the secondary-mortgage market. It, too, has helped put consumers in houses. The closely watched Federal Reserve also deeply affects the housing market by steering interest rates. Fed policies have increased homeownership since the abnormally high interest rates of the early 1980s.

Coauthor John Burns and his wife, Anne, benefited tremendously from the Federal Reserve's decisions to drop interest rates over time. Purchasing their first townhome in 1991, they chose an 8.5% adjustable-rate mortgage to keep the payment low while Anne returned to school to get her MBA. The interest rate could have risen to as high as 13.5% per the loan agreement, but rates fell throughout the six years they owned the home. Even though they sold the home in 1997 at a loss, they moved into a larger home for their growing family and eventually accomplished their goal of paying off their mortgage by the age of 50. Many people born before 1975 share similar stories, while few born after 1975 experienced the same government-induced wealth creation.

Government policies can backfire too. The 1992 Government-Sponsored Enterprises (GSE) Act continued the trajectory of past government policies by boosting affordable homeownership, especially among underserved populations. The GSE policy looked successful initially, growing the homeownership rate another 4%+. But many of those helped by the policy eventually could not pay their mortgage payments, resulting in huge foreclosures from 2009 through 2012. Intended to increase homeownership, the GSE Act ultimately contributed to the opposite effect. 1970s Balancers suffered the most devastating impact. Balancers went from having the highest homeownership rate for their age group in their early 20s to the lowest homeownership rate in the post-World War II era for those aged 36 to 45.

THE 1992 GSE ACT MANDATED MORE MORTGAGES TO LOW-INCOME BORROWERS, KICK-STARTING A 12-YEAR SURGE IN HOMEOWNERSHIP THAT COMPLETELY UNRAVELED, HURTING THE 1970s BALANCERS THE MOST.

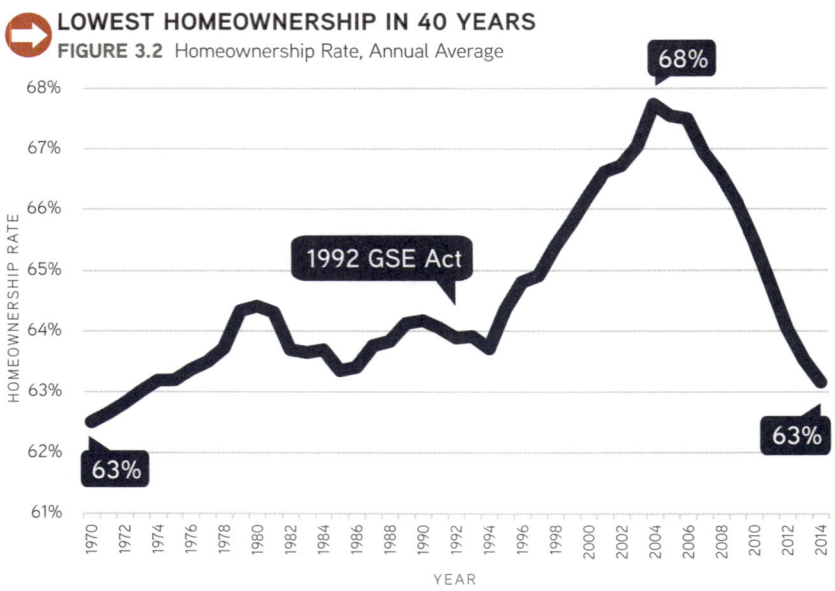

LOWEST HOMEOWNERSHIP IN 40 YEARS
FIGURE 3.2 Homeownership Rate, Annual Average

Source: John Burns Real Estate Consulting based on US Census Bureau data

In response to the 2008 financial crisis, government created new requirements that now make it more difficult to achieve homeownership than it was during the 2000s. These new policies continue to push the US homeownership rate lower and will prevent many of today's renters from becoming homeowners. Some policy experts believe that today's mortgage policies are far too tight, preventing millions from becoming homeowners. Other policy experts believe today's policies are still too loose and will result in many foreclosures during the next recession. All we can say for sure is that mortgage policy has significant demographic implications. Future changes in policy will impact millions of households.

Government immigration policy provides another clear example of this Big Influencer at work. The Immigration and Nationality Act of 1965 and three subsequent laws passed between 1980 and 1990 changed the criteria for new immigrants. The new laws opened the doors to a massive wave of newcomers after 60 years of low immigration. As a result, the government issued more green cards in the 20-year period from 1990 to 2009 than in the prior 60 years combined.

The massive immigration in the 1990s and 2000s filled in the 1970s Baby Bust. Thanks to immigration, today's population of people born in the 1970s includes 23% born in another country, and is only 6% less than those born in the 1960s. Immigration history shows just how dramatically US population growth can change with the stroke of the legislative pen.

MORE IMMIGRANTS LEGALLY MOVED TO THE US FROM 1990-2009 THAN THE PRIOR 60 YEARS, RESULTING IN 23% OF THE 1970s BALANCERS BEING FOREIGN-BORN.

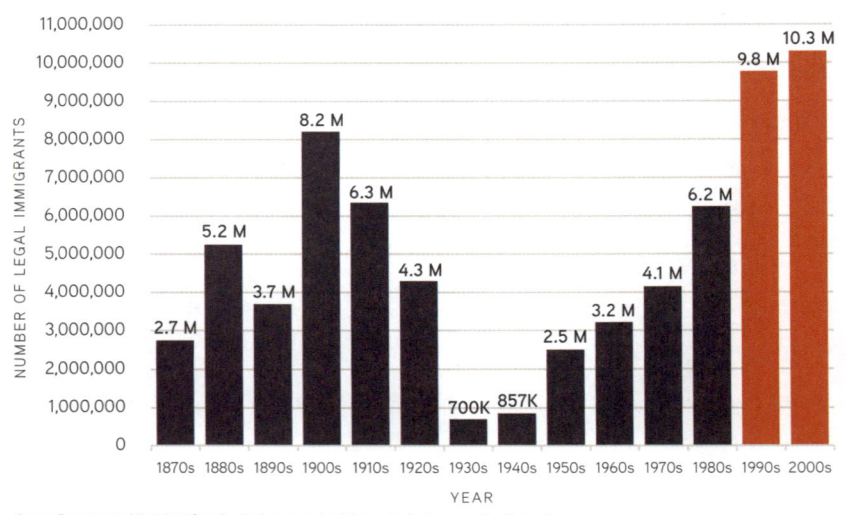

SURGING LEGAL IMMIGRATION
FIGURE 3.3 Legal Immigration by Decade

Decade	Number of Legal Immigrants
1870s	2.7 M
1880s	5.2 M
1890s	3.7 M
1900s	8.2 M
1910s	6.3 M
1920s	4.3 M
1930s	700K
1940s	857K
1950s	2.5 M
1960s	3.2 M
1970s	4.1 M
1980s	6.2 M
1990s	9.8 M
2000s	10.3 M

Source: Department of Homeland Security, legal green card recipients only, fiscal years ending September

Immigration has changed even more dramatically since 2010. Many of today's recent newcomers hail from India and China—which recently surpassed Mexico as the top source of new immigrants. Growing numbers of recent immigrants arrive with college degrees and plenty of money. The affluent foreign-born now purchase one of every seven homes sold in the US. The less-affluent are more difficult to find. The construction and agriculture industries that have historically relied on Mexican labor complain of huge labor shortages. We devoted chapter 5 of the book to these immigration shifts.

Other long-established programs many now take for granted impact demographic trends substantially. Social Security and Medicare, for example, have enabled millions of seniors to live independently from their families. Around 62% of those 75 or older head households today, compared to just 45% in 1950. This massive shift, which created demand for millions of additional houses, could not have occurred without government entitlement programs. Similarly, welfare, Medicaid, unemployment insurance, disability insurance, and the earned income tax credit have helped millions continue to head households who otherwise would have lived with others or on the streets. Since many of these programs have not been properly funded, significant policy changes will almost certainly occur. Stay tuned for future shifts in how and where people live.

38 MILLION PEOPLE RECEIVE SOCIAL SECURITY BENEFITS TODAY, COMPARED TO JUST 13 MILLION IN 1970.

RAPIDLY RISING SOCIAL SECURITY RECIPIENTS
FIGURE 3.4 Retirees Receiving Social Security Benefits (Millions)

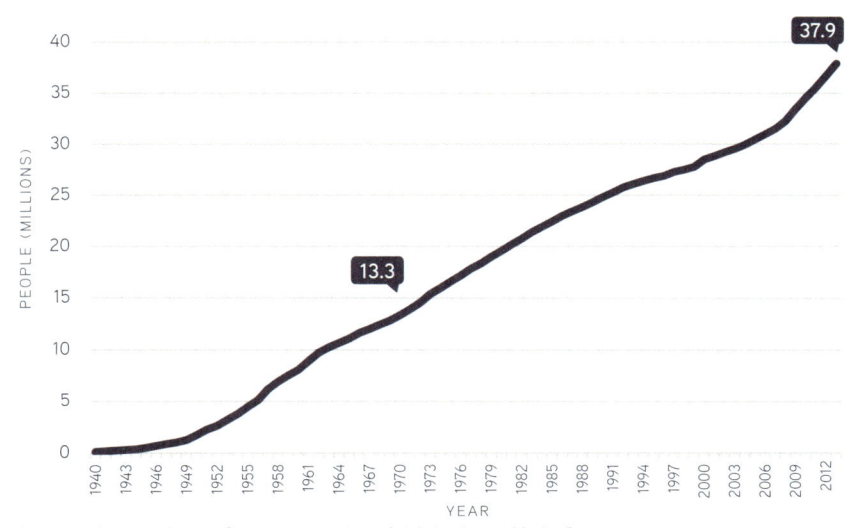

Source: Social Security Administration. Retired workers only—does not include dependents receiving benefits

The judicial branch of government also influences demographics, particularly through the Supreme Court's interpretation of the US Constitution. The legalization of abortion in 1973, coupled with the approval of the birth-control pill in 1960, resulted in far fewer children born in the 1970s. The 1970s saw 9.3 million abortions, and the next three decades 12 million to 16 million each, before the numbers began to fall. Think of the massive demographic impact of the *Roe v. Wade* abortion ruling—a single action by a Big Influencer—in terms of lower population numbers, fewer shotgun marriages, and higher percentages of wanted children. Would 50 million more people live in the US today?

State and local government decisions likewise drive big demographic shifts. For years, income- and property-tax policies pushed retirees out of New Jersey, New York, Connecticut, and Illinois. Those migrants flocked to Florida, Texas, and Nevada, where residents pay less taxes. Seniors simply don't want to pay high local taxes, particularly to fund schools attended by other peoples' children. But seniors aren't the only migrants. City investments in urban revitalization grew the populations in downtown San Diego and New York. Arizona's passage of Senate Bill 1070 in 2010 contributed to a massive out-migration of the Mexican foreign-born population. Colorado's 2014 legalization of marijuana contributed to an increase in migration of young adults. Coincidentally or not, apartment rents surged in Denver in 2014 and 2015. As you can see, local government decisions can alter demographics.

We continuously track government policy changes to note their possible effects on demographics. In our forecasts in coming chapters, we will make certain assumptions about future government policy—interest rates, homeownership, immigration, and other topics. We will assume what we consider the most likely scenario today, knowing full well that these assumptions will need to change over time.

Government will continue to influence the answers to the 6 Key Consumer Questions. How will immigration policy affect population growth? What mortgage qualifications will be necessary to purchase a home? When will marijuana become legal, if at all? Where will infrastructure investments shift development? Will more LGBT people live together now that same-sex marriage is legal? Why will certain ethnic restaurants grow faster than others?

ECONOMY

Most people understand the important role the economy plays each year, but rarely do they look at the impact over one decade or longer. Strategic long-term thinkers reflect on the economy's deeper demographic influences, the effects that can last many generations.

In one way or another, every American feels the effects of America's anemic economic growth since 2000. The economic growth rate during people's working years heavily impacts major life decisions: getting married, having children, taking vacations, renting or buying a home, and retiring.

The economic performance of 2000 to 2015 resembled the 1930s Depression era more closely than any intervening period. From 2007 to 2010, stock and home prices fell dramatically, negatively impacting every generation. The conservatively positioned 1930s Savers saw their net worth fall by 12%. Those born in the 1940s through the 1960s lost 25% to 28% of their

> **IN ONE WAY OR ANOTHER, EVERY AMERICAN FEELS THE EFFECTS OF AMERICA'S ANEMIC ECONOMIC GROWTH SINCE 2000.**

net worth. The 1980s Sharers felt the most pain, suffering high rates of unemployment and underemployment for many years.

THOSE BORN IN 1980 AND LATER STRUGGLED IN AN ECONOMY MORE SIMILAR TO THE 1930s THAN ANY DECADE SINCE THEN.

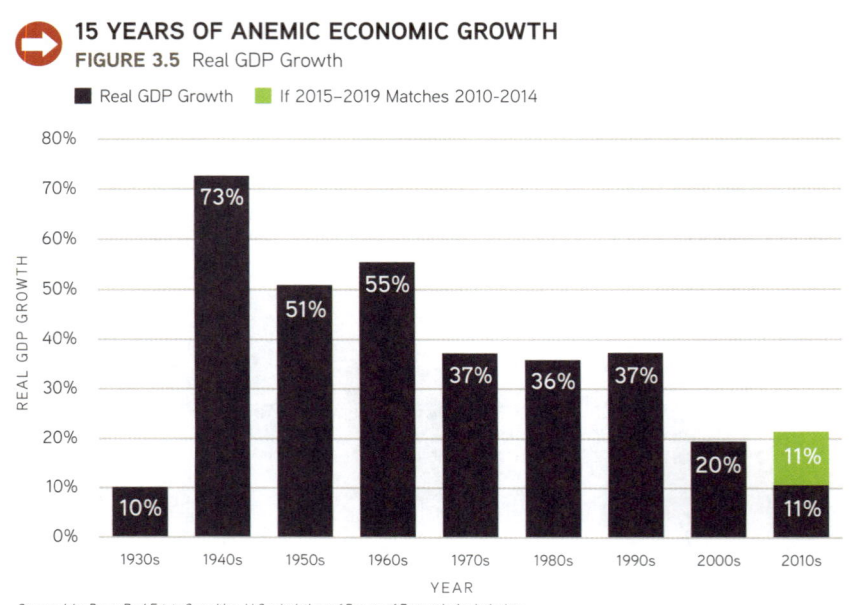

15 YEARS OF ANEMIC ECONOMIC GROWTH
FIGURE 3.5 Real GDP Growth

■ Real GDP Growth   ■ If 2015–2019 Matches 2010-2014

Decade	Real GDP Growth
1930s	10%
1940s	73%
1950s	51%
1960s	55%
1970s	37%
1980s	36%
1990s	37%
2000s	20%
2010s	11% (11% + projected 11%)

Source: John Burns Real Estate Consulting, LLC calculations of Bureau of Economic Analysis data

To put the recent lackluster economy into perspective, consider an analysis we did comparing the 1930s and 2000s, accounting for similarities and differences (such as today's more favorable mortgage environment). People born in 1922 who lived through the Great Depression as children formed very few households in their 20s. In fact, they formed 10% fewer households per person by age 28 than someone born 30 years later. A 10% decline in household-formation rate across one decade of pop-

A 10% DECLINE IN HOUSEHOLD-FORMATION RATE ACROSS ONE DECADE OF POPULATION RESULTS IN 4 MILLION FEWER HOUSEHOLDS.

ulation results in 4 million fewer households. We forecast household formations and locations in chapters 8 through 10 because so many businesses depend on new households to grow.

Compare the brutal economy of the 1980s Sharers' early working years with the economic experiences of prior generations. The 1930s Savers and the 1940s Achievers enjoyed robust economic growth during their careers. Most Savers retired affluent and early as a result, around 63 years old. Many in the 1970s Balancer and 1980s Sharer generations anticipate having to work past 65 to maintain a reasonable lifestyle.[18]

Each generation from the 1930s Savers through the 1990s Connectors has experienced slower economic growth than the generation before them. We calculated 2.4% average annual real GDP growth per person during their working lives. GDP growth per generation has steadily fallen, culminating in a paltry 1.0% per person per year for the 1980s Sharers. The Achievers, Innovators, Equalers, and Balancers compensated for the lower growth per person by increasing the number of dual-income households. Since 2001, however, fewer people work per household, compounding the effect of the poor economy on the 1980s Sharers. A shrinking workweek has also contributed to slower growth. Every generation has worked less than the previous one. The bottom line is that those born in the 1980s and later have had horrible economic luck. We should not be surprised that they have been delaying major life events and should not be surprised if they end up with far less wealth than their predecessors.

---

18   Andrew Duggan, "Retirement Remains Americans' Top Financial Worry," Gallup, April 22, 2014, http://www.gallup.com/poll/168626/retirement-remains-americans-top-financial-worry.aspx.

ECONOMIC GROWTH HAS DECLINED FOR EACH GENERATION. EARLIER GENERATIONS COMPENSATED WITH RISING DUAL-INCOME HOUSEHOLDS.

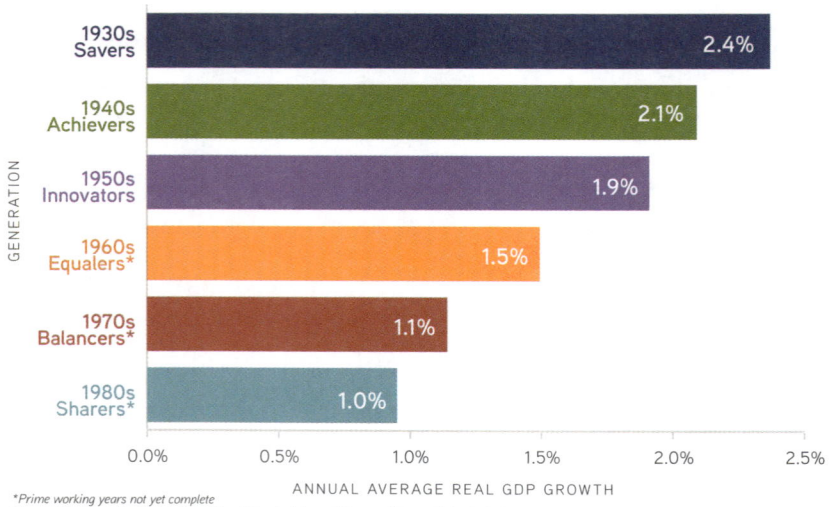

DECLINING GROWTH PER PERSON
FIGURE 3.6 Average Real GDP Growth per Person during Prime Working Years (25 to 54)

Generation	Annual Average Real GDP Growth
1930s Savers	2.4%
1940s Achievers	2.1%
1950s Innovators	1.9%
1960s Equalers*	1.5%
1970s Balancers*	1.1%
1980s Sharers*	1.0%

*Prime working years not yet complete
Source: John Burns Real Estate Consulting, LLC calculations of Bureau of Economic Analysis data

We hope this economic primer provides a broad demographic context for decision makers to project growth. Recalling the vastly different economic experiences of each generation in their childhood and early careers helps us understand their spending attitudes. Economic growth over the course of a decade or multiple decades makes a lasting impact on each generation, influencing people's behaviors as they move through life.

The economy will continue to influence the answers to the 6 Key Consumer Questions. How much will people earn? What investments will have the best returns? When will young families be able to save enough for a down payment? Where will people relocate for a good job? Who will get raises? Why will people buy instead of rent?

TECHNOLOGY

Most recognize how technology has completely transformed society. Technology's impact on how long people live garners less attention. Reviewing some of the ways technology has impacted demographics will provide helpful context as future technological developments shift where people live and how they spend.

Transportation technology offers a ready-made example. What would Denver, Charlotte, and Indianapolis look like today if rail lines hadn't stopped there in the late 1800s? How did subway car technology in the early 1900s transform New York, Boston, and Chicago? What would Los Angeles look like today without mass production of low-cost automobiles? Affordable automobiles changed how and where Americans lived beginning in the 1950s, ushering in decades of suburban growth and commutes that kept parents away from their families.

Air transportation tells a similar story. Boeing created the first passenger jet in 1958. Domestic air travel exploded in the 1960s and 1970s. Cities that invested heavily in airports—Dallas, Houston, Chicago, Charlotte, and Denver, for example—saw their populations grow at more than twice the national rate. With the exception of Denver, well-situated as a domestic travel hub, the busiest airports in the country now reside in the warm-weather states of the South or the international gateways for foreign travel (San Francisco, Chicago, New York). These areas experienced hefty permanent rent and price appreciation when builders

> **CITIES THAT INVESTED HEAVILY IN AIRPORTS—DALLAS, HOUSTON, CHICAGO, CHARLOTTE, AND DENVER, FOR EXAMPLE—SAW THEIR POPULATIONS GROW AT TWICE THE NATIONAL RATE.**

couldn't keep up with the demand for more homes. More recently, affordable airfares on new long-distance jets fuel immigration from all over the world. International air travel also created new customer bases and moved jobs overseas—huge positive and negative impacts on American residents.

Consider how quickly Uber has transformed travel in major cities. In 1947, a taxi medallion cost $2,500 in New York City, according to a story in *Bloomberg Businessweek*. After half a century of appreciation, the same medallion went for $1.32 million. Since the arrival of Uber, medallions now sell as low as $650,000—less than half their recent value.[19] Uber has changed the game for city dwellers, making it easier for those with cars to earn extra money and encouraging others to forego owning or leasing a car altogether. For both driver and passenger, city dwelling became more financially viable.

We wonder about the future impacts of technology and the sharing economy on household formation and spending patterns. Craigslist and Airbnb make it simple to rent out a room, something that might present a great solution for senior homeowners living in big houses on fixed incomes, as well as single parents looking for an affordable house in a good school district. Renting empty rooms could steal demand from hotels, apartments, homebuilders, and local municipalities who rely on hotel taxes and development fees. A rising number of residents per house could place strain on municipal services. New online businesses allow people to rent what they previously purchased, ranging from a bike to a dress

---

19   Simon Van Zuylen-Wood, "The Struggles of New York City's Taxi King," *Bloomberg*, August 27, 2015, http://www.bloomberg.com/features/2015-taxi-medallion-king/.

and, yes, even a casket.[20] The sharing economy will create many opportunities for consumers to live more financially efficient, damaging the outlook for many businesses along the way.

Technology has caused even bigger demographic changes in the realm of health. The invention of the birth-control pill and its approval by the FDA in 1960 directly coincided with the nation's peak birth year. In the 1980s, schools closed and businesses dependent on children struggled.

Today, birth technology pushes in the opposite direction. Because of IVF technology, women increasingly choose to start a family later in life. Women 40 or older now give birth to nearly 3% of all children, almost triple the percentage recorded in 1987. And that percentage is growing. Controversially, Apple and Facebook now offer "egg freezing" as a benefit to valuable female employees. As we'll document in the chapter on the dramatic shifts in female roles, technology has certainly aided many women in establishing and prolonging careers.

Babies born today can expect to live 79 years, thanks to health technology that has increased life expectancy by more than 50% during the last century.[21] Consider the demographic impact of technology-induced longer lives on pension plans, Social Security, and fields ranging from geriatric care to assisted living. Employers will create many jobs to serve the needs of an aging population. Conversely, someone will have to fund the costs of Social Security and Medicare. We can't help but wonder if technology

---

20   Jamie Joseph, "Caskets for Rent, and we're not kidding," Today, July 31, 2012, http://www.today.com/money/caskets-rent-were-not-kidding-917459.

21   Jiaquan Xu, MD; Sherry Murphy, BS; Kenneth Kochaneck, MA; and Brigham Bastian, BS, "Deaths: Final Data for 2013," Centers for Disease Control and Prevention, vol. 64, February 2016, http://www.cdc.gov/nchs/data/nvsr/nvsr64/nvsr64_02.pdf.

will continue to prolong life or if repercussions of the quadrupling of obese children from the 1970s to the 1990s will eventually shorten life.

LIFE EXPECTANCY HAS ALMOST DOUBLED IN THE LAST CENTURY THANKS IN PART TO HEALTH TECHNOLOGY.

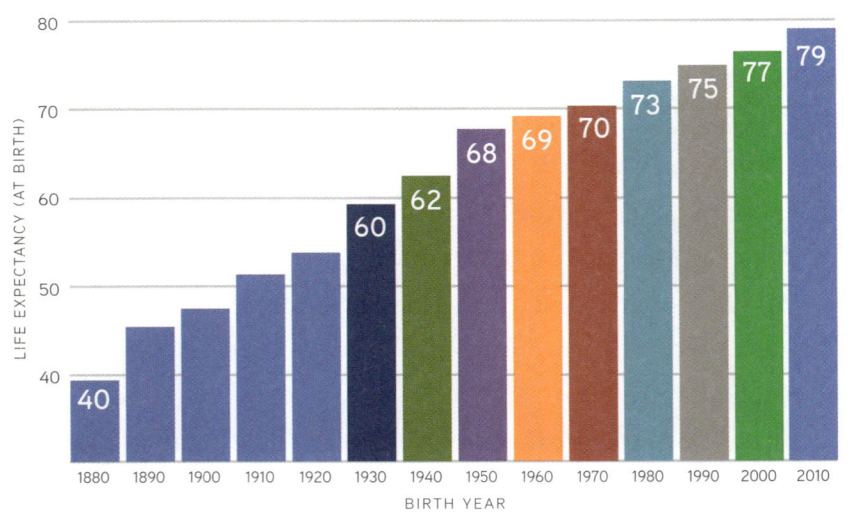

LIVING LONGER THAN EVER BEFORE
FIGURE 3.7 US Life Expectancy at Birth

Birth Year	Life Expectancy
1880	40
1890	45
1900	47
1910	51
1920	54
1930	60
1940	62
1950	68
1960	69
1970	70
1980	73
1990	75
2000	77
2010	79

Source: Mapping History, University of Oregon (1880–2000); Centers for Disease Control and Prevention, National Vital Statistics Reports, 2010

The Internet and computer chip qualify as the most obvious transformative technologies of recent decades. The Internet has enabled far more telecommuting. Our company, for instance, has talented employees all over the country who work from home. We could not have recruited them or enabled them to be productive if the Internet hadn't made telecommuting an option. For many of them, proximity to family drives where they will live, and virtually no job at any income could get them to move. This phenomenon rang far less true for the 1940s Achievers and 1950s Innovators, a fact that we will explore in depth in chapter 6. Homeowners move about half as often as they did in the 1980s and renters about a third as often.

AMERICANS NOW MOVE EVERY 9 YEARS COMPARED TO EVERY 6 YEARS IN THE 1980s.

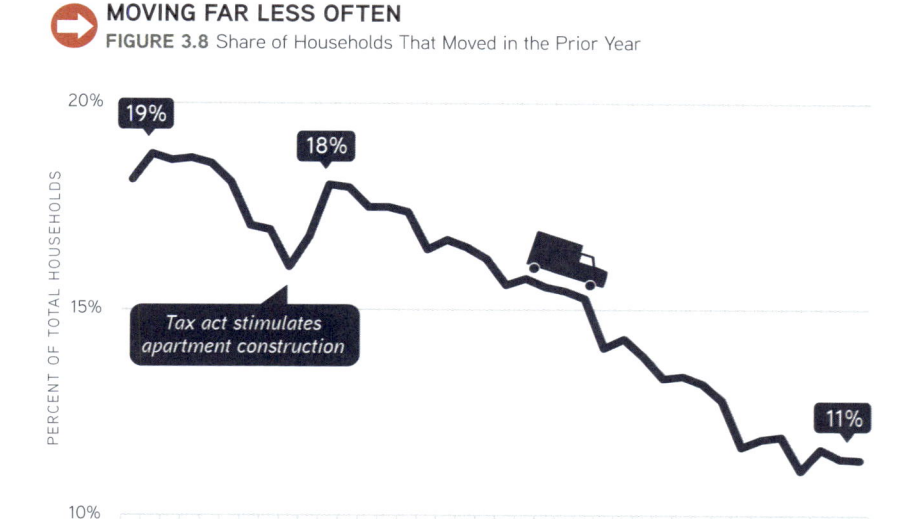

MOVING FAR LESS OFTEN
FIGURE 3.8 Share of Households That Moved in the Prior Year

Source: John Burns Real Estate Consulting, LLC calculations of US Census Bureau, Current Population Survey, Annual Social and Economic Supplements via IPUMS-CPS

While the Internet has made working more flexible in many ways, Internet technology has eliminated or raised barriers to employment for some. Around 69% of companies run criminal background checks on job candidates for a nominal fee, for instance.[22] Today,

---

22 Gary Fields and John Emshwiller, "As Arrest Records Rise, Americans Find Consequences Can Last a Lifetime," *The Wall Street Journal*, August 18, 2014, http://www.wsj.com/articles/as-arrest-records-rise-americans-find-consequences-can-last-a-lifetime-1408415402.

34% of unemployed men have a criminal record.[23] These criminal databases limit job prospects for millions.

While machines continue to replace humans in manufacturing jobs, computers now replace service jobs too. Banks need fewer tellers. Hospitals need fewer doctors. Computers trade stocks. When was the last time you met a travel agent? Technology threatens many jobs today.

The Internet has both helped and hurt retail sales. Online shopping brings retail access to all locations. Small businesses can now reach more customers, and rural dwellers can now purchase more easily. However, brick-and-mortar stores such as Borders Books, J.C. Penney, and Radio Shack struggled greatly because of Internet competition. Mom-and-pop retailers that don't adapt suffer, while other businesses and individuals cost effectively sell billions of dollars of goods and services on websites such as Amazon, eBay, and Etsy.

The rise in online shopping has resulted in the demise of many malls, many of which are being redeveloped into brand new places to live. Developers are tearing down retail centers all over the United States, replacing them with dynamic entertainment centers that include housing, developments historically known as mixed use. We coined the word surban™ for these developments—bringing the best of urban living to a suburban environment. This trend is shaping the US so profoundly today that we devoted chapter 10 to the topic.

Recently, smartphone technology has made the most significant impact. Sixty-four percent of American adults owned smartphones in 2015, up from just 35% four years earlier. GPS (location tracking), online payment, Internet search, and social media tech-

---

23   Binyamin Appelbaum, "The Vanishing Male Worker: How America Fell Behind," *The New York Times*, December 11, 2014, http://www.nytimes.com/2014/12/12/upshot/unemployment-the-vanishing-male-worker-how-america-fell-behind.html.

nologies embedded in smartphones have disrupted business models everywhere.[24] People take more pictures than ever, yet camera sales have plunged. Banks and retailers need a strong mobile presence to retain their customers.

Great companies will continue to use technology to disrupt the way people currently conduct business. Businesses should expect that future generations will spend very differently thanks to technology.

Technology will continue to influence the answers to the 6 Key Consumer Questions. How long will most people live? What jobs will robots replace? When will people purchase if they believe technology will make things cheaper? Where will people live if cars drive themselves? Who will move to cities with free wi-fi? Why will people buy from one online vendor instead of another?

SOCIETAL SHIFTS

Attitudes, values, and principles prove difficult to quantify, partly because they shift so quickly. The amount of time from an issue's "trigger point"—say, an individual state legalizing a practice—to federal action on that issue has steadily declined from nineteen years (for interracial marriage, in 1967) to two years (for same-sex marriage, in 2015[25]). The Internet and other technologies that make detailed information so quickly and universally available play an important role in the quickening pace of societal change.

---

24   Aaron Smith, "U.S. Smartphone Use in 2015," Pew Research Center, April 1, 2015, http://www.pewInternet.org/2015/04/01/us-smartphone-use-in-2015/.

25   Alex Tribou and Keith Collins, "This Is How Fast America Changes Its Mind," *Bloomberg*, June 26, 2015, http://www.bloomberg.com/graphics/2015-pace-of-social-change/.

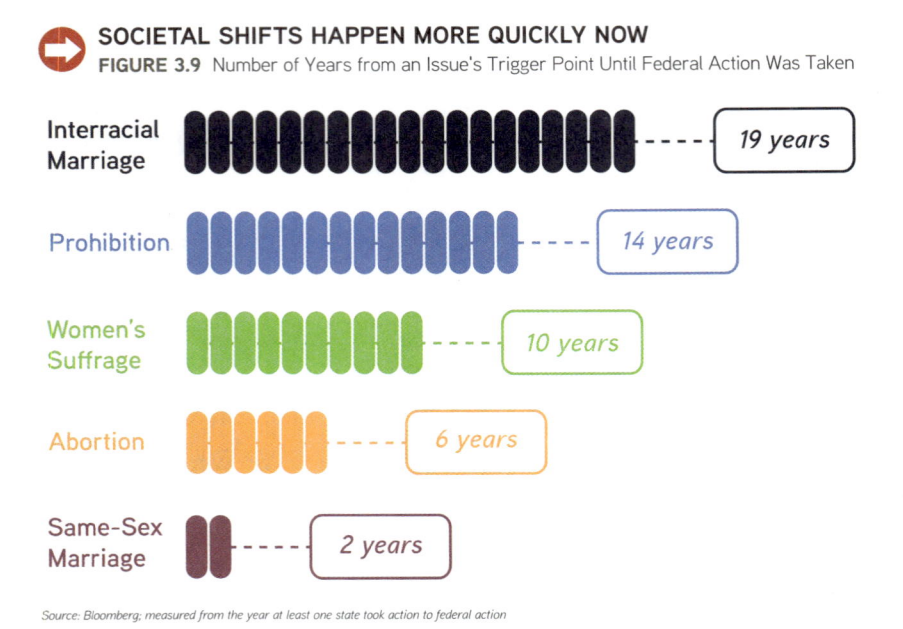

SOCIETAL SHIFTS HAPPEN MORE QUICKLY NOW.

SOCIETAL SHIFTS HAPPEN MORE QUICKLY NOW
FIGURE 3.9 Number of Years from an Issue's Trigger Point Until Federal Action Was Taken

- Interracial Marriage — 19 years
- Prohibition — 14 years
- Women's Suffrage — 10 years
- Abortion — 6 years
- Same-Sex Marriage — 2 years

Source: Bloomberg; measured from the year at least one state took action to federal action

The rapidity of societal shifts makes it all the more imperative that decision makers watch them closely and react nimbly. Our other Big Influencers might appear easier to study and quantify, but societal influence has concrete demographic consequences that deeply affect Americans' decisions.

The value we place on college education, for instance, has risen steadily over the last century. The 1980s Sharers and 1990s Connectors constitute the most-educated generations ever. Employers relying on a highly educated workforce will welcome this news, but many of the employees who took on tremendous debt for all that schooling have far less money to spend.

The shift in education appears especially prominent in women. By 2012, 37% of women aged 25–29 held a bachelor's degree or higher, compared to just 31% of men. Women's higher education levels have narrowed the wage gap and somewhat shifted gender roles. Most Americans know from experience that men now contribute to childcare, housework, and general domestic duties much more than their fathers or grandfathers did. However, the rise in stay-at-home dads, the steady increase in women earning more than their husbands, and other related shifts might surprise many. Businesses that cater to busy, affluent women have thrived.

Higher education levels and dramatically improved career opportunities for women delay the ages when people marry and have kids. Sharer couples now marry four years later than their parents did—women at 27 and men at 29. At 26, women start a family later in life, too—three years later than their mothers did and five years later than their grandmothers did. We will cover this transformation in greater depth in the next chapter.

1980s SHARER WOMEN GIVE BIRTH 3 YEARS LATER THAN THEIR MOM AND 5 YEARS LATER THAN THEIR GRANDMOTHER.

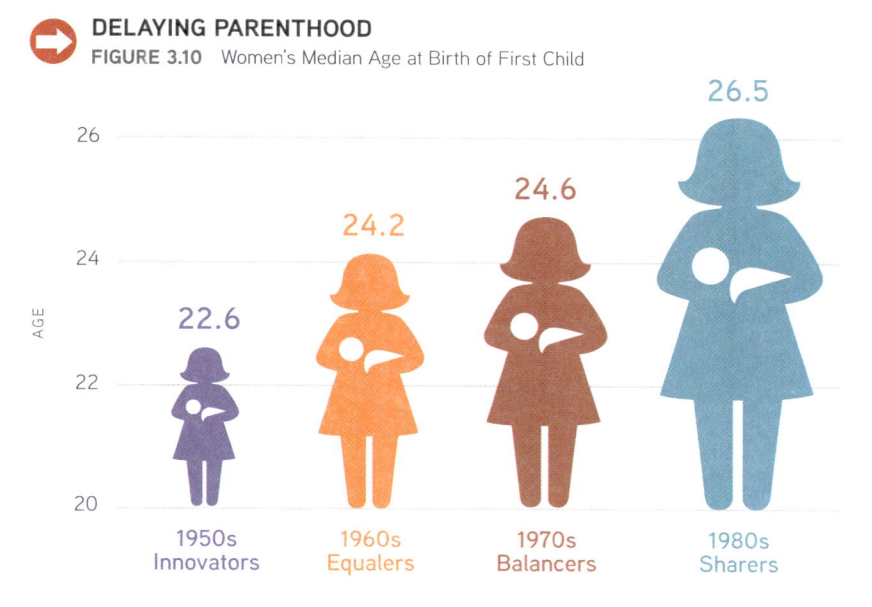

DELAYING PARENTHOOD
FIGURE 3.10 Women's Median Age at Birth of First Child

1950s Innovators	1960s Equalers	1970s Balancers	1980s Sharers
22.6	24.2	24.6	26.5

Source: John Burns Real Estate Consulting, LLC calculations of Centers for Disease Control and Prevention data

At age 35–39, only 65% of 1970s Balancers have married, compared to 84% of 1930s Savers at the same age. Even considering the rise in cohabitation, people increasingly delay living together.

LESS THAN 2/3 OF 1970s BALANCERS ARE MARRIED IN THEIR LATE 30s, COMPARED TO 84% OF 1930s SAVERS.

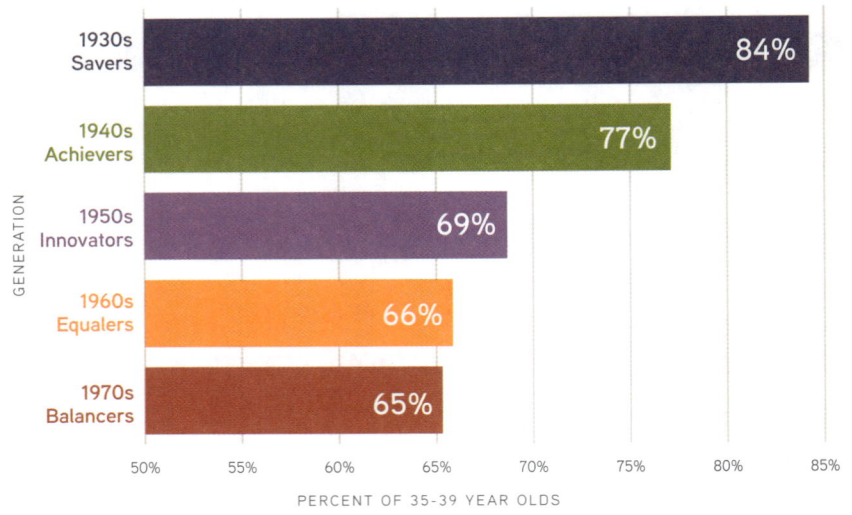

STAYING SINGLE FOR LONGER
FIGURE 3.11 Percent of People Married by Age and Birth Year, Age 35–39

Generation	Percent
1930s Savers	84%
1940s Achievers	77%
1950s Innovators	69%
1960s Equalers	66%
1970s Balancers	65%

PERCENT OF 35-39 YEAR OLDS

Source: John Burns Real Estate Consulting, LLC calculations of US Census Bureau, Current Population Survey, Annual Social and Economic Supplements via IPUMS-CPS

Decision makers tracking these changes have capitalized on them. Since parenting now occurs later in life, demand for urban housing has increased. Urban apartment owners have been able to raise rents quickly due to the demand/supply imbalance. Homebuilders know that women have their first child at age 26, and most will relocate to a good school district by age 31, when their oldest turns five. Surging urban demand is a leading indicator for future suburban demand. Couples will be far more willing than their Achiever and Innovator parents to live in a smaller, even attached home with a small yard in order to avoid a commute and to live closer to their friends and entertainment. Due to the economy, more of them will rent too.

Over 60 years, from 1950 to 2010, society shifted from 77% of households led by couples living together to only 55%—6% cohabitating and 49% married. That 6% cohabitation rate, by the way, doubled during the last 20 years. What does that say about the younger generations' desire for flexibility in life? If they won't sign the marriage paperwork, will they cosign a mortgage together?

The growing societal acceptance of the now-common term LGBT (lesbian, gay, bisexual, transgender) shifts demographics, too. In 2010, 9.1 million LGBT adults (3.8% of the adult population) reportedly lived in America. Following the Supreme Court's 2015 ruling protecting marriage rights for same-sex partners, we suspect that more LGBT couples will choose to live together, turning two households into one.

The TV show *Modern Family* probably best represents recent societal shifts, prominently featuring a gay couple with an adopted daughter, a dual-income household with smartphone-connected teens, and a grandfather's second marriage to a much younger Columbian woman with a child from her previous marriage. We suggest you pay attention to new TV shows, as the entertainment industry seems to do a great job of capturing societal shifts. Looking forward, we expect the number of nontraditional family households to grow and ethnic identity to blur as multiracial children rise in numbers.

Societal shifts will continue to influence the answers to the 6 Key Consumer Questions. How many children will be born? What will stay-at-home dads purchase differently than stay-at-home moms? When will college graduation rates plateau? Where will immigrant groups be most welcome to live? Who will live with three or more generations under the same roof? Why will people marry or cohabitate?

PART TWO

THE BIGGEST DEMOGRAPHIC OPPORTUNITIES

4: RISE OF THE WORKING WOMAN

The 1960s Equaler women drove one of the most important demographic shifts we found. Equaler women surpassed male education levels for the first time. For 25 years in a row, more women have graduated from college than men. In 1970, men received 58% of college degrees. In a complete reversal, women now earn 58% of all bachelor's and master's degrees.

58% OF TOTAL COLLEGE DEGREES NOW GO TO WOMEN.

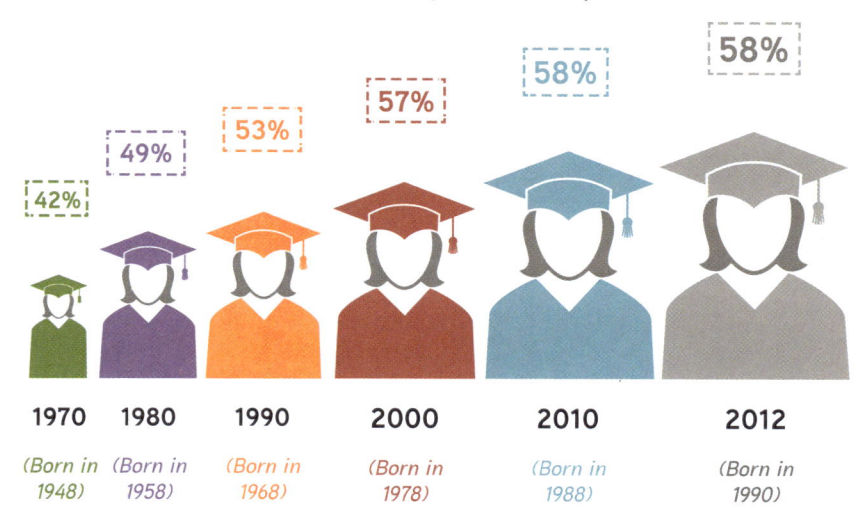

WOMEN RECEIVE 58% OF COLLEGE DEGREES TODAY
FIGURE 4.1 Bachelor's and Master's Degrees Conferred by Females

1970	1980	1990	2000	2010	2012
42%	49%	53%	57%	58%	58%
(Born in 1948)	(Born in 1958)	(Born in 1968)	(Born in 1978)	(Born in 1988)	(Born in 1990)

Source: John Burns Real Estate Consulting, LLC calculations of National Center for Education Statistics data

The surging divorce rates in the 1960s and 1970s wreaked havoc on poorly educated women, showing their young daughters the importance of being able to take care of themselves financially. Enabled by government's 1972 passage of Title IX, requiring equal education opportunities for women, women took full advantage. Dramatic shifts resulted:

- **Double the work**: Women nearly doubled their workforce participation from 37% working in 1950 to 73% in 1999.

- **Almost half of all jobs**: Women hold nearly 47% of all jobs in America today, up from less than 38% in 1970.

- **Sharply rising incomes**: Young adult female incomes rose 34% over the last 40 years, whereas male incomes fell 5%, adjusting both for inflation. Disparities still exist, but the gap certainly narrowed.

- **Primary breadwinners**: Around 38% of married women now earn more than their spouse, up from just 24% in the early '80s.

- **Delaying families**: Forty years ago, 68% of women in their late 20s had both a husband and child. That number has tumbled to 22%.

- **Going it alone**: Women also opt to parent alone more often. Approximately 18% of all newborns go home from the hospital to a single-parent household (41% of all births are to single women, 44% of whom do not live with the father).

In the 1970s, social attitudes toward women's roles continued to change. Gloria Steinem founded *Ms.* magazine in 1971 partially because she realized that no women actually controlled women's magazines. Women's studies programs sprang up at universities. Popular TV shows such as *The Mary Tyler Moore Show* and *One Day at a Time* celebrated independent, single, working women.

Economic factors also played a pivotal role. Educational opportunities opened up for women just as the switch from a manufacturing economy to a service economy accelerated. Jobs that required physical strength or manual skills—learned in shop classes and apprentice programs—faded. Jobs requiring education and interpersonal skills grew.

BETTER EDUCATED

Expanding women's educational opportunities influenced other shifts we will explore in this chapter—changes in income, marriage, parenting, and childbirth. Today, 39% of 1980s Sharer women and 32% of men own a bachelor's degree. With women 7% more likely to graduate from college than men, the workplace and home life will continue to change dramatically.

BETTER EDUCATED: 39% OF 1980s SHARER WOMEN AND 32% OF MEN HELD BACHELOR'S DEGREES IN 2013.

EQUALER WOMEN WERE THE FIRST TO ATTAIN THE SAME EDUCATION LEVEL AS MEN

FIGURE 4.2 Difference between US Women & Men Aged 25–34 with Bachelor's Degree or Higher

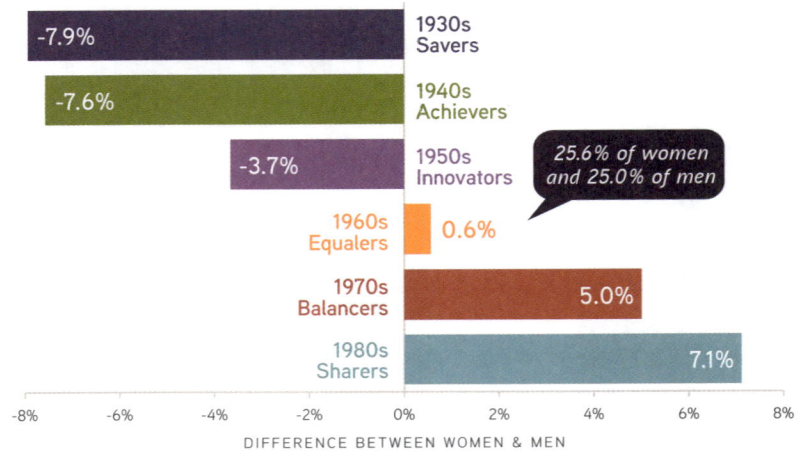

Generation	Difference
1930s Savers	-7.9%
1940s Achievers	-7.6%
1950s Innovators	-3.7%
1960s Equalers	0.6%
1970s Balancers	5.0%
1980s Sharers	7.1%

25.6% of women and 25.0% of men (1960s Equalers)

DIFFERENCE BETWEEN WOMEN & MEN

Source: John Burns Real Estate Consulting, LLC calculations of US Census Bureau, Current Population Survey, Annual Social and Economic Supplements via IPUMS-CPS

The rise in college graduation rates, particularly for women, contributes to the household income inequality so frequently cited by the media. Among married couples, 23% have both graduated from college—a percentage that has steadily risen for decades. When more households contain dual-income, college-educated workers, income growth rises faster at the top income levels.

23% OF MARRIED COUPLES EARNED COLLEGE DEGREES, UP FROM 3% IN 1960.

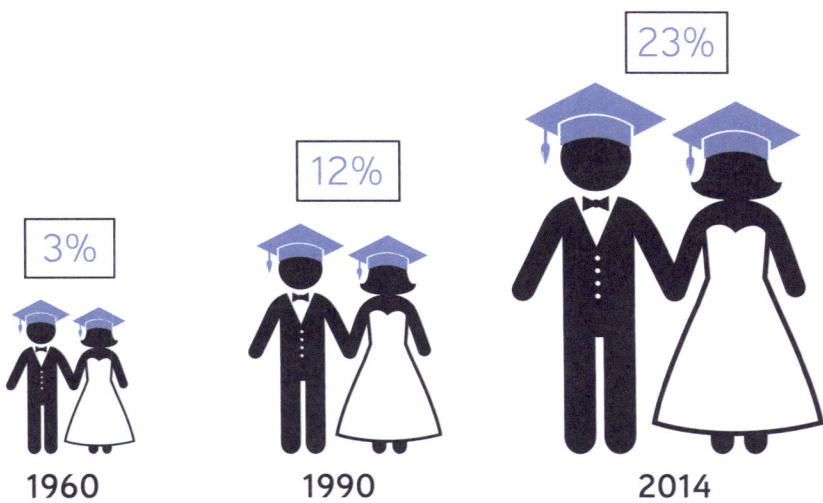

➡ MORE WELL-EDUCATED COUPLES
FIGURE 4.3 Share of Married Couples Where Both Spouses Have a College Degree

1960	1990	2014
3%	12%	23%

Source: US Census Bureau, Decennial Census 1960-2010, American Community Survey via IPUMS-USA

Lisa Marquis Jackson, a 1960s Equaler, provides a great example of the educational shifts experienced by women. The education of Jackson's parents, her own experience, and that of her daughters, varies dramatically from generation to generation. Jackson left for college in the early '80s, the pivotal time when a higher percentage of women than men began earning college degrees. She and her sisters never doubted they would go to college, but her opportunities differed from those of her Achiever parents, born in the 1940s. Her father took a difficult route to college, first joining the military, and later finishing his degree at Purdue. Her mother, who worked for a bank, didn't go to college.

Jackson noted: "It was a different world then. My parents got married young, and my mom supported my dad while he was in school. I was born early in the marriage."

Jackson, a 49-year-old Dallas resident, spent her formative years outside Peoria, Illinois, where her father worked for Caterpillar. Though educational opportunity for women expanded in the '80s, Jackson was the only woman from the small graduating class at her rural high school to go directly to a four-year college. Her background, career, and eventual divorce made her hyperaware of the importance of education for her own daughters.

"Education was the key to my getting ahead, so it's a priority for me with my daughters," Jackson said. Her oldest daughter attends a private college, and the youngest, at 16, attends the same private high school in Dallas that her older sister did.

"In my wildest dreams, I never thought my kids would go to private school. It's not part of my past. I didn't plan or budget for that, but it just ended up being very clear when they hit middle school in the public-school system that it was not the best I could do for them, and education is really important to me. As a parent, I feel like it's one of the most important investments I can make."

While Jackson considers education one of her most important investments, she also names it one of the priciest. Education's generational shift has significant financial implications. "I think I'm being accurate, or close to it, when I say that maybe one semester of tuition for my daughter's college would equal the cost of my entire college education," Jackson said. "It is a totally different animal." Her oldest daughter contemplated premed as a freshman in 2016, while the youngest, who loves animals, considered becoming a veterinarian.

Cynthia Laguna, a 30-year-old member of the 1980s Sharer generation, provides another great example of the educational shifts for women. When she started at the University of California, Irvine, Laguna chose a course of study heavy on science and math: aerospace engineering. After a couple of years, she switched to a double major of sociology and international studies. Her current job doesn't relate to those disciplines, but like Jackson, Laguna understood early on the importance of education. At three years of age, she came to America with her parents from Cuernavaca, Mexico. As a girl, she accompanied her mother on her job, cleaning houses.

"I would go with her and see how much work or what type of work you have to do if you don't go to college," Laguna said. "She taught me that to be a successful person, you should put as much effort as you can into going to school, getting good grades, and doing good things for yourself. I mean, it's not a bad job, cleaning houses. A job is a job, but that's not something my mom had as a goal for me, and I definitely didn't want to do it."

CLOSING THE INCOME GAP

Like Jackson and a growing number of women since the '60s, Laguna translated her education into income. She got her current accounting job right out of school after interning for the company during college and has worked there for a decade. She lived with her parents postcollege and, in five years, saved enough to buy—in her mid-20s—a $370,000 three-bedroom house. She lives in that house today, with her husband and their infant daughter, Quetzally.

Contrast the employment opportunities available to 1960s Equaler Lisa Marquis Jackson and 1980s Sharer Cynthia Laguna with the aforementioned challenge faced by one of the most successful female 1930s Savers, Supreme Court Justice Sandra Day O'Connor. Justice O'Connor overcame huge biases against hiring female lawyers and helped pioneer the opportunities available to women today. Numerous women today continue the fight to create even more opportunities.

From the 1970s through the 2000s, women's incomes grew much faster than men's, partly because of rising education levels. In real dollars, female incomes rose 35% from 1970 to 2000, while male incomes rose only 7%. Growth for both genders has stalled in the tough economy of the last decade, but we believe women's income growth will likely continue to outpace men's, given the gender disparity in higher education.

REAL FEMALE INCOMES GREW MUCH FASTER THAN MEN'S FROM 1970 THROUGH 2000, PARTIALLY DUE TO RISING FEMALE EDUCATION LEVELS.

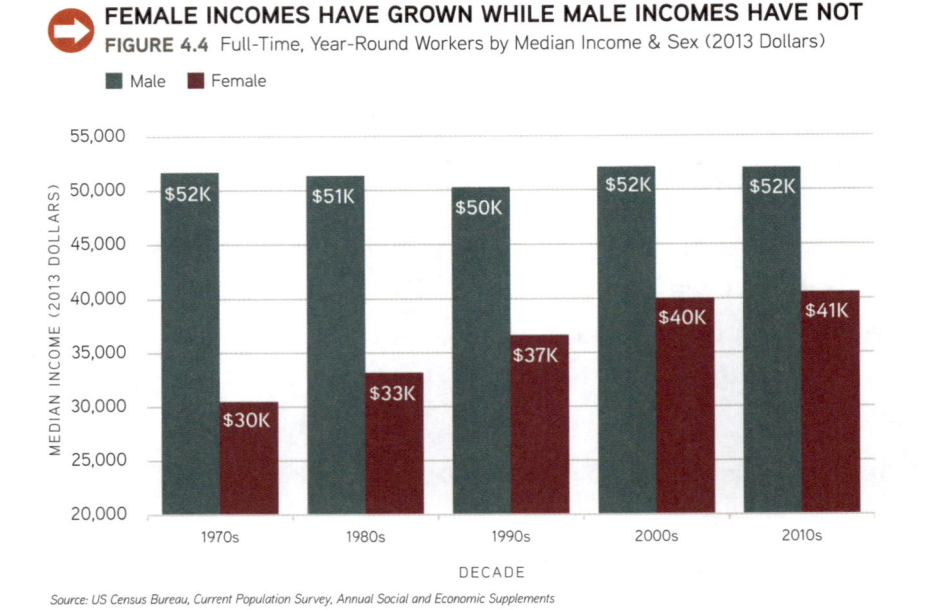

FEMALE INCOMES HAVE GROWN WHILE MALE INCOMES HAVE NOT
FIGURE 4.4 Full-Time, Year-Round Workers by Median Income & Sex (2013 Dollars)

Decade	Male	Female
1970s	$52K	$30K
1980s	$51K	$33K
1990s	$50K	$37K
2000s	$52K	$40K
2010s	$52K	$41K

Source: US Census Bureau, Current Population Survey, Annual Social and Economic Supplements

Even more dramatically, just looking at the prime earning years of 35–44, women's incomes rose 59% while men's incomes plunged 19%, adjusting for inflation.

4: RISE OF THE WORKING WOMAN

Laguna the accountant shopped for a year before she found a house she liked. By then, she'd become engaged, so she added her husband's name to the loan. However, she alone made the down payment and received the mortgage approval for the purchase.

BY 2025, WE EXPECT THAT AT LEAST 40% OF WOMEN WILL EARN MORE THAN THEIR HUSBANDS WHO WORK.

She earns more than her husband, an alarm-service technician who attended a technical school. As primary breadwinner, she's part of another growing trend. Thirty-five years ago, 24% of women earned more than their spouses. Today, 38% earn more, a number that likely will grow. By 2025, we expect that at least 40% of women will earn more than their husbands who work.

WOMEN NOW EARN MORE THAN THEIR HUSBANDS 38% OF THE TIME, PARTIALLY DUE TO RISING EDUCATION LEVELS.

➡ **38% OF WOMEN EARN MORE THAN THEIR HUSBANDS TODAY**
FIGURE 4.5 Married Households with Wife Earning More Than Husband

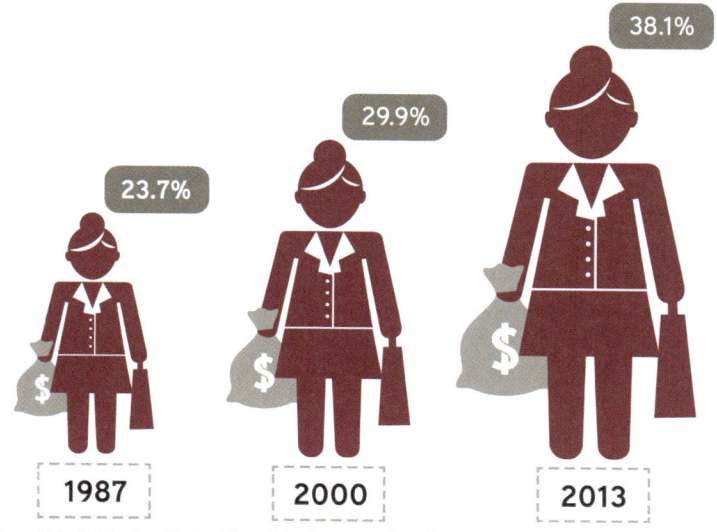

1987: 23.7%
2000: 29.9%
2013: 38.1%

Source: Bureau of Labor Statistics, Annual Social and Economic Supplements to the Current Population Survey

The percentage of working-age women who work skyrocketed from the mid-1970s into the late 1980s, before decelerating beginning around 2001—right around 9/11. Meanwhile, participation rates for working-age men began a long-term decline in the mid-1950s that continues to this day. Eighty-three percent of working-age men and 70% of working-age women work today.

THE PERCENTAGE OF WOMEN AGED 20–64 WITH A JOB HAS DOUBLED SINCE 1950, WHILE THE PERCENTAGE OF MEN WORKING HAS DECLINED 11%.

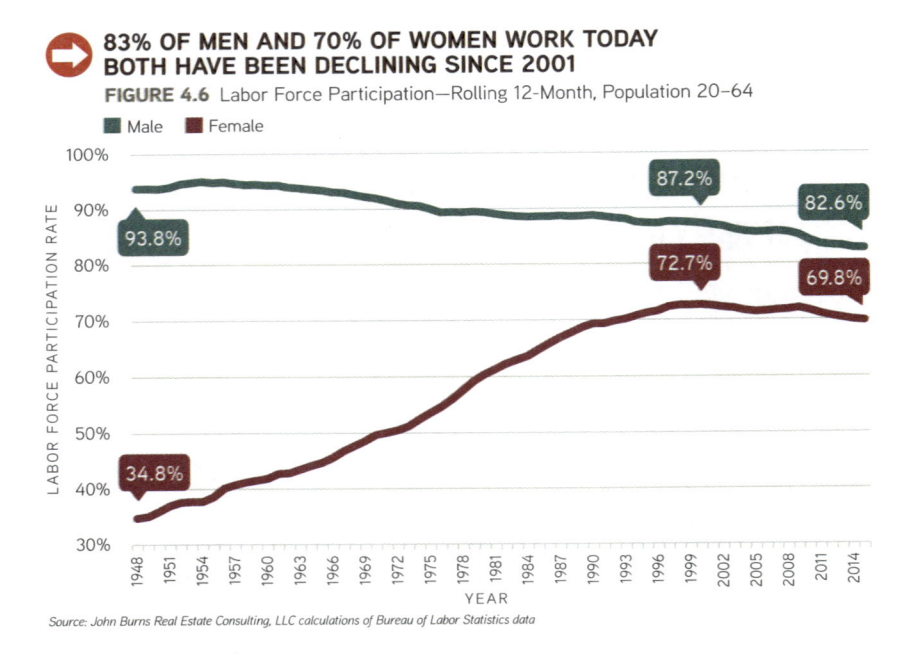

83% OF MEN AND 70% OF WOMEN WORK TODAY BOTH HAVE BEEN DECLINING SINCE 2001

FIGURE 4.6 Labor Force Participation—Rolling 12-Month, Population 20–64

Source: John Burns Real Estate Consulting, LLC calculations of Bureau of Labor Statistics data

Increasingly, women such as Lisa Marquis Jackson and Cynthia Laguna position themselves to meet the demands of work and family. They marry later, start a family later, and enjoy longer careers. Laguna married in 2011 at the age of 25, a little below today's female median marriage age of 26 years and 7 months, but she said peers in her Mexican-American community saw that as quite late. Jackson married at 27. By the time Laguna and Jackson had their first child at age 30, both had completed their bachelor's degrees, bought a house, and worked for nearly a decade.

COUPLES MARRY 4 YEARS LATER THAN THEIR PARENTS AND 6 YEARS LATER THAN THEIR GRANDPARENTS.

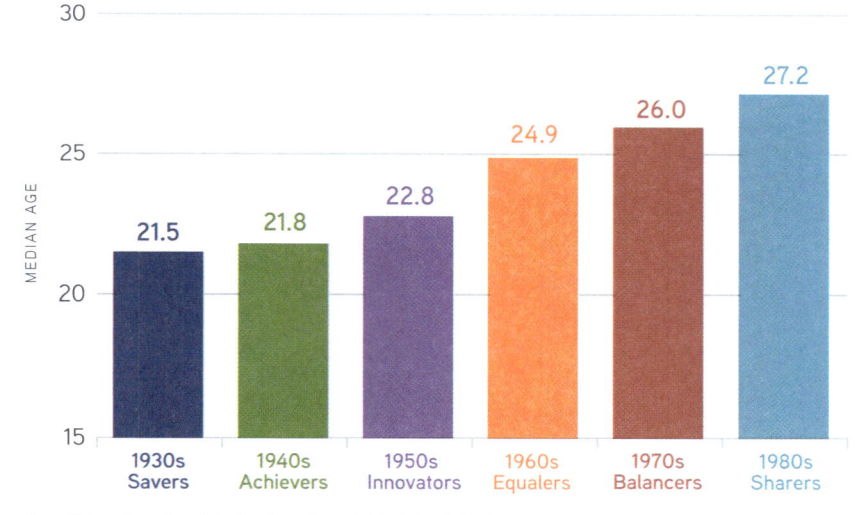

MARRYING MUCH LATER
FIGURE 4.7 Median Age at First Marriage

Decade	Median Age
1930s Savers	21.5
1940s Achievers	21.8
1950s Innovators	22.8
1960s Equalers	24.9
1970s Balancers	26.0
1980s Sharers	27.2

Source: US Census Bureau Current Population Survey, Annual Social and Economic Supplements

Top companies work to help these highly educated workers prolong their careers, and technology often provides the means. IVF and other medical advances make it more common for women to give birth later in life. Facebook and Apple announced in 2014 that they would pay the $20,000+ cost of egg freezing for select employees. In 1980, slightly more than 0.5% of newborns had a 40+ year-old mom. By 2012, that number rose to nearly 3%, a trend we expect to continue.

FERTILIZATION TECHNOLOGY NOW ENABLES WOMEN TO WORK LONGER AND DELAY CHILDBIRTH. MOMS AGED 40 YEARS AND OLDER GIVE BIRTH TO 3% OF TODAY'S BABIES.

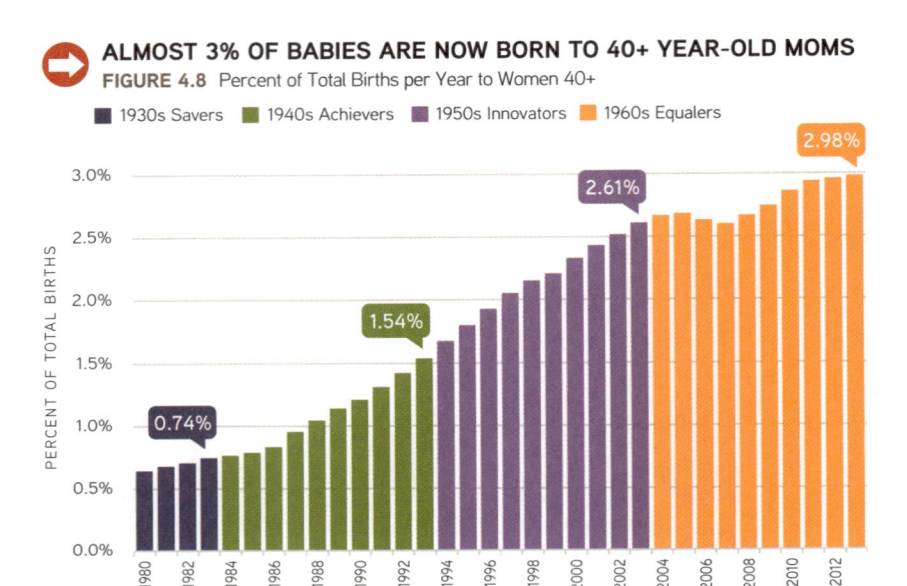

ALMOST 3% OF BABIES ARE NOW BORN TO 40+ YEAR-OLD MOMS

FIGURE 4.8 Percent of Total Births per Year to Women 40+

■ 1930s Savers   ■ 1940s Achievers   ■ 1950s Innovators   ■ 1960s Equalers

Source: Centers for Disease Control, National Vital Statistics Report

IVF has removed some of the sense of urgency to start a family early. Over the 15 years from 1994 to 2009, the age a woman had her first child rose by one year, to age 25. Just five years later, however, that age rose all the way to 26.5. The delay appears at least partly related to the Great Recession, but 1980s Sharers have clearly said, "We are in no hurry to have kids."

WOMEN DELAY THEIR FIRST CHILD UNTIL AGE 26, A SIGNIFICANT 1-YEAR DELAY SINCE THE 2009 RECESSION BEGAN.

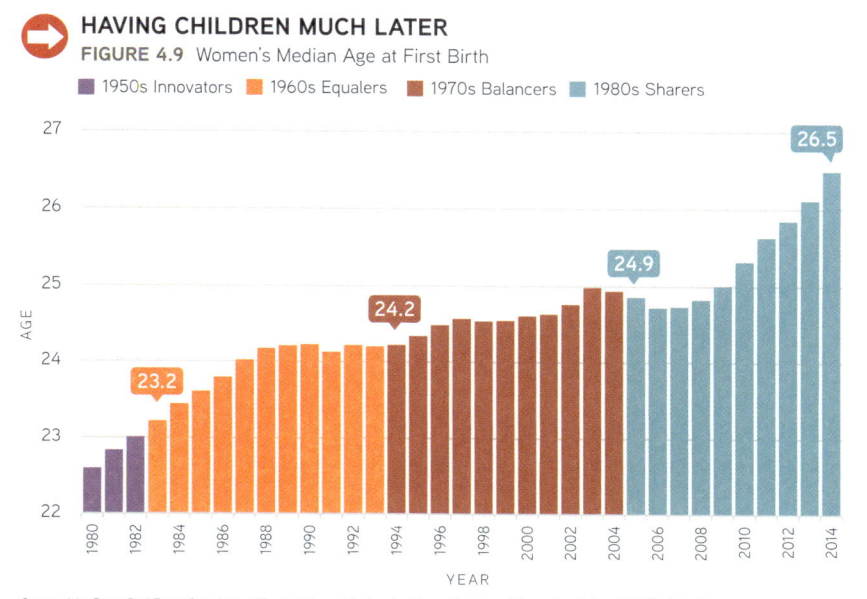

HAVING CHILDREN MUCH LATER
FIGURE 4.9 Women's Median Age at First Birth

■ 1950s Innovators ■ 1960s Equalers ■ 1970s Balancers ■ 1980s Sharers

Source: John Burns Real Estate Consulting, LLC calculations of Centers for Disease Control and Prevention, National Vital Statistics Report

By the time Jackson gave birth to her first daughter, her knowledge, reputation, and industry contacts as a reporter were sufficient to allow her to work from home.

> *"When the kids were born, I realized quickly that I wanted to be in a place where I could have both job and family,"* Jackson said. *"I didn't want to have my first daughter in a traditional daycare setting. Nothing against people who do that—it was maybe the control freak in me. But I was able to balance the career that I wanted with the time I needed with my kids and was able to take on more or less work depending on what the kids needed."*

As her children got older, Jackson could take on more work and adapt her schedule to theirs. Her work-from-home schedule sometimes meant getting up at 4:30 a.m. and working for hours before they woke so that she could shuttle kids or attend school events. This proved much harder in the 1990s than today, she said. Back then, corporate culture didn't consider the needs of working mothers. Today, a long list of companies such as Abbott, IBM, and Verizon offer longer paid maternity leave, flextime, on-site daycare, lactation rooms, wellness coaching, benefits for fertility treatment, and other measures to help working women. Businesses have adapted to their employees' needs.

As corporate culture evolved, technology and the Internet made telecommuting commonplace. Working mothers who previously might have taken long leaves or perhaps ended careers kept working. Jackson remembers sending floppy disks via FedEx in the early days working at home and fearing that domestic noise would interrupt phone calls, revealing that she worked at home. Jackson recalls,

> *"It's the barking-dog index. I've always had dogs, and you were terrified to have a dog bark then because it was a sign you were in a home office. It was this big, complicated thing to have the dogs somewhere else, or you were shoving them into a bathroom or a closet or something. Now I'm on calls where someone's in a coffee shop or their car; there are babies crying. If anything, people now think more of those working at home because it is often senior people with the flexibility who are doing it. Often, I say, 'Full disclosure, you may hear a dog barking here, I'm at home'—and they'll say, 'Me too. There might be a baby crying here any minute.'"*

Despite workplace progress, for women such as Jackson and Laguna, balancing careers and childcare remains a challenge.

"That's the elusive goal, the main challenge in life," Jackson said. "It has its pros and cons. The pros are I have been a mom who is present, and I have been able to somehow navigate through a lot of challenges that I never anticipated I would have, but at the same time, it's hard to separate work and life. It's not something where you kind of turn work off at 5:00 p.m."

As women surpassed men in college degrees and rapidly gained in income, a shift—not always smooth—occurred in domestic gender roles. While women work more, men work more around the house. That balance grew especially tricky for Jackson in the late 2000s. Her now ex-husband worked in telecomm in Dallas, and when the industry downsized, he moved to a home office. Jackson said this allowed him to do more domestic chores, but a disproportionate share of that burden still fell on her. "There was the traditional stereotype that that was the woman's role, and there was a lot of conflict in our marriage over that, too," Jackson said.

BALANCER AND SHARER DADS SPEND MORE THAN TWICE AS MUCH TIME WITH THEIR KIDS AS THEIR DADS DID.

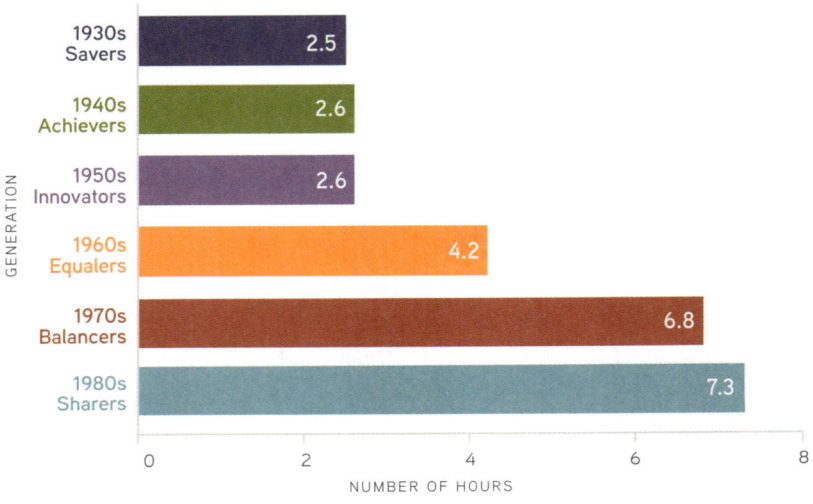

MORE-INVOLVED FATHERS

FIGURE 4.10 Average Number of Hours Spent on Childcare per Week by Fathers

Generation	Number of Hours
1930s Savers	2.5
1940s Achievers	2.6
1950s Innovators	2.6
1960s Equalers	4.2
1970s Balancers	6.8
1980s Sharers	7.3

Source: Pew Research Center

Cynthia Laguna gets plenty of help around the house from her husband, splitting domestic work and childcare. Her mother, a professional housecleaner, does most of the cleaning—for the same rate she charges all customers. Laguna does whatever spot cleaning circumstance demands, and her husband does all the yard work, painting, and other maintenance. They split cooking and childcare duties—showering, feeding, and changing—in half, although imbalance creeps into that last chore.

"We have a deal: whoever gets home first, cooks—and I never get home first," Laguna said, laughing. "Not intentionally! I have to go pick up my daughter or stop somewhere, always something. But he's a good cook, and I honestly think he enjoys doing that."

This arrangement differs significantly from that of Laguna's parents. Her dad, rarely home, worked three jobs for years as Laguna grew up. Her mother handled all the housework and childcare. Increasingly, though, the husband stays home, tending to the house and children while his wife goes out to work.

Men increasingly embrace the new role, blogging about how they shop, keep house, and care for their kids. The Dad 2.0 Summit, an annual conference, focuses on shopping, parenting, and other concerns involving stay-at-home fathers. *Modern Dads,* a reality show on A&E, follows a group of stay-at-home dads in Austin, TX, as they buy groceries, shuttle kids to soccer games, and change diapers. Dads who work also work more at home. Facebook actually offers its employees up to four months of paid maternity or paternity leave, which they can take throughout the year. In 2016, Facebook CEO Mark Zuckerberg took advantage of the new policy.

Changing social attitudes along with higher levels of education, income, and independence for women contribute to another seismic shift in demographics—a steep increase in the number of unmarried women giving birth. Women now marry at a median age of 26 years and 7 months and give birth to their first child at one month past their 26th birthday. Yes, women are now more likely to marry after having a child than before.

When the 1930s Savers became parents, 5% gave birth while unmarried. That percentage has grown with each succeeding generation. By 2012, 41% of moms (mostly 1980s Sharer moms) gave birth unmarried. While slightly more than half of the fathers still live with the mother at the time, this constitutes a dramatic shift in household composition, with a variety of implications.

UNMARRIED WOMEN GIVE BIRTH TO 41% OF BABIES, A 766% INCREASE SINCE 1960.

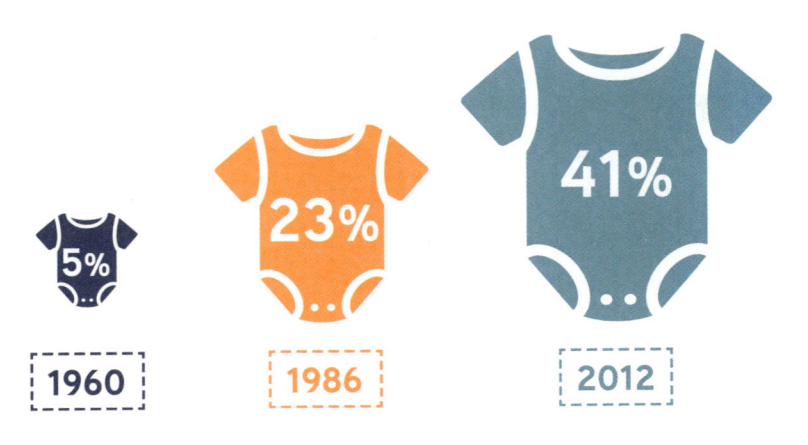

➡ **SINGLE MOMS HAVE EXPLODED IN NUMBERS**
FIGURE 4.11 Percent of Births to Unmarried Women

5% — 1960
23% — 1986
41% — 2012

Source: Centers for Disease Control and Prevention, National Vital Statistics Report

Parents increasingly raise their children on their own. In 1960, fewer than two million women raised kids on their own. Today, that number has more than quadrupled to 8.4 million. Single fathers raising kids have increased ninefold over the same period, from 0.3 million to 2.8 million. This trend points to less disposable income—childcare gets pricey—and a high demand for products and services that save time and add flexibility for single parents.

SINCE 1960, SINGLE PARENTING HAS QUADRUPLED FOR WOMEN AND INCREASED NINEFOLD FOR MEN.

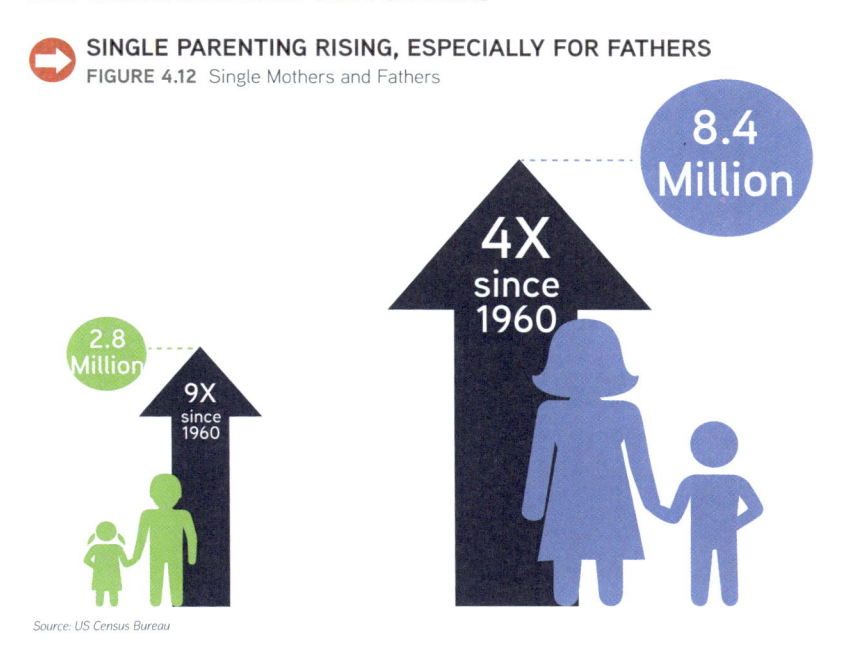

SINGLE PARENTING RISING, ESPECIALLY FOR FATHERS
FIGURE 4.12 Single Mothers and Fathers

8.4 Million

4X since 1960

2.8 Million

9X since 1960

Source: US Census Bureau

Almost one in three kids now live with just one biological parent—24% living primarily with Mom and 8% living primarily with Dad. This trend has grown steadily for decades, with huge implications. The childcare business has boomed, for example, along with all businesses catering to single, working parents. Single-income households forced to pay for childcare find it much harder to save a down payment for a house or money for a college education.

ALMOST 1/3 OF CHILDREN LIVE WITH ONE PARENT, COMPARED TO 9% IN 1960.

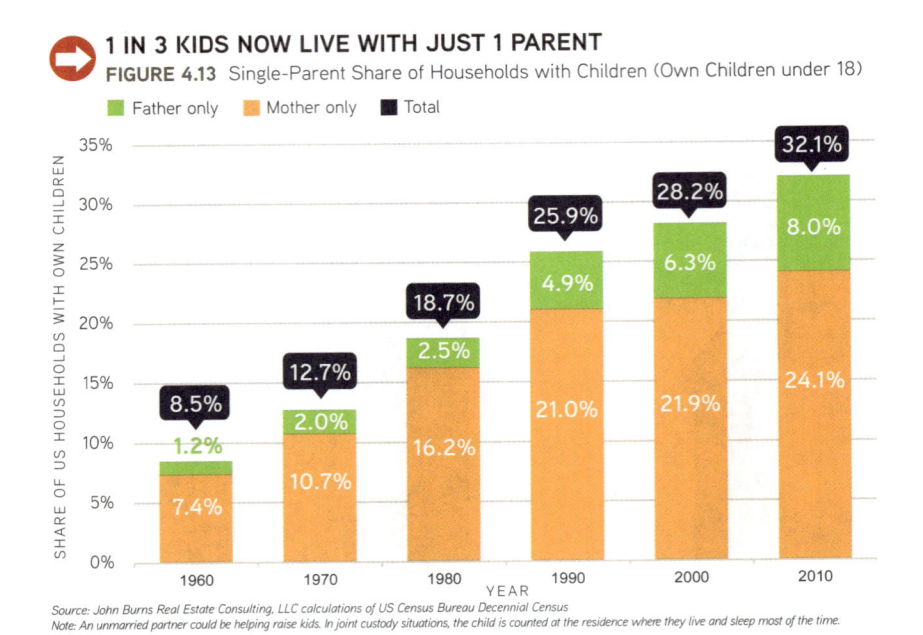

1 IN 3 KIDS NOW LIVE WITH JUST 1 PARENT

FIGURE 4.13 Single-Parent Share of Households with Children (Own Children under 18)

■ Father only　■ Mother only　■ Total

Year	Mother only	Father only	Total
1960	7.4%	1.2%	8.5%
1970	10.7%	2.0%	12.7%
1980	16.2%	2.5%	18.7%
1990	21.0%	4.9%	25.9%
2000	21.9%	6.3%	28.2%
2010	24.1%	8.0%	32.1%

SHARE OF US HOUSEHOLDS WITH OWN CHILDREN

Source: John Burns Real Estate Consulting, LLC calculations of US Census Bureau Decennial Census
Note: An unmarried partner could be helping raise kids. In joint custody situations, the child is counted at the residence where they live and sleep most of the time.

Female roles have shifted dramatically from the days when Sandra Day O'Connor could not get a job interview. A much higher percentage of women work. Far more complete college. They marry later and have children later or not at all. They increasingly opt to parent alone. They earn more and enjoy longer careers. They receive more help with childcare and housework from male partners, a rising number of whom earn less than their wives. Businesses that continue to strategically cater to these shifts, hiring more women and allowing more flexibility for both men and women, will have an advantage over their competition.

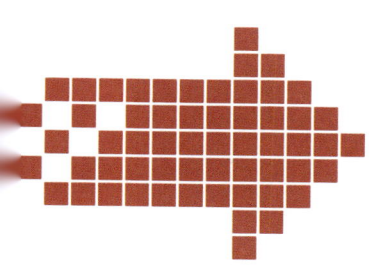

5: A WAVE OF AFFLUENT IMMIGRANTS

America's foreign-born population quadrupled in 40 years, from almost 10 million in 1970 to almost 40 million in 2010. Recently, immigration has dramatically shifted away from impoverished people crossing the US-Mexican border to affluent people arriving via airplane. Hundreds of thousands of Chinese, Indian, and other immigrants now arrive here by plane, enabled by wealth created in their recently robust economies. Conversely, after decades of significant immigration, more Mexican-born people actually left the United States than entered by 2013.[26]

---

26   US Census Bureau, "China Replaces Mexico as the Top Sending Country for Immigrants to the United States," May 1, 2015, http://researchmatters.blogs.census.gov/2015/05/01/china-replaces-mexico-as-the-top-sending-country-for-immigrants-to-the-united-states/.

THE FOREIGN-BORN POPULATION DOUBLED IN 20 YEARS TO 40 MILLION PEOPLE.

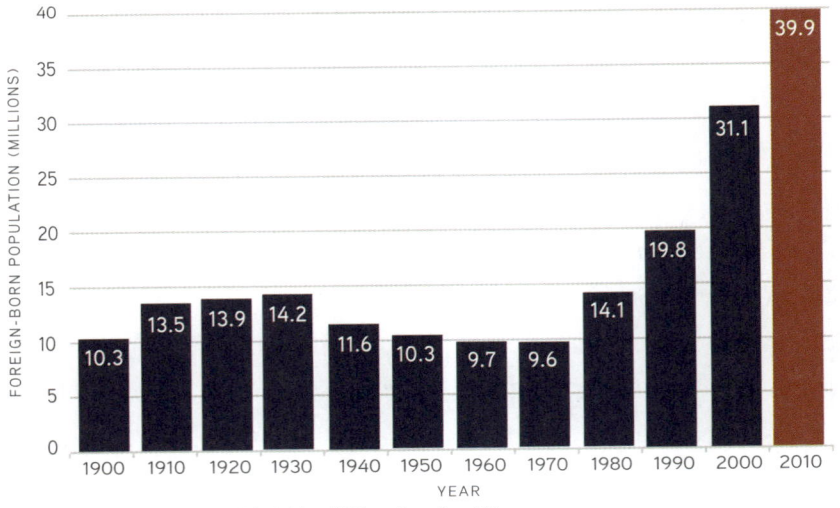

HIGHEST IMMIGRANT POPULATION EVER
FIGURE 5.1 Foreign-Born Population in the United States, 1900–2010

Year	Foreign-Born Population (Millions)
1900	10.3
1910	13.5
1920	13.9
1930	14.2
1940	11.6
1950	10.3
1960	9.7
1970	9.6
1980	14.1
1990	19.8
2000	31.1
2010	39.9

Source: John Burns Real Estate Consulting, LLC calculations of US Census Bureau Decennial Census

A strong desire for better economic, freedom, and lifestyle opportunities in America drives immigration demand. The sources of demand can fluctuate dramatically from year to year, based on political and economic activities in other countries, making immigration demand very difficult to forecast. In turn, the US government regulates immigration supply through visa limits. This complicated international web of immigration demand and supply caused the percentage of American residents born in other countries to plummet from 15% in 1910 to 5% in 1970 and then rebound to 13% by 2010. Nearly one in seven American residents moved from elsewhere. Businesses who respond most quickly to demand shifts find a brand-new customer with different tastes and preferences.

13% OF AMERICANS IMMIGRATED HERE—THE MOST IN 90+ YEARS.

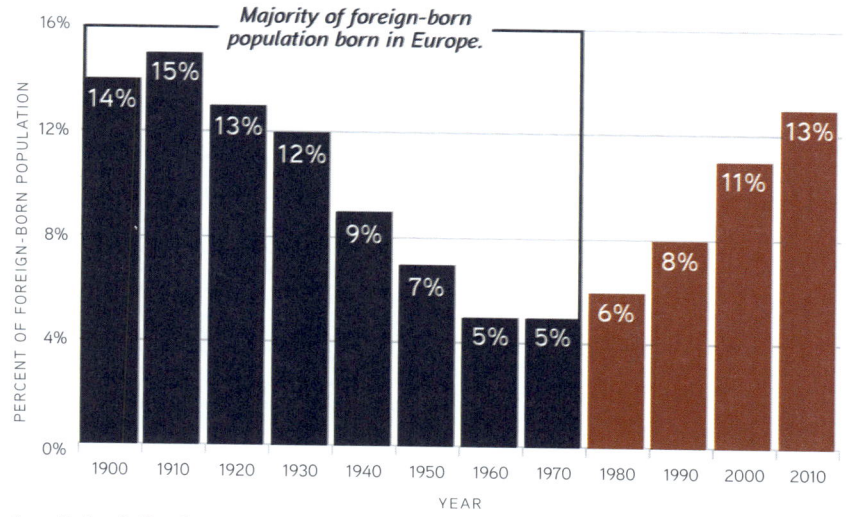

RISING DIVERSITY
FIGURE 5.2 Foreign-Born Share of US Population

Majority of foreign-born population born in Europe.

Year	Percent
1900	14%
1910	15%
1920	13%
1930	12%
1940	9%
1950	7%
1960	5%
1970	5%
1980	6%
1990	8%
2000	11%
2010	13%

Source: John Burns Real Estate Consulting, LLC calculations of US Census Bureau Decennial Census

Immigrants, such a profound part of this country's history and identity, once again play a powerful role in American life. At its current pace, immigration will account for more than half of our population growth by 2023.

In 1987, Manuel Laguna became a part of this wave of immigration when he legally came to California from Cuernavaca, Mexico, to work, save, and get a feel for *el otro lado,* or "the other side." He left behind a young wife, Elena, and a two-year-old daughter, Cynthia. He didn't want to live apart from his family, even temporarily, but in Mexico, his income barely covered food. In 1980s America, Manuel quickly realized, companies needed workers and paid them much higher wages than he earned back home.

The following year, Manuel moved his wife and three-year-old daughter, Cynthia, to California. A friend from home encouraged them to move to Costa Mesa, an Orange County community adjacent to Newport Beach. His friend claimed he had a nice house with two empty rooms for them.

"He painted a nice picture," Manuel said, "but when we got there, 27 people were living in the small house. They even rented the garage. Eleven of us, including Cynthia, slept in the living room."

During the next five months, the Lagunas saved a little money and met people who pointed them to a better apartment, where they shared a bathroom but at least had their own bedroom. Though they only spoke Spanish, making contacts who could help them proved easy. A large Mexican-born community resided in Costa Mesa in 1988.

US immigration has occurred in waves. A large influx of German and Irish came during the westward expansion of the mid-nineteenth century, while southern and eastern Europeans flocked to America as industrialization picked up at the turn of the century.

Immigration tapered during the Depression of the 1930s. The four subsequent decades saw comparatively low levels of people moving to the US. This trend, combined with the death or departure of immigrants already here, caused the foreign-born share of the US population to decline in the late '60s. But over the next 40 years immigration surged, reaching as high as 35% of population growth during the 1990s before dipping slightly to 32% from 2000 to 2010.

Not since the 1920s, a period that followed decades of strong immigration, has America experienced such diversity.

IMMIGRATION HAS RECENTLY FUELED 1/3 OF POPULATION GROWTH.

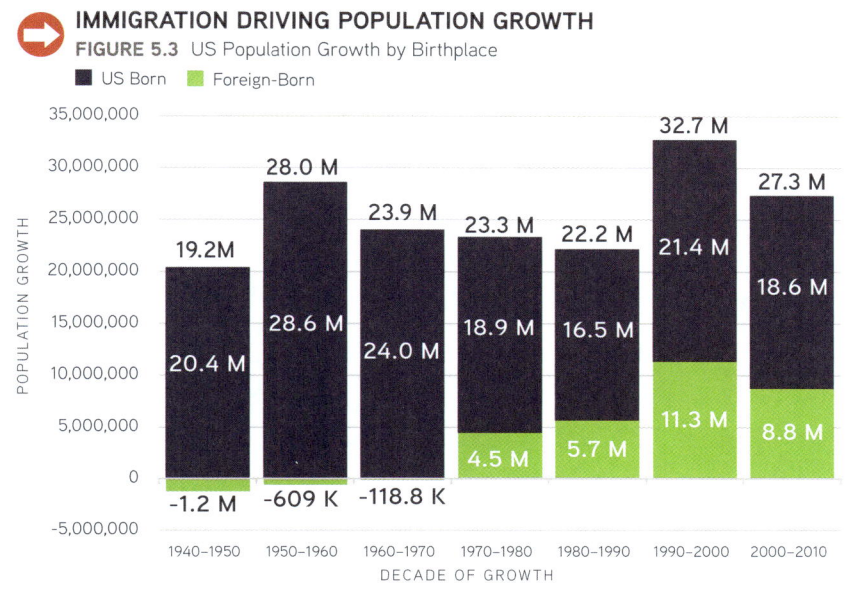

IMMIGRATION DRIVING POPULATION GROWTH
FIGURE 5.3 US Population Growth by Birthplace
■ US Born ■ Foreign-Born

Decade	Total	US Born	Foreign-Born
1940–1950	19.2M	20.4 M	-1.2 M
1950–1960	28.0 M	28.6 M	-609 K
1960–1970	23.9 M	24.0 M	-118.8 K
1970–1980	23.3 M	18.9 M	4.5 M
1980–1990	22.2 M	16.5 M	5.7 M
1990–2000	32.7 M	21.4 M	11.3 M
2000–2010	27.3 M	18.6 M	8.8 M

Source: John Burns Real Estate Consulting, LLC calculations of US Census Bureau Decennial Census

What caused this major shift? Government policy proved a powerful catalyst. The architects of the Immigration and Nationality Act of 1965 designed the law to promote more equal immigration opportunities across the globe. The prior quota system in place for almost half a century favored northern Europeans. The new law, also known as the Hart-Celler Act, privileged family connections and certain categories—those with needed skills or refugee claims, for instance. Congress ostensibly killed the old quota system, though it did impose caps for individual countries, as well as an overall limit.

Government's new approach opened the doors to large numbers of immigrants from Asia, Africa, Latin America, and Eastern Europe. Some sought economic opportunity. Others fled Cold War conflicts in Southeast Asia or oppressive regimes in Cuba and behind the Iron

Curtain. Three subsequent laws (the Refugee Act of 1980, the Immigration Reform and Control Act of 1986, and the Immigration Act of 1990) boosted the numbers further. The shift in government policy set the stage for almost a million net immigrants per year during the 1990s and 2000s. More legal immigrants entered the US during those two decades than in the prior 60 years combined.

Technology has played a significant role, thanks to more affordable international air travel and the Internet. Using the Internet, people from all over the world can research where they might relocate and easily contact friends and family already in the US.

These changes in immigration policy left a big stamp on recent generations. The 1970s Balancers boast the greatest international diversity, with 23% born internationally. Almost 1/4 of employees and customers in the prime working and spending years of 36–45 immigrated here. Those include some of our country's most successful entrepreneurs, such as South African-born Tesla founder Elon Musk and Russian-born Google founder Sergey Brin.

The dramatic increase in immigration has shaped the cities that, historically, evolved as ports of entry for newcomers. At Senn High School, on Chicago's North Side, students speak 44 languages. More than 60% speak a language other than English at home.[27] A 2011 *New York Daily News* article chronicled three blocks in the New York borough of Queens where residents represented 51 countries—India, Pakistan, Colombia, Guyana, Mexico, and many more.[28] Visitors to Miami's Little Havana these days will find cuisine from Central America, South America, Vietnam, and elsewhere alongside

---

27 Senn High School, "Ethnic Diversity," http://www.sennhs.org/apps/pages/index.jsp?uREC_ID=167284&type=d&pREC_ID=343573.

28 Sam Levin, "Three Queens blocks house immigrants from 51 countries making nabe most diverse in NYC," *New York Daily News*, August 25, 2011, http://www.nydailynews.com/new-york/queens/queens-blocks-house-immigrants-51-countries-making-nabe-diverse-nyc-article-1.946795.

the famous Cuban fare. All of these shifts create and destroy local businesses, which either adapt or shut their doors. New ethnic restaurants and churches provide the most visible signs of a shifting neighborhood.

America's typical immigrant narrative revolves around an economic motive, and the Lagunas' story bears that out. "In Mexico, my parents said we just had enough money to eat, pretty much," Cynthia said. "Everything was tough. I only wore my cousin's hand-me-downs, and my mom only had three outfits."

In the US, Manuel and Elena each worked multiple jobs. They arranged their shifts to take turns watching Cynthia, catching a few hours of sleep whenever they could. A bicycle purchased at Goodwill and equipped with a baby-seat provided their only transport, often carrying all three Lagunas at once.

They saved and eventually bought a comfortable one-story home in Costa Mesa. They found better jobs—Elena cleaning upscale houses, Manuel driving a bus for the Orange County Transportation Authority—and eventually went from a family of three sharing a bicycle to a three-car family of four. Cynthia graduated from UC Irvine and her younger brother currently studies aerospace engineering at San Diego State University.

Many immigrants tell similar stories of fleeing poverty for financial success in the US, but the rise of significant wealth abroad creates new kinds of immigrant stories and new motives for people who earned plenty in their native lands. This rings especially true for those leaving the so-called BRIC countries (Brazil, Russia, India, and China). The US economy grew 69% in nominal dollars from 2000 to 2014. Compare that growth with the expansion of some of the world's fastest-growing economies during the same fourteen-year period, led by China's phenomenal 763% growth!

ECONOMIC PROSPERITY IN OTHER COUNTRIES HAS CREATED THE WEALTH NEEDED TO MIGRATE TO THE US.

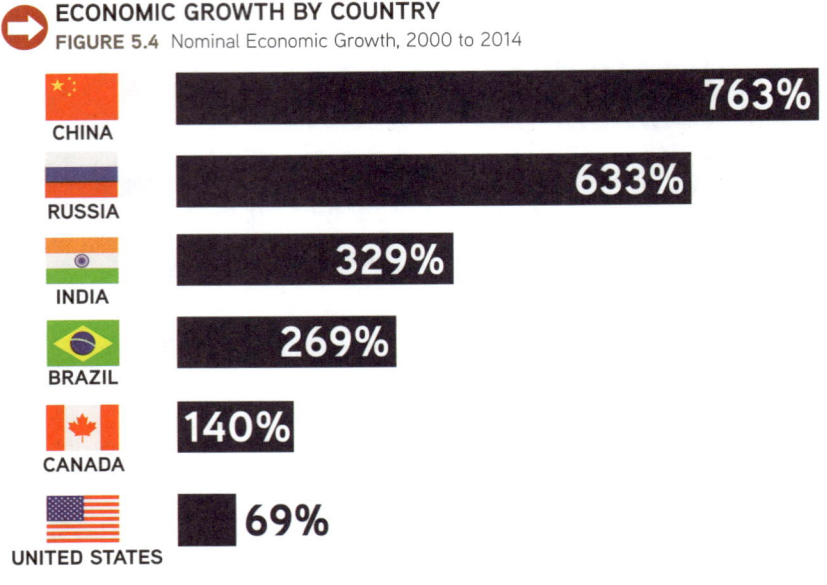

ECONOMIC GROWTH BY COUNTRY
FIGURE 5.4 Nominal Economic Growth, 2000 to 2014

Country	Growth
CHINA	763%
RUSSIA	633%
INDIA	329%
BRAZIL	269%
CANADA	140%
UNITED STATES	69%

Source: International Monetary Fund, World Economic Outlook Database

The shift from mostly impoverished immigrants seeking a better life in the United States to affluent individuals leaving their countries behind marks a very significant shift in migration. Many of these new residents seek democracy, lower pollution levels, an English-speaking education for their children, and a stable legal framework enforcing ethical behavior. The number of airline passengers originating from other countries has grown from 41 million in 1990 to 91 million today.

As CEO of the California region for Brookfield Residential, a $4.5-billion-dollar-per-year homebuilder, Adrian Foley counts many buyers from the Pacific Rim among his clientele. The factors that influence their decisions to come to America vary, he said, depending on their country of origin.

"For European buyers, the expectations of the standard of living are significantly lower than what California actually provides, so it's a stark realization when they get here and realize they can get so much more than they thought," Foley said. "Also, the education network around you is strong. The European one is strong, too, but for Chinese and Indian buyers, perhaps that's not the case. Another big issue is the rule of law. It's not a concern for Europeans, but for Chinese buyers, the US is a safe haven."

> **THE NUMBER OF AIRLINE PASSENGERS ORIGINATING FROM OTHER COUNTRIES HAS GROWN FROM 41 MILLION IN 1990 TO 91 MILLION TODAY.**

Foley knows something about European buyers. He grew up in Britain and moved to California 25 years ago, immigrating to California after the Connecticut woman he married spent a year with him in rainy London.

Historically, problems abroad create demand to move to the US. Religious persecution, war, pollution, corruption, and recessions create demand for immigrants to flock to the US. For example, Cuba became the top source of immigration during the upheaval of the Fidel Castro regime's early years in the 1960s. Few Cubans move here today. In the 1970s, when the Immigration and Nationality Act of 1965 had fully taken effect, Asian countries moved up in the rankings. Eventually, Asia accounted for five of the top ten countries of origin. Mexican immigration surged in the 1990s due to economic opportunities in the US. Recent economic growth in China and India created well-off buyers who can afford the considerable expense of flying here.

MORE MEXICANS NOW LEAVE AMERICA THAN ENTER—A HUGE SHIFT.

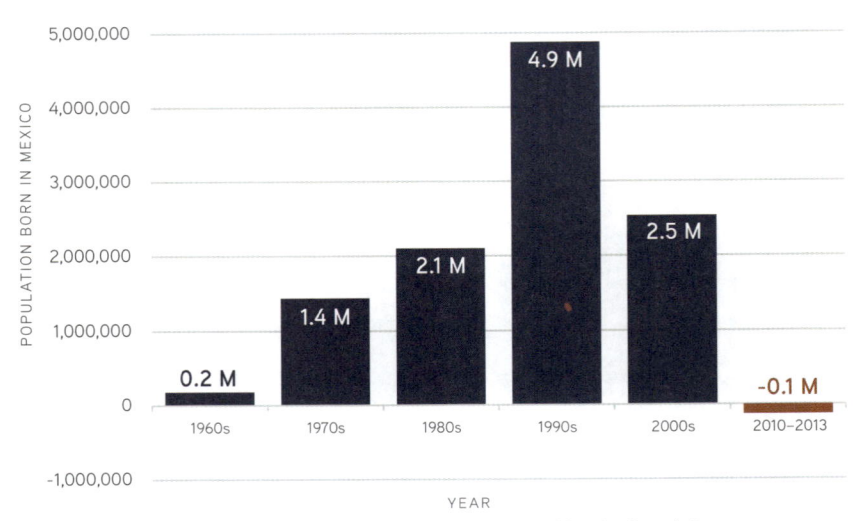

➡ MEXICAN IMMIGRATION HAS ENDED
FIGURE 5.5 Net Increase in US Residents Born in Mexico

Decade	Population Born in Mexico
1960s	0.2 M
1970s	1.4 M
1980s	2.1 M
1990s	4.9 M
2000s	2.5 M
2010–2013	-0.1 M

Source: John Burns Real Estate Consulting, LLC calculations of US Census Bureau Decennial Census, 2013 American Community Survey

In 2013, the US included 11.6 million people born in Mexico. Thirty-seven percent live in California and 22% live in Texas. The greatest numbers reside in Los Angeles County, CA; Harris County, TX (Houston); and Cook County, IL (Chicago). After surging in the '70s and '90s, Mexican immigration slowed in the 2000s. In part, the Great Recession and improved opportunities in Mexico caused the slowdown.

Hundreds of thousands of people fled Mexico each year to the United States when the Lagunas moved. "That seemed like a peak time when everyone wanted to come to the US," Manuel said. That massive demographic shift, however, has ended. Approximately half as many Mexicans moved to the US in the 2000s as in the 1990s. This shift heavily impacts businesses that rely on Hispanic labor, such as construction and agriculture, and cater to Mexican-born consumers. In 2014, 570,000 fewer Mexican-born construction workers worked in the US than in 2007. Homebuilders from coast to coast complained of labor shortages and rising construction costs.

A report from Pew in 2012 noted that reasons for the decline in Mexican immigration to the US from Mexico included:

- weakened US job and housing construction markets
- heightened border enforcement
- a rise in deportations
- growing dangers associated with illegal border crossings
- a long-term decline in Mexico's birth rate
- better economic conditions in Mexico[29]

The Lagunas said they noticed evidence of this downward trend. "It used to be easier [in the US]," Elena said. "There was a ton of work here. People crossed more easily. Now, you need a Social Security card, a green card, a whole bunch of stuff. Also, based on what we hear, things are way better in Mexico than before. People seem to live more comfortably. They aren't as desperate to come to the US."

---

29 Jeffrey Passel, D'Vera Cohn, and Ana Gonzalez-Barrera, "Net Migration from Mexico Falls to Zero—and Perhaps Less," Pew Hispanic Center, April 23, 2012, http://www.pewhispanic.org/2012/04/23/net-migration-from-mexico-falls-to-zero-and-perhaps-less/.

INDIANS FLOCK TO THE US.

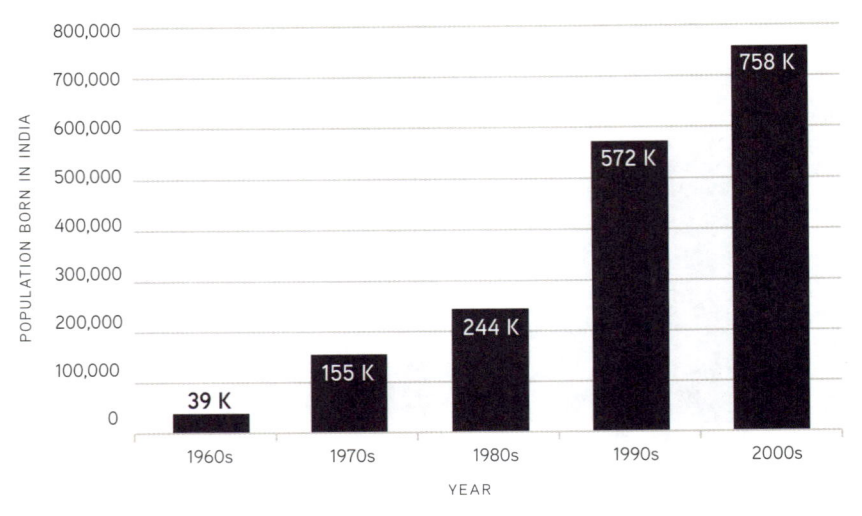

SURGING IMMIGRATION FROM INDIA
FIGURE 5.6 Net Increase in US Residents Born in India

Year	Population Born in India
1960s	39 K
1970s	155 K
1980s	244 K
1990s	572 K
2000s	758 K

Source: John Burns Real Estate Consulting, LLC calculations of US Census Bureau Decennial Census, 2010 American Community Survey

In 2013, two million Indian-born people lived in the US. About 20% live in California, 12% in New Jersey, and 9% in Texas, especially in the Houston area. The greatest numbers reside in Santa Clara County, CA; Middlesex County, NJ; and Cook County, IL. Today, immigrants from India receive the majority of visas (H-1B) for skilled technology workers sponsored by US employers.

CHINESE INCREASINGLY RELOCATE TO THE US.

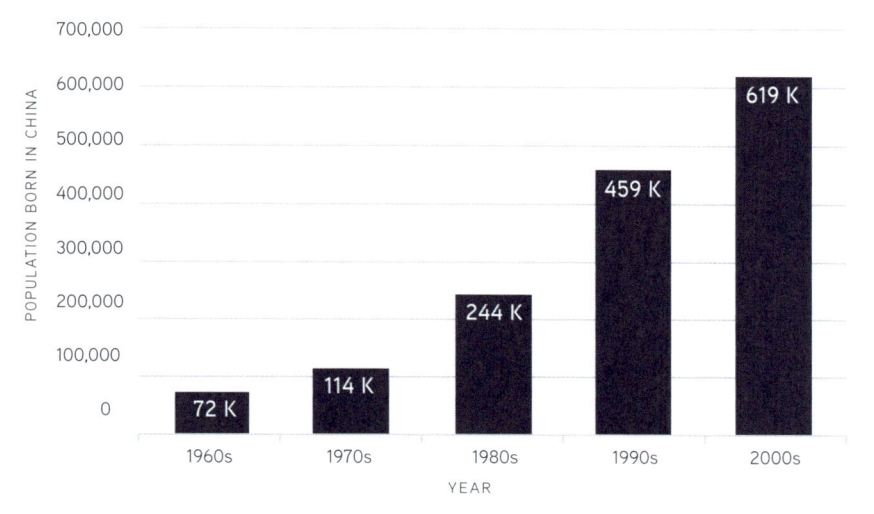

SURGING IMMIGRATION FROM CHINA
FIGURE 5.7 Net Increase in US Residents Born in China

Year	Population Born in China
1960s	72 K
1970s	114 K
1980s	244 K
1990s	459 K
2000s	619 K

Source: John Burns Real Estate Consulting, LLC calculations of US Census Bureau Decennial Census, 2010 American Community Survey

The US included 1.8 million people born in China in 2013. About 30% live in California and 21% in New York. Midcentury Chinese immigration largely originated from Taiwan. The restoration of diplomatic relations between China and the US in 1978—another example of government's impact on demographics—paved the way for more immigration of college students and professionals from mainland China. In addition to educational opportunities, Chinese immigrants (especially the upper-middle class and wealthy in recent years) seek a better quality of life and economic opportunities.

Like the European immigrants of earlier generations, today's newcomers from China and India often choose communities where their compatriots settled years ago. There, they find food, products, customs, and culture that provide a sense of familiarity. After the Tiananmen Square protests of 1989 and ahead of the return of Hong

Kong to Chinese sovereignty in 1997, Chinatowns in San Francisco and New York received a burst of vitality as immigrants moved their families and opened businesses there. An Indian immigrant who moves to the towns of Iselin or Edison in New Jersey will as likely hear Hindi as English on Oak Tree Road, where one restaurant reviewer counted more than fifty Indian restaurants on a four-mile stretch.[30]

Highly educated Chinese and Indian immigrants also gravitate to areas with high levels of tech sector employment, such as San Jose and Seattle, and medical employment, such as Houston and Los Angeles.

This concentration effect helps explain why more than half the surge in immigration between 1990 and 2010 occurred in just five states: California, Texas, Florida, New York, and New Jersey. Texas and New Jersey rose in the rankings during those 20 years, while the bottom 25 states (plus Washington, DC) accounted for just 8% of the foreign-born growth. Today, California has 12% of the US population but welcomes 18% of the immigrant arrivals. Texas has 8% of the population but houses 13% of new immigrants.

---

30 "Crazy! 56 Indian Restaurants Crowd 4-Mile Oak Tree Road Stretch in Edison/Iselin, NJ," SearchIndia, http://www.searchindia.com/2012/02/28/crazy-56-indian-restaurants-crowd-4-mile-oak-tree-road-stretch-in-edisoniselin-nj/.

48% OF RECENT FOREIGN-BORN POPULATION GROWTH TOOK PLACE IN JUST 4 STATES.

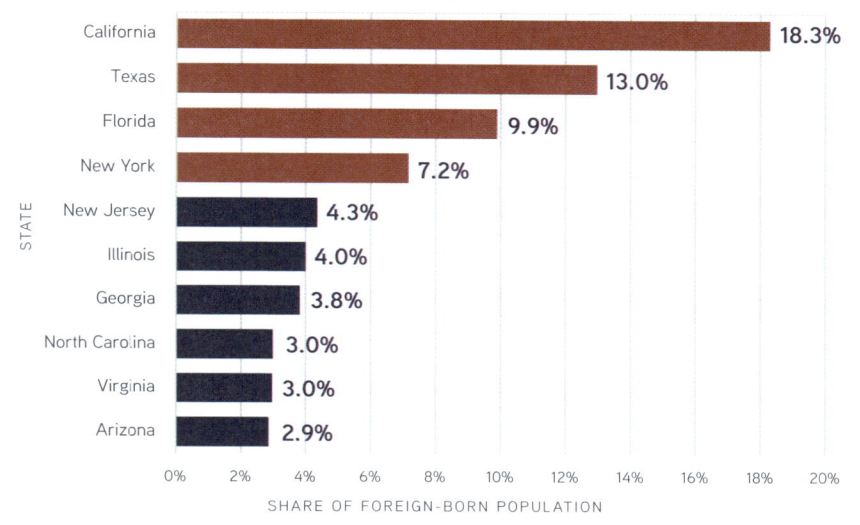

IMMIGRANT CONCENTRATIONS
FIGURE 5.8 1990–2010 Share of US Foreign-Born Population Growth

State	Share of Foreign-Born Population
California	18.3%
Texas	13.0%
Florida	9.9%
New York	7.2%
New Jersey	4.3%
Illinois	4.0%
Georgia	3.8%
North Carolina	3.0%
Virginia	3.0%
Arizona	2.9%

Source: US Census Bureau—1990 Decennial Census, 2010 American Community Survey

These states house the "gateway cities" with major airports offering convenient, affordable international flights. San Francisco, Los Angeles, Houston, Seattle, New York, Miami, Dallas, and Chicago offer many international flights each day.

Immigrants increasingly move inland as well, to places with strong economies. Cities such as Las Vegas, Atlanta, and Austin offer plenty of employment opportunities. Demand for goods and services has changed in these areas due to the newly diverse makeup of the population.

Foreign-born households continue to rise in many markets throughout the South and on the coasts. Southern border-states saw the biggest increases, while southeast Florida and Washington, DC experienced huge growth in immigrant populations. Harris County, which includes Houston, leads the pack, with 287,462 new foreign-born residents, primarily of Mexican origin. Texas accounts for five of the top twenty foreign-born counties.

Miami-Dade County in Florida now has more foreign-born residents than US-born. The counties surrounding Manhattan Island in New York are not far behind. Foreign-born residents account for 48% of residents in Queens County, New York; 39% in Hudson County, New Jersey; and 38% in Brooklyn's King County.

5: A WAVE OF AFFLUENT IMMIGRANTS

TEXAS'S WELCOMING ATTITUDE TO IMMIGRANTS HAS CONTRIBUTED TO ITS STRONG POPULATION GROWTH.

BIGGEST IMMIGRANT COUNTIES
FIGURE 5.9 *Growth of Foreign-Born Population by County, 2000–2010*

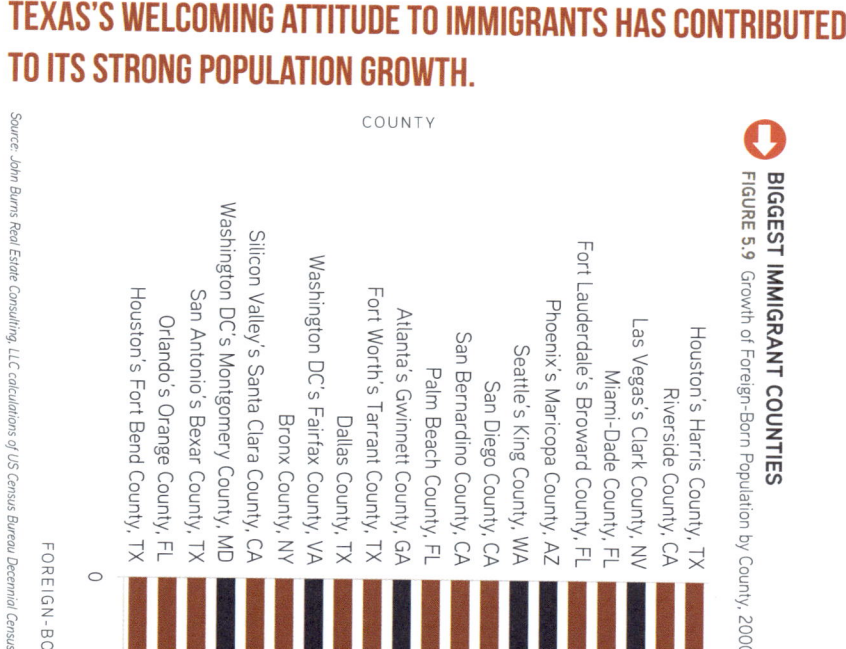

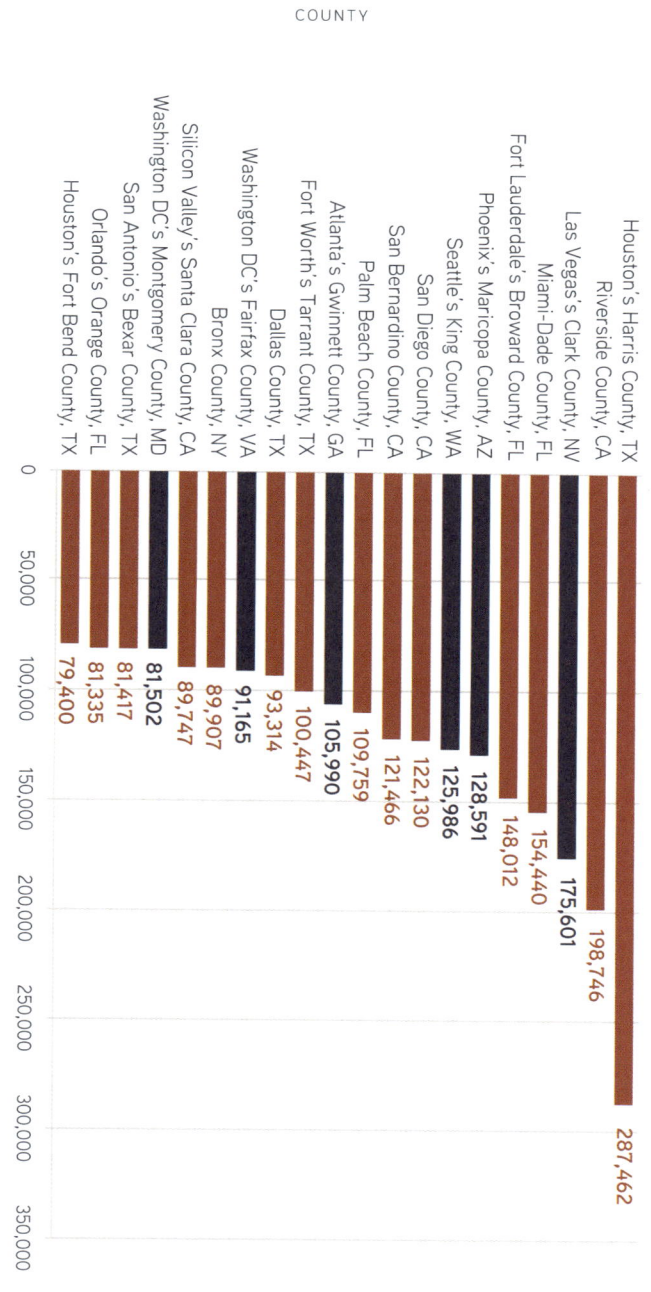

County	Foreign-Born Population Growth, 2000–2010
Houston's Harris County, TX	287,462
Riverside County, CA	198,746
Las Vegas's Clark County, NV	175,601
Miami-Dade County, FL	154,440
Fort Lauderdale's Broward County, FL	148,012
Phoenix's Maricopa County, AZ	128,591
Seattle's King County, WA	125,986
San Diego County, CA	122,130
San Bernardino County, CA	121,466
Palm Beach County, FL	109,759
Atlanta's Gwinnett County, GA	105,990
Fort Worth's Tarrant County, TX	100,447
Washington DC's Fairfax County, VA	93,314
Dallas County, TX	91,165
Bronx County, NY	89,907
Silicon Valley's Santa Clara County, CA	89,747
Washington DC's Montgomery County, MD	81,502
San Antonio's Bexar County, TX	81,417
Orlando's Orange County, FL	81,335
Houston's Fort Bend County, TX	79,400

Source: John Burns Real Estate Consulting, LLC calculations of US Census Bureau Decennial Census

BIG SHIFTS AHEAD

MORE THAN 1/2 OF MIAMI'S RESIDENTS MOVED HERE FROM ANOTHER COUNTRY.

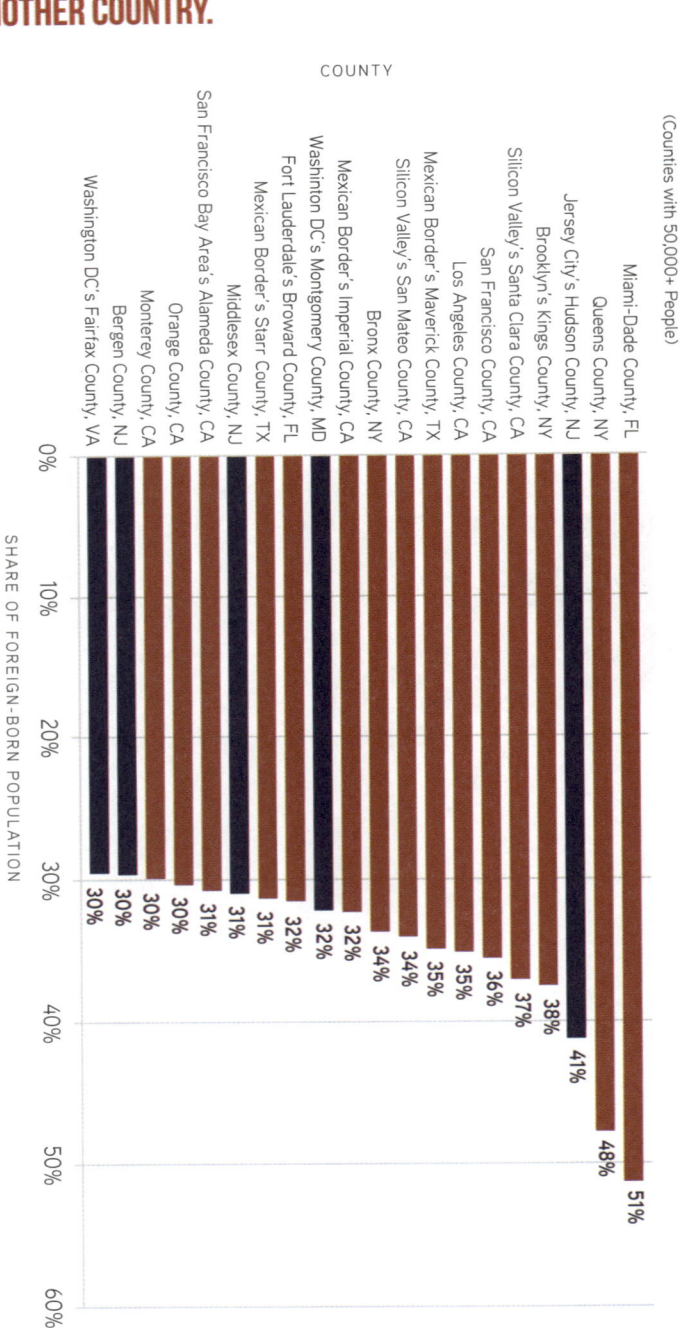

HIGHEST IMMIGRANT CONCENTRATIONS
FIGURE 5.10 Highest Share of Foreign-Born Population, 2009–2013
(Counties with 50,000+ People)

County	Share of Foreign-Born Population
Miami-Dade County, FL	51%
Queens County, NY	48%
Jersey City's Hudson County, NJ	41%
Brooklyn's Kings County, NY	38%
Silicon Valley's Santa Clara County, CA	37%
San Francisco County, CA	36%
Los Angeles County, CA	35%
Mexican Border's Maverick County, TX	35%
Silicon Valley's San Mateo County, CA	34%
Bronx County, NY	34%
Mexican Border's Imperial County, CA	32%
Washington DC's Montgomery County, MD	32%
Fort Lauderdale's Broward County, FL	32%
Mexican Border's Starr County, TX	31%
Middlesex County, NJ	31%
San Francisco Bay Area's Alameda County, CA	30%
Orange County, CA	30%
Monterey County, CA	30%
Bergen County, NJ	30%
Washington DC's Fairfax County, VA	30%

Source: John Burns Real Estate Consulting, LLC calculations of US Census Bureau, 2009–2013 American Community Survey

Business leaders ignore immigration's seismic demographic shift and the enormous marketing opportunities it creates at their peril. Adrian Foley, the California-based COO of Brookfield Residential, said that in 2015 his company sold about half of its new homes to buyers who probably came from another country, though some might have lived in the US for decades.

Given the high percentage of foreign-born homebuyers in California, Brookfield's success rests on understanding and catering to these potential clients on a "macro and micro level," Foley said. "We do market differently to ethnic audiences," Foley said. "How we choose to advertise, where we advertise, how we position our product in terms of floor plans, the community offering, the specifications—it's all different. There are a lot of strategic specification shifts, depending on the buyer profile and the ethnicity of buyers."

For example, Foley said, in Chinese and Indian culture, the parents of buyers often live in the home and care for their grandchildren. Brookfield designs particular rooms or suites of rooms for "the hierarch" in the family. "That's a very important role, and it's treated that way," Foley said. "It's not appropriate for those rooms to be in locations that are inferior, and they need privacy. There are also different styles of cooking, so Brookfield includes the appropriate kitchen appliances and layout. There are elements relating to good karma or good luck—design components, as well as things like the number of houses in a community, for example. *Feng shui* [design principles] can play a role, especially for an earlier generation of overseas buyers."

Brookfield markets its product in a variety of languages and in ethnic media outlets, and it runs multilingual sales centers, even though most of its foreign-born buyers either speak English or use a broker who does. "We have speakers of Hindi or Mandarin or Spanish on our sales staff," Foley said. "Someone might say, 'Everyone should speak English here.' But we have a much better experience with buyers this way because even if their English is pretty good, a lot of subtleties can get lost."

Even the food Brookfield serves at grand openings reflects the target ethnicities for various communities, with samosas and shumai as common as prosciutto and brie. Considering the demographics of his market and the maturing of the California buyer, Foley anticipates that the foreign-born share of his clientele—already half his buyers—will continue to grow and diversify.

The foreign-born population also impacts data that many often rely on. For example, foreign-born households drag the homeownership rate down almost 3%. Only 51% of foreign-born households own a home, compared to 67% of US-born. Therefore, strong immigration accounts for a portion of the massive recent homeownership rate decline. With the recent shift to more affluent immigrants, we expect this 16% gap to narrow.

51% OF THE FOREIGN-BORN POPULATION OWN HOMES.

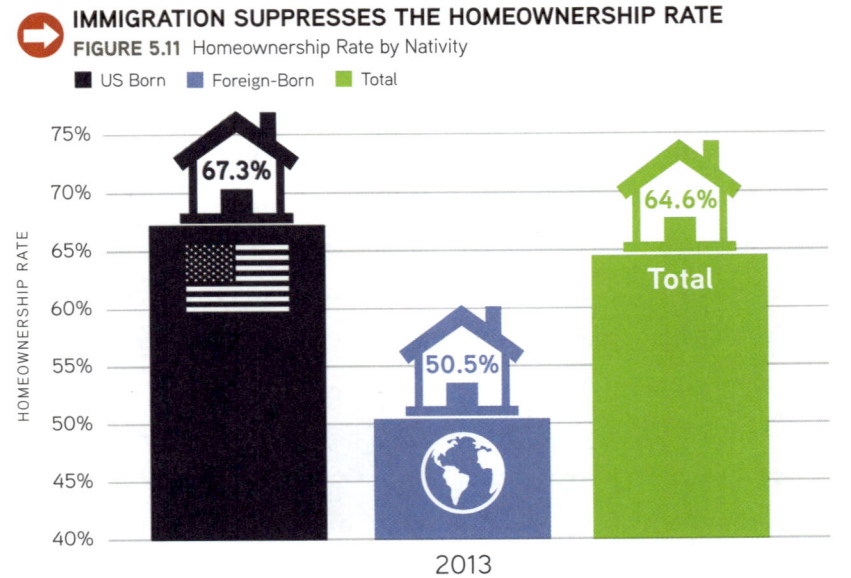

IMMIGRATION SUPPRESSES THE HOMEOWNERSHIP RATE

FIGURE 5.11 Homeownership Rate by Nativity

- US Born: 67.3%
- Foreign-Born: 50.5%
- Total: 64.6%

2013

Source: John Burns Real Estate Consulting, LLC calculations of US Census Bureau, Current Population Survey, Annual Social and Economic Supplements via IPUMS-CPS

Immigrants also tend to live with others for a while, forming new households at a slower rate than those born in the US. Immigrants also tend to live with multiple generations of adults in the home. Only 22% of immigrants aged eighteen or older head a household during their first year in the US.

IMMIGRANTS OFTEN LIVE WITH MORE THAN 2 ADULTS IN THE HOME, CREATING FEWER HOUSEHOLDS PER ADULT AND DESIRING HOMES WITH MORE BEDROOMS AND BATHROOMS.

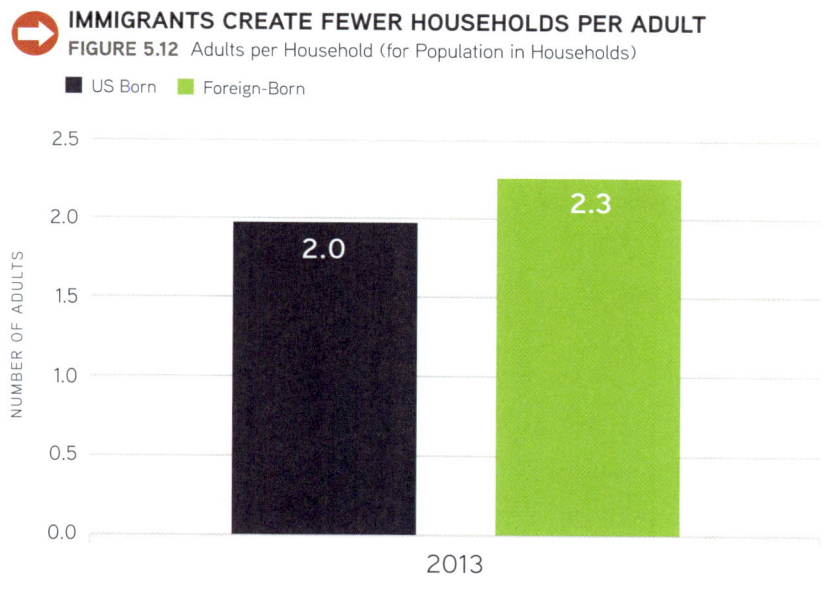

IMMIGRANTS CREATE FEWER HOUSEHOLDS PER ADULT
FIGURE 5.12 Adults per Household (for Population in Households)

	US Born	Foreign-Born
2013	2.0	2.3

Source: John Burns Real Estate Consulting, LLC calculations of US Census Bureau, 2013 American Community Survey via IPUMS-USA

The 1970s Balancers easily rank as the most diverse of our generations, with 23%—nearly one in four—foreign-born. The influx of young people continuing to arrive means that the percentage of foreign-born 1980s Sharers and 1990s Connectors will rise as well. Most people immigrate to the US in their 20s and 30s. Census Bureau forecasters project rising diversity for the younger generations.

THE 1970s BALANCERS BOAST THE GREATEST FOREIGN DIVERSITY, WITH 23% FOREIGN-BORN.

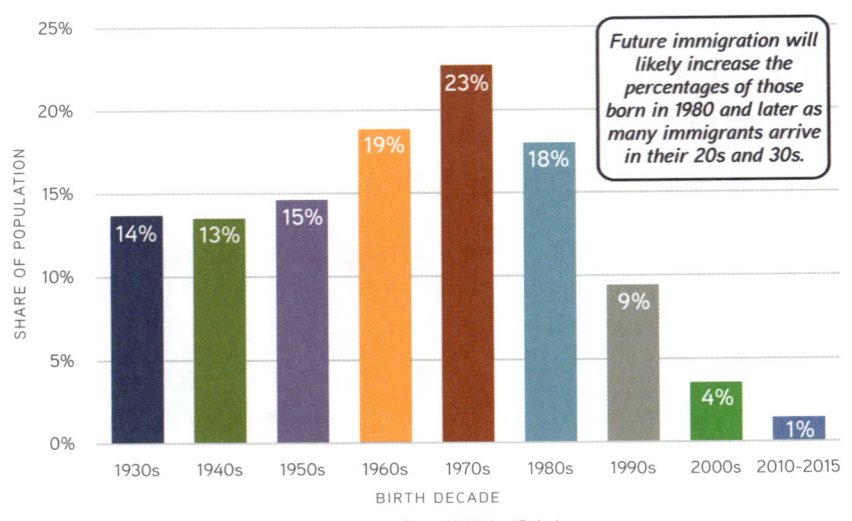

THE BALANCERS ARE THE MOST DIVERSE GROUP
FIGURE 5.13 Percent of 2015 Population That Is Foreign-Born

Birth Decade	Share of Population
1930s	14%
1940s	13%
1950s	15%
1960s	19%
1970s	23%
1980s	18%
1990s	9%
2000s	4%
2010–2015	1%

Future immigration will likely increase the percentages of those born in 1980 and later as many immigrants arrive in their 20s and 30s.

Source: John Burns Real Estate Consulting, LLC calculations of US Census Bureau 2014 National Projections

We can't predict much about those born in the 2000s. They're simply too young. But we do know that diversity has surrounded these children in many ways. With almost 25% of their parents born overseas, diversity has infused their classrooms, play dates, soccer teams, and first jobs. We named those born in the 2000s "Globals" for this reason. They know people from cultures all over the world and accept international cultures more easily than any children before them.

With 30% of the population growth born in another country, businesspeople must identify and target these consumers similar to the way Brookfield Residential does. As shown very clearly by history, changes in government policy can cause immigration to ebb and flow. Changes in economic opportunity both in America and in other countries can also cause immigration to shift. Recent economic improvements in China have created enough affluence to allow people to move to the US, while economic improvements in Mexico have reduced the urgency to move. People are staying in Mexico because the US opportunities are not that much better. America's growing diversity creates plenty of opportunity for those able to capitalize on the big immigration shifts.

6: RETIREE EXPLOSION UNDERWAY

In ten short years, from 2005 to 2015, the number of people turning 65 each year exploded from 2.2 million to 3.5 million. In 2022, 4 million residents will celebrate their 65th birthday. The current surge in retirement is depleting the labor force of millions of 1950s-born workaholics. In 2025, 66 million Americans will have celebrated their 65th birthday, a 38% increase in only a ten-year period. For ease of reading, we will refer to this group as retirees, although we know full well many will continue working.

The 1950s Innovators will redefine retirement, just like they redefined everything else. A far greater percentage than ever before will work. They will reward themselves in retirement by doing work they enjoy and spending time with their children and grandchildren. Prior generations rewarded themselves in their golden years by moving away from the family they had worked so hard to support.

> **IN 2025, 66 MILLION AMERICANS WILL HAVE CELEBRATED THEIR 65TH BIRTHDAY, A 38% INCREASE IN ONLY A TEN-YEAR PERIOD.**

THE 1950s INNOVATORS WILL DRIVE AN EXPLOSION OF 18 MILLION MORE PEOPLE AGED 65+ OVER THE NEXT 10 YEARS.

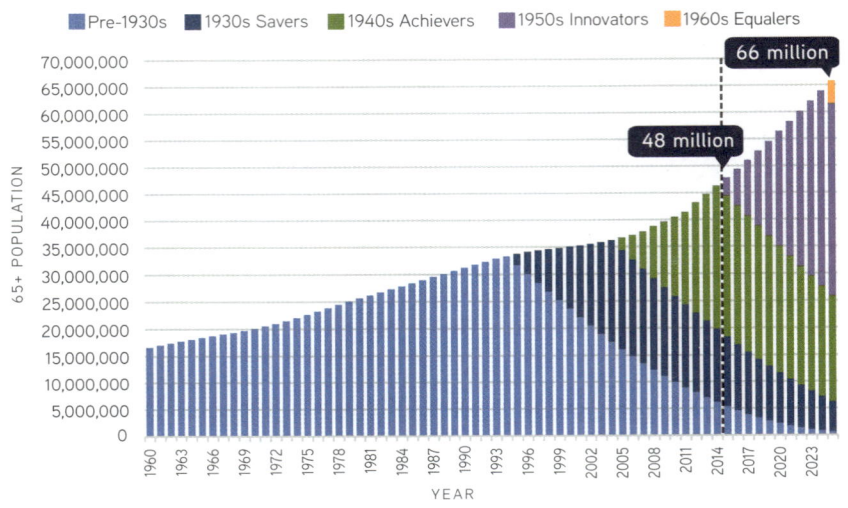

➡ SURGE IN 65+ POPULATION
FIGURE 6.1 65+ Population by Decade of Birth

■ Pre-1930s   ■ 1930s Savers   ■ 1940s Achievers   ■ 1950s Innovators   ■ 1960s Equalers

66 million
48 million

Source: John Burns Real Estate Consulting, LLC calculations of US Census Bureau Population Estimates and 2014 National Projections

Americans over 65 increasingly work. Exactly 18% of 65–69 year-old Achievers work full time, compared to 14% of Savers and 10% of the prior generation at the same age. Far more continue to work part time as well.

18% OF ACHIEVERS AGED 65–69 WORK FULL TIME TODAY, NEARLY DOUBLE THE PERCENTAGE THAT WORKED FULL TIME 20 YEARS AGO.

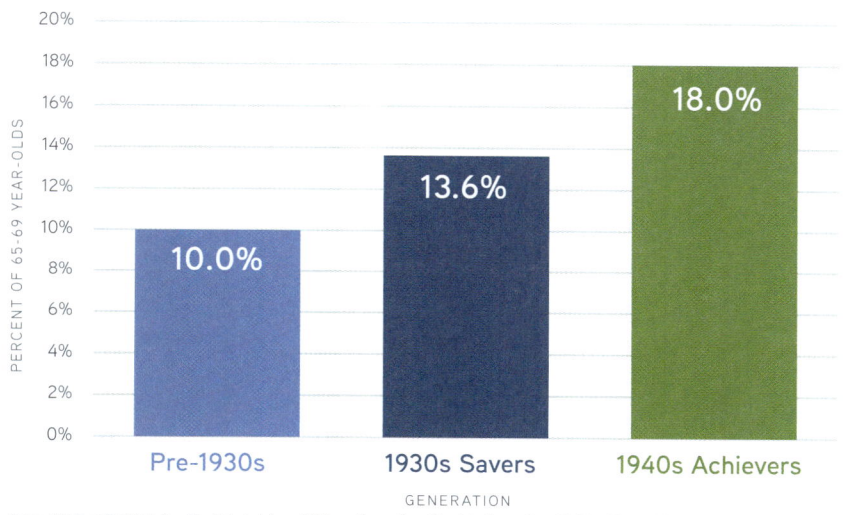

WORKING FULL TIME PAST 65
FIGURE 6.2 Percent of 65–69 Year-Olds Working Full Time

Generation	Percent
Pre-1930s	10.0%
1930s Savers	13.6%
1940s Achievers	18.0%

Source: John Burns Real Estate Consulting, LLC calculations of US Census Bureau, Current Population Survey, Annual Social and Economic Supplements via IPUMS-CPS

More 1950s Innovators—the oldest of whom are now in their early 60s—are in the labor force than the 1930s Savers and 1940s Achievers did at the same age. A whopping 56% of Innovators still work at least part time—a 7% higher rate than the Achievers and 11% higher than the Savers. They will continue to work hard well past 65, simultaneously collecting a paycheck and Social Security.

INNOVATORS ARE 7% MORE LIKELY THAN THE ACHIEVERS TO BE WORKING IN THEIR EARLY 60s.

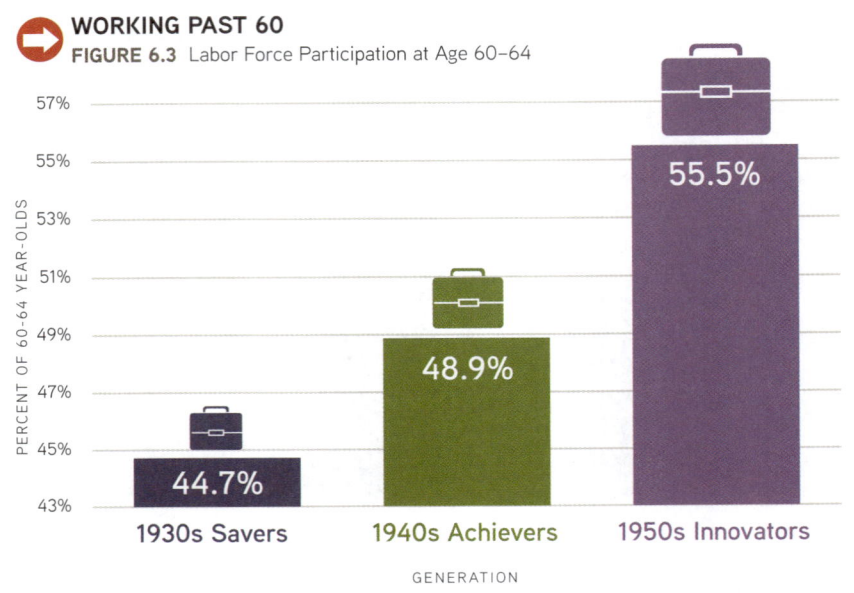

WORKING PAST 60

FIGURE 6.3 Labor Force Participation at Age 60–64

- 1930s Savers: 44.7%
- 1940s Achievers: 48.9%
- 1950s Innovators: 55.5%

PERCENT OF 60–64 YEAR-OLDS / GENERATION

Source: Bureau of Labor Statistics; John Burns Real Estate Consulting, LLC

Advances in medicine will also add to America's graying trend. Life expectancy at birth currently increases two to three months every year. Steady advances in medications and vaccines during the twentieth century prolonged life. Think of the ominous way the words "open-heart surgery" once rang in the air. Today, doctors routinely perform quadruple bypasses and organ transplants with tremendous success. 1950s Innovators replace hips and knees in record numbers, some returning to work in just a few short days.

LIFE EXPECTANCY INCREASES MORE THAN 2 MONTHS EVERY YEAR, AMPLIFYING THE NUMBER OF PEOPLE OVER 65 AND DEPLETING PENSION FUNDS THAT DID NOT PLAN FOR LONGER LIVING.

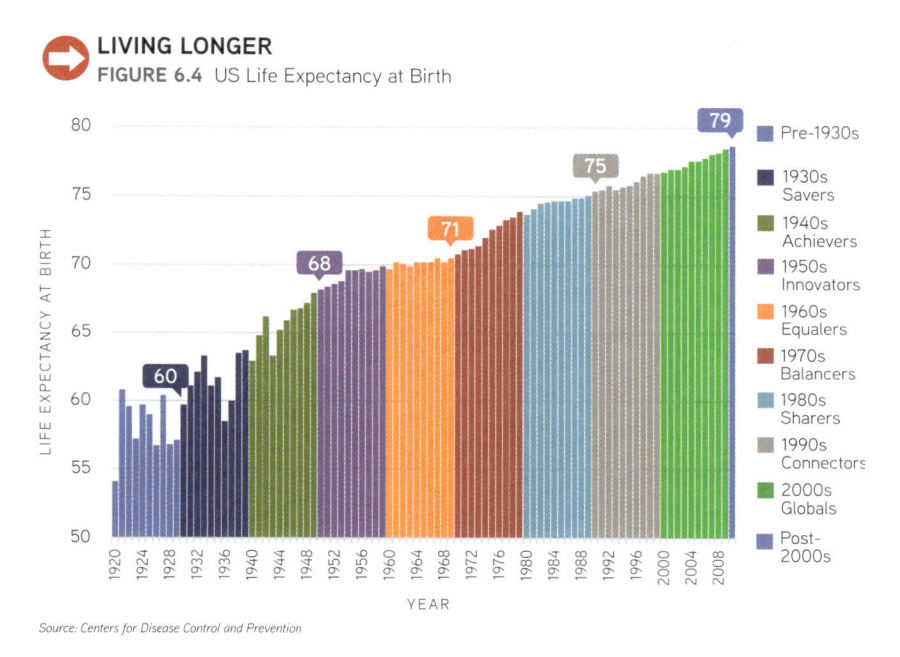

LIVING LONGER
FIGURE 6.4 US Life Expectancy at Birth

Source: Centers for Disease Control and Prevention

Virtually everyone knows about America's aging population. Because of that widespread knowledge, heavy investment in this perfectly predictable and well-known trend could very well result in an oversupply of many products or services. Look no further than the golf industry, which overinvested in new golf courses due to the easily quantifiable demographics that golfers play more rounds as they age. When the 1940s Achievers did not play as much golf as anticipated, a massive oversupply of very expensive golf courses resulted. While businesspeople love to quantify the demand, they often underestimate the competitive supply.

Today's retirees hold more money in the bank than previous retirees. Their strong work ethic played a huge role in their wealth creation. Luck played a huge role too, as they experienced a strong economy during most of their careers. Late in their careers, falling interest rates boosted home, stock, and bond values, creating even more wealth.

More than 75% of those aged 55 or older owned their homes in 2013. Companies selling products and services to today's affluent retirees see major opportunities ahead in remodeling, multiple generations of adults living in the same house, assisted living, healthcare, medicine, financial services, recreation, travel, mortality businesses, and other fields. Smart companies will also tap into retirees' desire to continue working, although perhaps at a somewhat slower pace as a tradeoff for less money.

Tremendous opportunities for customer segmentation abound. A 65-year-old body feels very different than an 85-year-old body. More than ever will retire affluent, but far more will retire on a budget. Many will move. Far more will stay in place.

New healthcare technologies, such as cancer drugs, as well as lifestyle changes, such as fewer smokers, help Americans live longer. Americans remain active well into what we once considered "old age." Waterskiing at 70? Taking a new job at 65? Why not? Moving into the heart of a big city after decades of tranquil suburban life? Sure. Those born during the 1940s and 1950s rewrote the rules during the '60s and '70s, changing the way we think about race, sex, gender, art, and

> **THOSE BORN DURING THE 1940s AND 1950s REWROTE THE RULES DURING THE '60s AND '70s, CHANGING THE WAY WE THINK ABOUT RACE, SEX, GENDER, ART, AND CAREERS. THAT THEY ARE CHANGING ATTITUDES ABOUT AGING SHOULD NOT SURPRISE ANYONE.**

careers. That they are changing attitudes about aging should not surprise anyone.

Steve Burch, the 63-year-old ex-Chrysler and Pulte executive who cannot imagine retiring, has dual motives for working past 65. Like many of the 1940s Achievers and 1950s Innovators, he always worked long hours and enjoyed a successful career that provided a healthy income. Like others in those generations—and perhaps partly because of the primacy of his career—he went through an expensive divorce after 20+ years of marriage. While working past 65 will delay the day he taps into savings, staying active recently became a more important part of the equation. Burch recently witnessed the sedentary lifestyle of his much younger fiancé's father, which triggered the new perspective.

"I underestimated the value of staying very active and really engaged in the workforce," Burch said. "I saw the way [not working] plays out in another guy's life and the way he spends his day. Staying engaged and continuing to work is a much more important piece [of life] than I originally thought. I don't feel old."

Lisa Marquis Jackson, the 49-year-old single mom from Dallas, looks at retirement much differently than her parents did. She expects to keep a busy calendar in retirement. With two daughters in school and expensive tuition bills to cover, however, Jackson worries more than Burch about paying for her golden years.

"Right now, I should be doing more for my retirement, and I'm doing more for education," Jackson said. "That part is very unbalanced, but I feel like it's the right investment for me to be making."

Far fewer Achievers struggle in their golden years than retirees of years past. The percentage of 65–69-year-olds living in poverty fell from 22% in the late 1960s to 9% today, the lowest percentage on record. We can thank government programs such as Social

Security for the change, as well as the work ethic of the 1940s Achievers. Dual-income households certainly contribute to a decline in poverty levels.

POVERTY AMONG EARLY RETIREES HAS PLUNGED FROM 22% TO 9%.

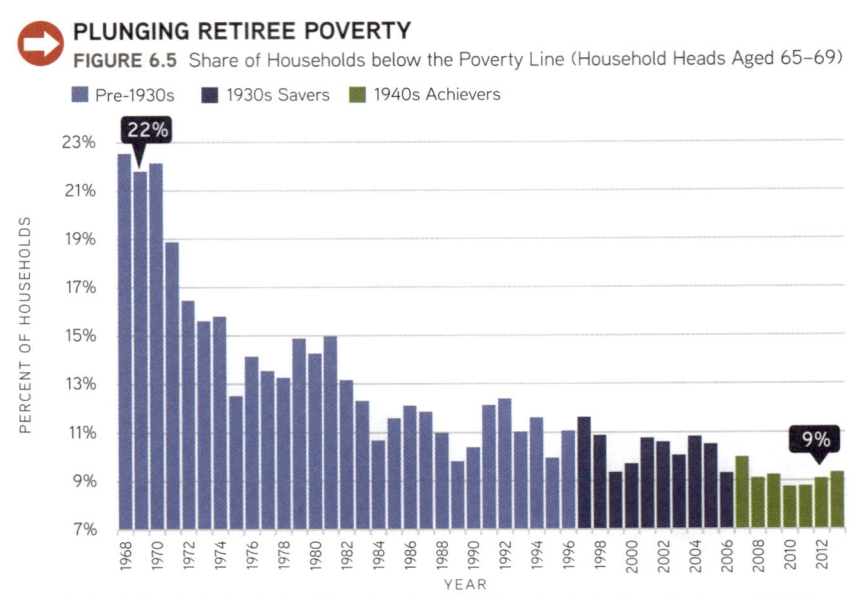

PLUNGING RETIREE POVERTY
FIGURE 6.5 Share of Households below the Poverty Line (Household Heads Aged 65–69)

Source: John Burns Real Estate Consulting, LLC calculations of US Census Bureau, Current Population Survey, Annual Social and Economic Supplements via IPUMS-CPS

Even 60-year-olds with substantial nest eggs now realize that they might live another 30 or 40 years and could use additional income. The stock market decline that came with the Great Recession took a big bite out of retirement savings. Historically low interest rates clearly changed the game too. Those who saved for retirement can no longer count on much interest income in retirement.

> **EVEN 60-YEAR-OLDS WITH SUBSTANTIAL NEST EGGS NOW REALIZE THAT THEY MIGHT LIVE ANOTHER 30 OR 40 YEARS AND COULD USE ADDITIONAL INCOME.**

Matching the Achievers' need to work with employers'

need for hard-working team members, a new type of job called "gig" employment emerged. Increasingly, companies offer part-time and flexible employment for seniors who bring invaluable experience to the workplace but might not want traditional 40-hour workweeks. Some companies pay low wages but offer healthcare, while others avoid paying for healthcare altogether.

The technology of the sharing economy creates many opportunities for retirees to earn money too. They can rent out a room in their home on Airbnb, drive for Uber or DoorDash, work part time in retail, or consult to small companies needing the help.

Government will continue to prolong work in other ways too. They have announced an increase in the age for collecting full benefits to 67 by 2027 and enhanced benefits for those who wait until they turn 70 to collect. As with many policies, this announcement has backfired by casting doubts on the system's long-term stability. Few wait until age 70 to begin drawing on Social Security.

The wealth of this rapidly growing group presents enormous opportunities for companies of all kinds. For example, we anticipate a surge in the remodeling business driven by those 65 and older. Homes need to be reconfigured from homes designed for young families to homes designed for older couples and singles. Assisted-living facilities will boom, as will healthcare, medical devices, and medications. Financial products that produce income and allow borrowing against assets will also prove popular. Reverse mortgages will allow retirees to continue spending. On a less sanguine note, the mortality business—such as funeral homes, coffin-makers, and crematoria—can also plan for an influx of new customers for many years to come. Already, 10% more people pass away per year than just one decade ago.

BY THE MID-2020s, TWICE AS MANY PEOPLE WILL CELEBRATE THEIR 65TH BIRTHDAY THAN CELEBRATED IN THE 1980s AND 1990s.

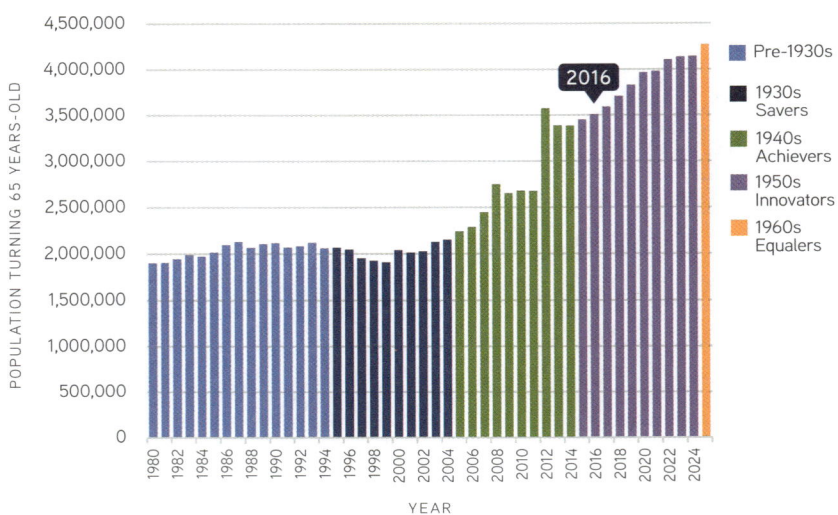

RETIREE EXPLOSION STARTED IN 2012
FIGURE 6.6 Population Aged 65

Source: US Census Bureau Population Estimates and 2014 National Projections. 65-year-old population as of July 1 each year

The retirement surge over the next decade means that by 2025, the number of people leaving the labor pool (the total number of people aged 20–64) will almost equal the number entering it. The labor pool's historical growth of 1.5 million+/- workers per year will drop below 500,000 by 2022—and stay there through at least 2025. And this forecast assumes that America's robust immigration continues. Because of this decline in the growth rate of workers, the economy almost certainly cannot experience sustained robust economic growth.

> **BECAUSE OF THIS DECLINE IN THE GROWTH RATE OF WORKERS, THE ECONOMY ALMOST CERTAINLY CANNOT EXPERIENCE SUSTAINED ROBUST ECONOMIC GROWTH.**

THE TRADITIONAL "LABOR POOL" OF THE WORKING-AGE POPULATION 20–64 WILL GROW MUCH MORE SLOWLY OVER THE NEXT DECADE.

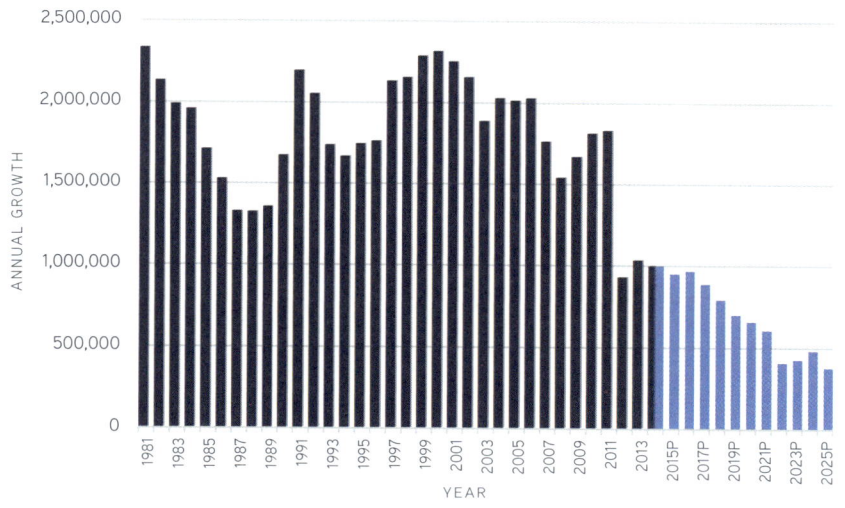

RETIREMENT WILL DRAMATICALLY SLOW JOB CREATION
FIGURE 6.7 Growth of US Resident Population Aged 20–64

Source: John Burns Real Estate Consulting, LLC calculations of US Census Bureau Population Estimates and 2014 National Projections

The surge in retirees will result in a shortage of workers and a dramatic rise in wages unless the economy only grows very slowly, immigration substantially increases, or new technologies successfully replace millions of workers. Because of the worker shortage, companies creating technologies that improve productivity will do well. Prefabricated houses assembled on-site will replace some construction workers, computers that read medical tests will replace some highly paid technicians, and lower-skilled labor will continue to struggle while highly skilled labor succeeds. Highly skilled labor shouldn't rest on its laurels, however, as developments in artificial intelligence begin to replace knowledge workers as well.

Technology has allowed companies to become far more efficient without having to pay people better. Advances in technology outpaced advances in wages over the last 40 years. Prior to 1975, wages rose and productivity improved at roughly similar rates. Since 1975—about the time that the 1950s Innovators started their first companies—technology has increased the output per hour 132%, while hourly wages grew just 54%.

Complicating the labor equation further, the workweek continues to decline as the workaholic Achievers and Innovators retire. The average workweek fell from 50 hours in 1920 to 34 hours in 2015.

THE AVERAGE WORKWEEK FELL FROM 50 HOURS IN 1920 TO 34 HOURS IN 2015.

Also, the nature of work continues to change. Uber, eBay, and other new companies empower people to work multiple jobs and choose flexible hours—often fewer than 40 per week. Younger generations, working parents, and retirees increasingly like the variety and flexibility of gig employment. Innovators will seek out gig jobs that offer flexible schedules and healthcare insurance.

The younger generations also strive for greater family-work balance than did earlier generations. The Innovator work ethic, "the primacy of work" in Burch's terms, will quickly fade as they retire, replaced by the work ethic of the 1990s Connectors. "It would be a very apt description to call me a workaholic through my whole life, both personally and professionally," Burch said. "Actually, one of my friends once said about me, 'With Burch, anything worth doing is worth overdoing.' If I have an epitaph on my headstone that probably should be it."

As his career developed, Burch made multiple moves, from Michigan to Arizona to Atlanta and back to Michigan, always working long hours. Better jobs and professional advancement prompted the moves. He barely consulted his wife about these decisions or considered other life factors. If a solid opportunity to advance in his career presented itself, of course they would move. Since the couple raised horses on the side and lived on farms with significant acreage, such shifts put considerable strain on the marriage and ultimately contributed to a divorce.

"As I work with younger kids in these businesses, moving is a huge and very meaningful decision for them," Burch said. "I've seen a number of guys who had really significant opportunities provided to them for professional advancement, and they turned them down because they didn't want to uproot their families and move them. That is a big generational difference."

Burch observed the difference closely when his son left a promising job in Washington, DC, because he didn't like the atmosphere there and missed his social circle in Michigan. "He never really developed a clique in DC that he was happy with, and he moved back to Michigan primarily for social reasons," Burch said. "In his case, it was a lateral move with the same company. He's done really well in that group [in Michigan], and I think he has potential for advancement there. Nevertheless, that's something that never would have occurred to me, I don't think—to move for social reasons. For me, it was always professional."

Each generation redefines retirement. Just as the Achievers did not play golf like their predecessors, the Innovators will not retire like the Achievers or Savers. Many will likely define age 65 to 74 as the next chapter in their working life and will seek out more activities with the kids and grandchildren. The Innovators' affluence and workaholic tendencies will help them continue to enjoy life, while their longevity will also create financial strains later in life. Plan now for three virtual certainties—18 million more people over the age of 65 in 2025, more older workers than ever before, and a future labor shortage due to significant retirement (even considering more technologies that replace workers).

> **PLAN NOW FOR THREE VIRTUAL CERTAINTIES—18 MILLION MORE PEOPLE OVER THE AGE OF 65 IN 2025, MORE OLDER WORKERS THAN EVER BEFORE, AND A FUTURE LABOR SHORTAGE DUE TO SIGNIFICANT RETIREMENT (EVEN CONSIDERING MORE TECHNOLOGIES THAT REPLACE WORKERS).**

Business leaders who fail to study these massive demographic shifts in detail will miss out on market share. A general awareness of the aging dynamic doesn't go far enough. Future retirees will behave differently than prior retirees because the 4 Big Influencers during their life were different. Government added substantial entitlement benefits during their lifetime and assisted asset appreciation by dropping interest rates. The Innovators benefited from a tremendous economy during most of their working lives. They led the development of many new technologies that will help them live longer. More than prior generations, they will live with their adult children and grandchildren too. Businesses of all kinds can capitalize on the coming wave of retirees.

7: FINALLY LEAVING THE NEST

Young adults now live at home in unprecedented numbers, thanks primarily to the negative impact of one of the 4 Big Influencers: the economy. The younger 1980s Sharers and older 1990s Connectors entered the workforce in the worst economy since the 1930s. For many, living at home makes the most financial sense. Partially for financial reasons, they have also delayed the main reason people leave home—to get married and start a family. We expect a boom in people leaving home in the next decade, forming households and starting families.

Warning! This chapter contains A LOT of statistics designed to help you forecast household formations. We show how we arrived at our forecasts in a way that allows you to compare each generation to prior generations and to adjust our forecast to arrive at your own numbers if you so decide. Those of you who don't want the details might want to skip to the last two paragraphs in the chapter. For those who love the details, we also provided appendix 2.

Today, 1950s Innovators through 1980s Sharers head 87 million of America's 121 million households, averaging 22 million households each. We expect the 1990s Connectors and 2000s Globals to head a similar number of households someday.

EACH DECADE BORN FROM 1950s THROUGH 1980s HEADS 22 MILLION+/- HOUSEHOLDS.

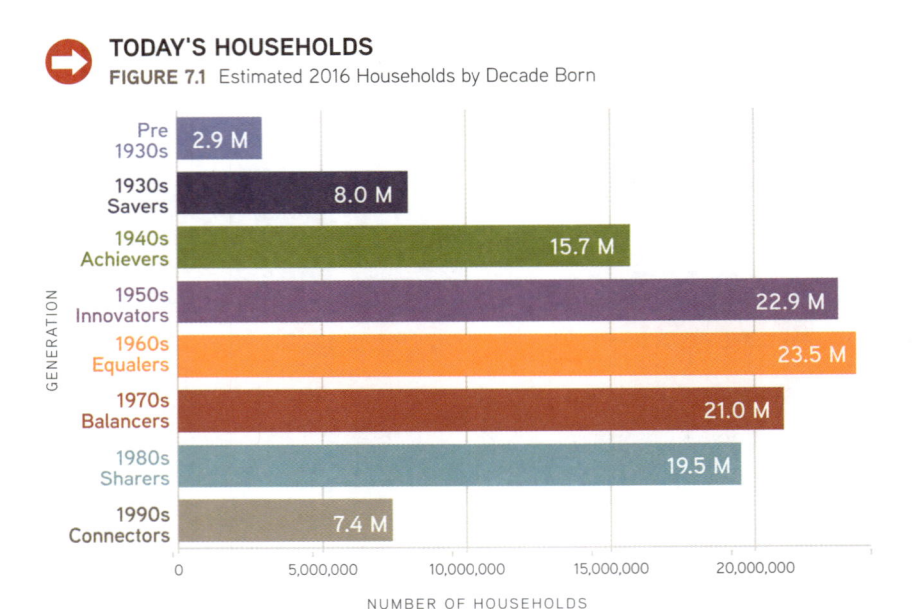

TODAY'S HOUSEHOLDS
FIGURE 7.1 Estimated 2016 Households by Decade Born

Generation	Households
Pre 1930s	2.9 M
1930s Savers	8.0 M
1940s Achievers	15.7 M
1950s Innovators	22.9 M
1960s Equalers	23.5 M
1970s Balancers	21.0 M
1980s Sharers	19.5 M
1990s Connectors	7.4 M

Sources: John Burns Real Estate Consulting, LLC based on US Census Bureau data

People will likely continue marrying later and having kids later. Sharers and Connectors know very well how expensive college and kids can be and will thus plan parenting quite carefully. Therefore, more than any generation before them, they will wait until they complete their education before starting a family. Living at home while working punches the ticket for many to start independent life unencumbered by debt.

We estimate that America will add 12.5 million more households from 2016 to 2025—86% more than added in the prior ten years but less than from 1996–2005. With a huge population of people born in the 1990s, plus pent-up household formation demand from the last decade, we could easily forecast more. However, the many factors discussed in this book and covered in more detail in the next four chapters, lead us to forecast far more conservatively. We included our forecasts for each generation in appendix 2.

12.5 MILLION MORE HOUSEHOLDS WILL BOOST THE ECONOMY.

HOUSEHOLD GROWTH BY DECADE
FIGURE 7.2 Household Growth by Decade (Millions)

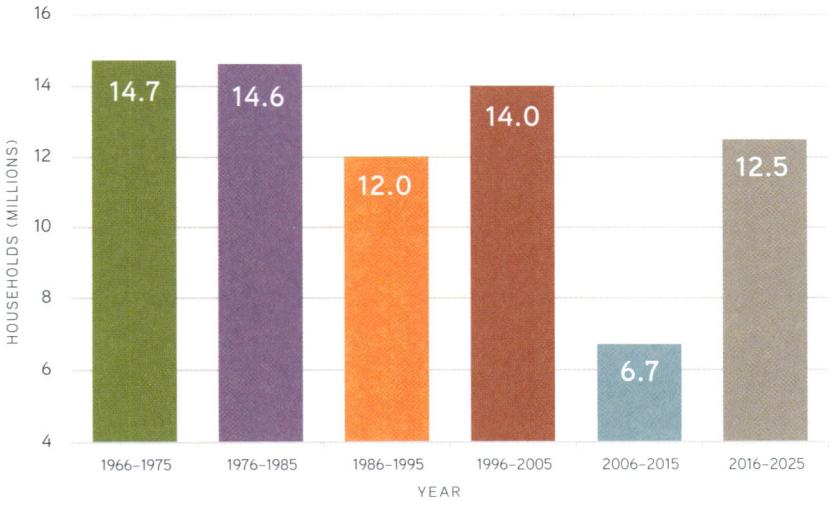

Year	Households (Millions)
1966–1975	14.7
1976–1985	14.6
1986–1995	12.0
1996–2005	14.0
2006–2015	6.7
2016–2025	12.5

Source: John Burns Real Estate Consulting, LLC based on US Census Bureau data. Note: colors based on generation in their 20s.

Household formations drive the economy. We devoted this entire chapter to household formations because new households play such a huge role in economic growth. Consider all the goods and services that new households need—appliances, furniture, utilities, bedding, cookware, etc. Virtually all retailers focus on future household growth for the site selection of their next store. More households also drive the need for more construction.

Every occupied home and apartment is considered one household, regardless of how many people live in the home or apartment. Households form when people move away from home or immigrate here from another country. The number of households declines when couples living separately decide to live together, when people move back in with their parents or with roommates, or when someone living alone dies or goes into an assisted-living facility or prison.

When Mexican-born Cynthia Laguna saved enough for a down payment and left her parents' house to buy her own, she formed a new household. Cynthia joined a rare group who owned their first household, as most people rent before owning. Consultant Steve Burch moved out and formed a new household when he got divorced. Mother-of-two Lisa Marquis Jackson's oldest daughter lives away from home most of the year, in a college dorm, which does not count as a separate household—officially, she still lives with Mom.

Our forecast for massive growth will result in fewer new households than formed in the 1970s, when the 1950s Innovator group came of age. For our forecast, we analyzed every age group, concluding that *America will lose 13.3 million households over the next ten years headed by someone born in the 1960s and earlier* (a record number of losses to assisted-living facilities and mortality), *and gain 25.8 million by those born later.* Most of the households lost currently own their home, which will result in a drag on the homeownership rate.

7: FINALLY LEAVING THE NEST

THOSE BORN IN THE 1980s AND LATER WILL DRIVE MOST FUTURE HOUSEHOLD FORMATIONS.

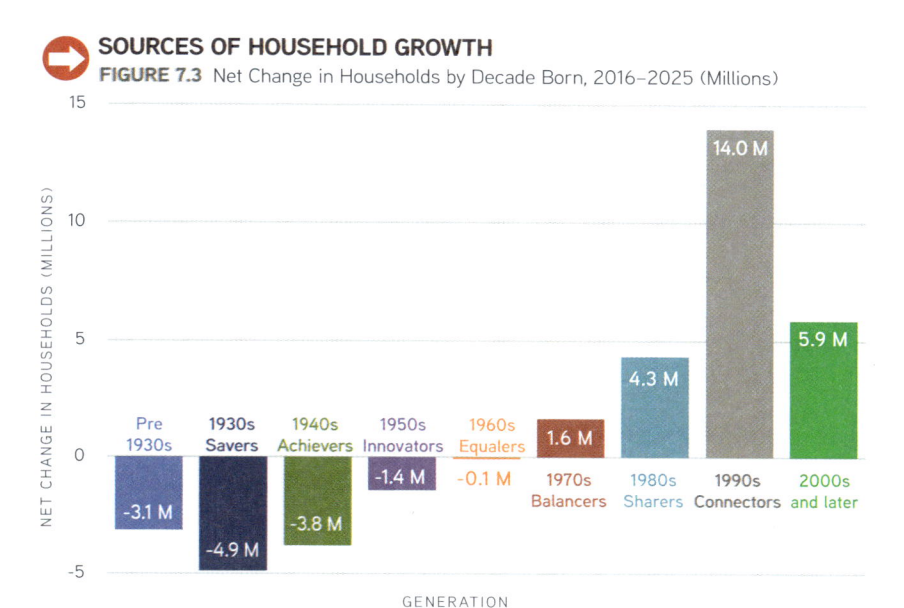

SOURCES OF HOUSEHOLD GROWTH

FIGURE 7.3 Net Change in Households by Decade Born, 2016–2025 (Millions)

Generation	Net Change (Millions)
Pre 1930s	-3.1 M
1930s Savers	-4.9 M
1940s Achievers	-3.8 M
1950s Innovators	-1.4 M
1960s Equalers	-0.1 M
1970s Balancers	1.6 M
1980s Sharers	4.3 M
1990s Connectors	14.0 M
2000s and later	5.9 M

Sources: John Burns Real Estate Consulting, LLC

Over the next decade, the

■	beleaguered 1970s Balancers should add 1.6 million households (reaching 22.4 million households);
■	delayed 1980s Sharers should add 4.3 million households (reaching 23.1 million households);
■	young 1990s Connectors should add 14.0 million households (reaching 19.9 million households); and
■	very young 2000s Globals should add 5.9 million households (reaching 5.9 million households by the time the oldest of this group reaches 25 years of age).

Clearly, the 1990s Connectors and 2000s Globals will drive most household growth. We assumed that both groups will form households slowly in comparison to their predecessors. We also believe both will continue to live at home longer than prior generations.

Let's highlight some of the trends involved in the forecasted household boom:

- **Pent-up demand**. The economic slowdown during the Great Recession dramatically slowed household formations, as adult children lived at home longer and families and friends doubled up in one house.

- **Permanent damage**. We calculate that America lost 6.7 million households to the Great Recession, many of them permanently. Those aged in their 30s, 40s, and 50s head households at lower rates today than during recent decades.

- **Economic recovery**. Household formation began returning to normal in 2016, seven years after the collapse of financial-services firm Lehman Brothers. We observed similar rates of recovery seven years after the 1980s economic collapse in Houston and the 1990s collapse in Southern California.

- **Rising deaths**. We now lose more than 1.2 million households every year to assisted-living facilities, retirees moving in with their adult children, and mortality. We lose 200,000+ more households each year to mortality than only one decade ago. This rarely reported surge in deaths drags on household growth.

We scrutinized all of the reasons people don't form households, uncovering some real eye-opening trends. For instance, almost 1 in 100 adults lived in prison or jail in 2013, around 2.2 million people, the vast majority of them men. This rapidly rising number has reduced household formation and contributed to female incomes rising faster than male incomes.

As with other demographic trends we've explored, household formation ebbs and flows under the influence of government, the economy, technology, and societal shifts. Of these 4 Big Influencers, the economy wields the most influence. For eight years after the Great Recession, America formed about half as many households as normal.

HOUSEHOLD FORMATIONS PLUNGED 50%+ AFTER THE GREAT RECESSION.

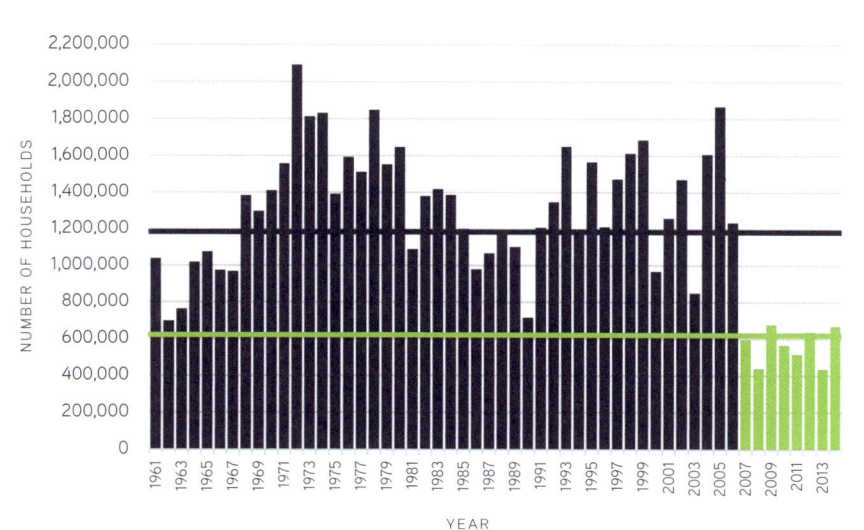

LOW RECENT HOUSEHOLD GROWTH
FIGURE 7.4 Net Household Formation, 1965–2014

Source: John Burns Real Estate Consulting, LLC based on US Census Bureau data

The 1990s Connectors and the 1980s Sharers create households more slowly than every generation since the 1930s. Living with one's parents for three, five, even ten years after school no longer seems odd—to twenty-somethings or their folks. Contrast this change with the societal biases in the 1970s and 1980s, when living at home as an adult was considered a huge failure. The extremely popular 1970s TV show, *All in the Family*, featured a character nicknamed "Meathead," partially because he lived with his in-laws. In the 1970s, nobody wanted to be "Meathead."

For more context, let's look at the 1980s Sharers alongside their 1950s Innovator parents. At 28, less than half of the Sharers lived with a spouse or partner. Contrast that with 85% of 1930s Savers coupled up at the same age. It wasn't that long ago that 25-year-olds faced pressure to marry before all the good partners were gone. Today, parents pressure many 25-year-olds to wait.

LESS THAN 1/2 OF PEOPLE AT THEIR 10-YEAR REUNION ARE MARRIED OR LIVING WITH A PARTNER.

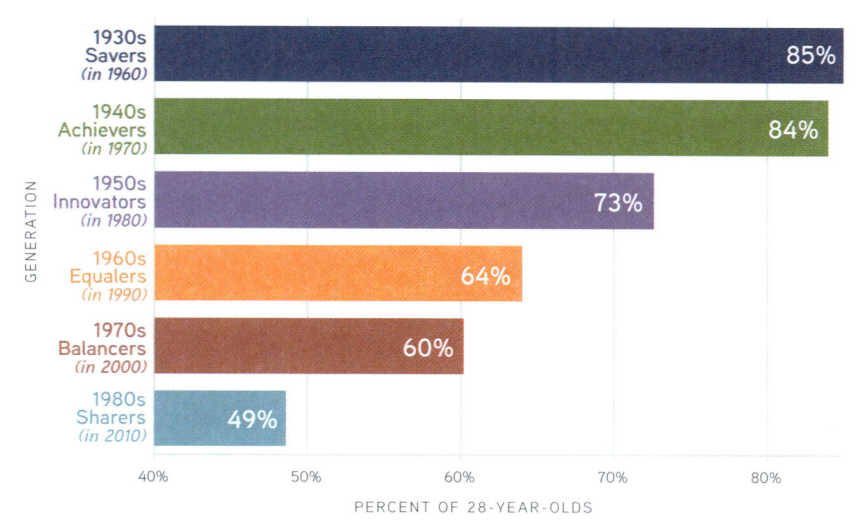

SINGLE 28-YEAR-OLDS NOW OUTNUMBER THE MARRIED
FIGURE 7.5 Percentage of 28-Year-Olds Living with a Spouse/Partner

Generation	Percent
1930s Savers (in 1960)	85%
1940s Achievers (in 1970)	84%
1950s Innovators (in 1980)	73%
1960s Equalers (in 1990)	64%
1970s Balancers (in 2000)	60%
1980s Sharers (in 2010)	49%

PERCENT OF 28-YEAR-OLDS

Source: US Census Bureau Decennial Census (1950–2000), American Community Survey (2010–2013) via IPUMS-USA, forecast by JBREC

Twice as many 1980s Sharers live with their parents than did the 1950s Innovators. Only 14% of 1950s Innovators lived with their parents at age 28, while 31% of 1980s Sharers did in 2010.

THE GREAT RECESSION RAMPED UP THE RATE OF YOUNG ADULTS LIVING WITH THEIR PARENTS AND ROOMMATES, FROM 23% IN 2000 TO 31% IN 2010.

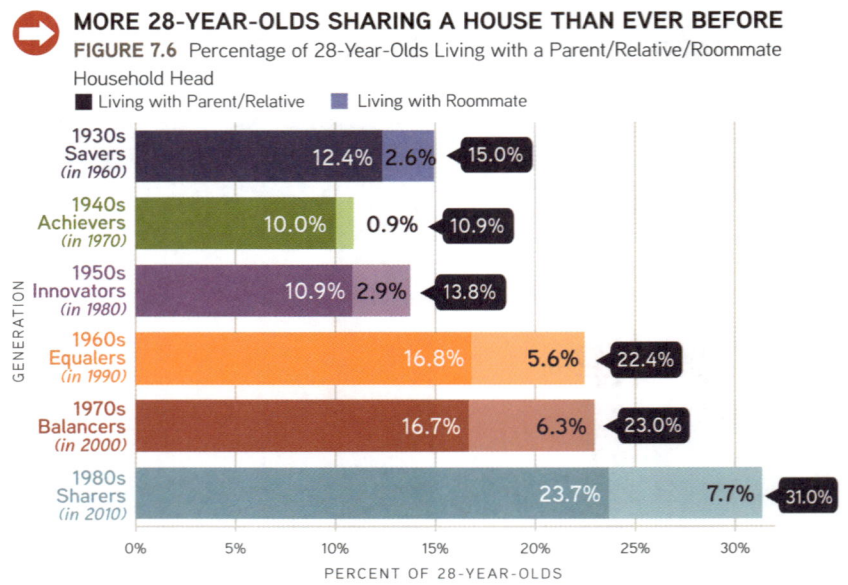

MORE 28-YEAR-OLDS SHARING A HOUSE THAN EVER BEFORE

FIGURE 7.6 Percentage of 28-Year-Olds Living with a Parent/Relative/Roommate Household Head

■ Living with Parent/Relative   ■ Living with Roommate

Generation	Living with Parent/Relative	Living with Roommate	Total
1930s Savers (in 1960)	12.4%	2.6%	15.0%
1940s Achievers (in 1970)	10.0%	0.9%	10.9%
1950s Innovators (in 1980)	10.9%	2.9%	13.8%
1960s Equalers (in 1990)	16.8%	5.6%	22.4%
1970s Balancers (in 2000)	16.7%	6.3%	23.0%
1980s Sharers (in 2010)	23.7%	7.7%	31.0%

Source: US Census Bureau Decennial Census (1950–2000), American Community Survey (2010–2013) via IPUMS-USA, forecast by JBREC

One of those Sharers living with his parents in 2016 was Kyle Zierer, a 29-year-old born in 1987. Zierer graduated from UC Irvine in 2009, in the depths of the Great Recession. Fortunately, given the economy, he found a job within six months. It paid poorly, though, and he spent the next year and a half searching for better-paid employment while treading water at his first job.

Many of Zierer's peers had a tougher time finding work. The US experienced 19.5% growth in real gross domestic product in the 2000s and 10.7% GDP growth from 2010 to 2014. These anemic growth statistics are closer to the level of growth during the Great Depression of the 1930s than to any other decade and applied a major brake to household formation.

"I have a lot of friends with college degrees who are working retail still," Zierer said. "They might be an assistant manager at a retail store, things like that. They haven't gotten the kind of job where you can get ahead."

Zierer, however, had two jobs during this period, and his income bumped up at the second one. In early 2016, with his thirtieth birthday approaching, he hoped to move out on his own soon, but why did he live with his parents for so long? Rent in his part of Orange County, California, ranged from $1,500 to $1,800 for a one-bedroom apartment, he said, and paying that would have felt like a waste.

"I've been living at home, trying to save up for a down payment for a house—that's the goal," Zierer said. "Rent is really expensive, and paying that much every month while trying to save a down payment is tough."

High rents hold back household formation, especially among 1980s Sharers such as Zierer and the 1990s Connectors. Rents rose from 17% of renter household income in 1984 to 24% in 2013—a steep increase, especially for those beginning careers or operating on tight budgets.

Student debt also hurt household formation for the heavily burdened Sharers and Connectors. Zierer was lucky to attend a state school where his parents could handle tuition, but many of his peers face steep monthly loan payments. In 2005, 2.2 million households paid student debt payments of $250 or more per month, a number that rose to 5.9 million households by 2014. We estimate that 414,000 fewer home sales occurred in 2014 due to the rise in student debt.[31]

---

31 John Burns Real Estate Consulting, LLC, "Student Debt and Delayed Homeownership," September 2014.

"Sometimes [living with parents] can get on your nerves, like when they ask, 'Where are you going?' Well, I'm 29, don't worry about it." Zierer laughed. "But we get along well. I do a lot with my dad—he's really into fishing, and so am I, so we fish sometimes."

Like Zierer's parents, most parents—63% of them in 2014—now prefer that their adult child live at home.[32] Archie Bunker, the lead character of the 1970s TV show *All in the Family*, would be appalled to learn that attitudes have shifted this much.

Several of Zierer's friends still live with their parents, and the stigma once attached to such arrangements has largely faded. This shocks some born during the Baby Boom, who don't realize that they were the aberrant generation. The 1940s Achievers and 1950s Innovators formed households early in life at unprecedented rates during good economic times.

Still, with age 30 around the corner, Zierer has concluded that now is the time to go it alone. Living with Mom and Dad still raises certain eyebrows, especially at age 30.

"I know a few friends who still live at home," Zierer said. "One just recently—he's a year older—lived at home like me, then bought a condo. Single women my age who have their stuff together don't want to date a guy who lives at home."

Those born in the 1980s, like Zierer, added up to 1.6 million households per year heading into the Great Recession. They have added far fewer since then. We expect the final remnants of pent-up demand from Sharers like Zierer to unleash over time. The 1980s Sharers represent 4.3 million of our forecast of 25.8 million new households formed by 2025.

---

32   Stephanie Postles, "Why Are Young Adults Living with Their Parents and When Will They Move Out?," http://www.fanniemae.com/portal/about-us/media/commentary/072914-postles.html.

We analyzed headship rates—the percentage of adults who head households—for every generation at the ages when they would attend their high school reunions (10-year reunion at age 28, 20-year reunion at age 38, 30-year reunion at age 48, and so on over the decades). These very important charts make for a textbook-like read, so we put them in appendix 2. The charts offer a wealth of information for anyone striving to understand particular generations, such as the 1990s Connectors, who will soon form their first household, or the 1940s Achievers, who will consider assisted-living facilities as they turn 80. The charts also provide a bird's-eye view of historical trends in household formation, an invaluable tool for understanding generational shifts.

Demographers call the percentage of adults who head households the "headship rate." It provides the most important tool in household-formation forecasts, and we'll refer to it frequently, so let's show how the math works. In 2015, 250 million adults lived in 120 million households. Therefore, 48% of adults headed a household, calculated as 120 million household heads divided by 250 million adults. 48% headed a household, and 52% lived in a household headed by someone else, or in an institution like prison or an assisted-living facility. A 1% shift in the headship rate across all ages would equal 2.5 million more or fewer households.

THE HEADSHIP RATE PEAKED AROUND 2000 AND HAS STEADILY TRENDED DOWN SINCE, RESULTING IN MORE ADULTS PER HOUSEHOLD.

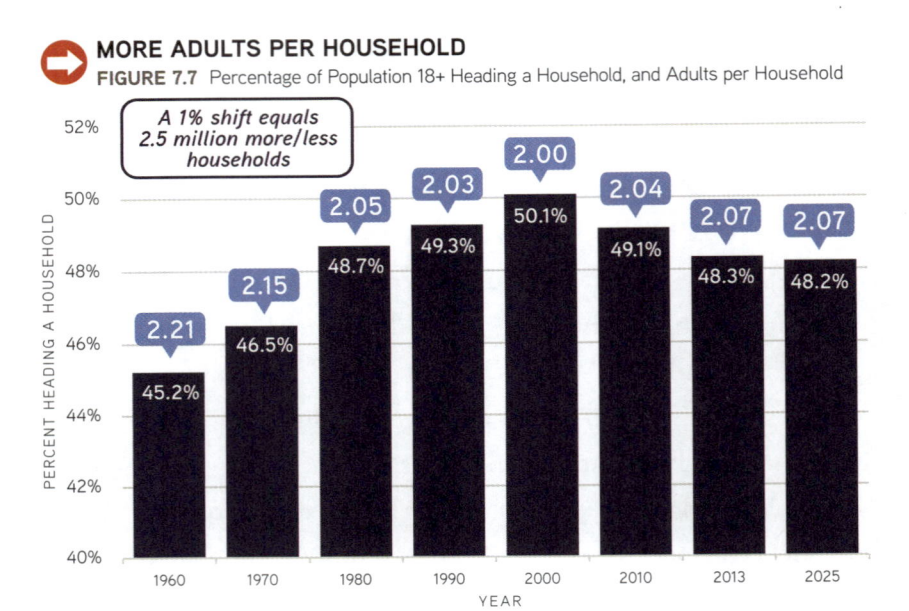

MORE ADULTS PER HOUSEHOLD

FIGURE 7.7 Percentage of Population 18+ Heading a Household, and Adults per Household

A 1% shift equals 2.5 million more/less households

Year	% Heading a Household	Adults per Household
1960	45.2%	2.21
1970	46.5%	2.15
1980	48.7%	2.05
1990	49.3%	2.03
2000	50.1%	2.00
2010	49.1%	2.04
2013	48.3%	2.07
2025	48.2%	2.07

Source: John Burns Real Estate Consulting, LLC based on US Census Bureau data

For demographic purposes, every household has a "head." A wife, husband, or the roommate who signed the lease heads the household—a somewhat arbitrary label in many situations. For our purposes, we don't care which person heads the household—just that a household exists.

In just a few decades, headship rates can change dramatically, resulting in millions of unexpected household formations, or millions fewer. Let's contrast people at their ten-year high school reunion in 1960 with a ten-year reunion in 1980. In 1960, 28-year-olds born in 1932 had only achieved a 42% headship rate. Their high marriage rates reduced headship, and the thrifty 1930s Savers tended to live with their parents until they got married. Contrast that with 1980, when 28-year-old Innovators born in 1952 reached a 49% headship rate. They left home as soon as possible, resulting in 280,000+/- more households than would have been created with a 42% headship rate.

We forecast a 38.2% headship rate in 2025 for 28-year-old Connectors, the lowest rate for 28-year-olds since the 1930s Savers. The Savers headed few households because so many lived with their spouse rather than their parents—a completely different reason than today.

1990s CONNECTORS WILL FORM THE FEWEST HOUSEHOLDS PER PERSON OF ANY GENERATION WE STUDIED.

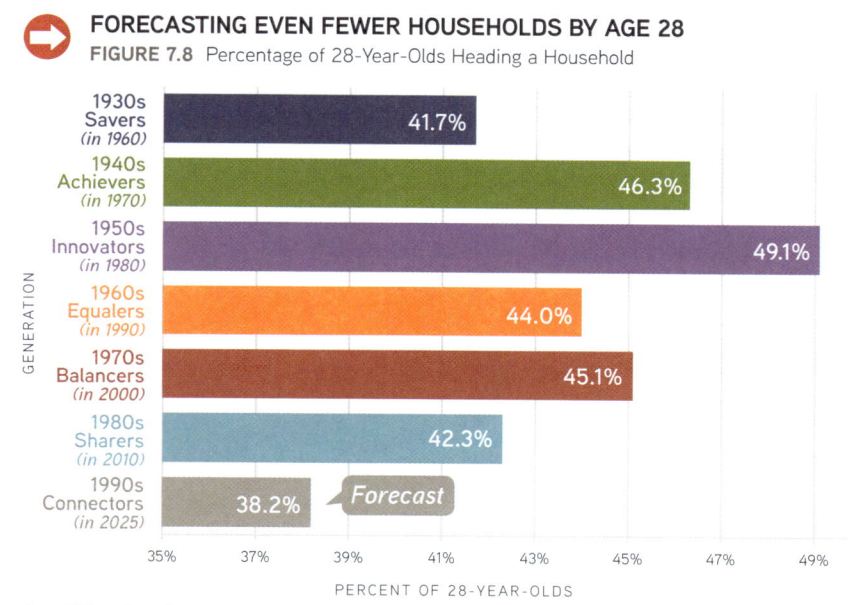

FORECASTING EVEN FEWER HOUSEHOLDS BY AGE 28

FIGURE 7.8 Percentage of 28-Year-Olds Heading a Household

Generation	Percent
1930s Savers (in 1960)	41.7%
1940s Achievers (in 1970)	46.3%
1950s Innovators (in 1980)	49.1%
1960s Equalers (in 1990)	44.0%
1970s Balancers (in 2000)	45.1%
1980s Sharers (in 2010)	42.3%
1990s Connectors (in 2025)	38.2% Forecast

Source: US Census Bureau Decennial Census (1950–2000), American Community Survey (2010–2013) via IPUMS-USA, forecast by JBREC

To determine the 38.2% forecasted headship rate for Connectors in 2025, we studied and forecasted every major reason people do not head households by the age of 28. Some of these changes opened our eyes wide.

Marital/cohabitation rates should continue to plunge. Rates fell from 43% of the 1930s Savers heading a household with their spouse/partner at age 28 to only 24% of the 1980s Sharers doing the same in 2010. We estimate that only 23% of 1990s Connectors will head a household with their spouse or partner at age 28. Since living together involves two people, let's do the math. Since two people live in these households, this means that approximately 86% of 1930s Savers lived with their partner at age 28, compared to just 48% of 1980s Sharers at the same age today.

MARITAL/COHABITATION RATES SHOULD CONTINUE TO PLUNGE FOR 28-YEAR-OLDS.

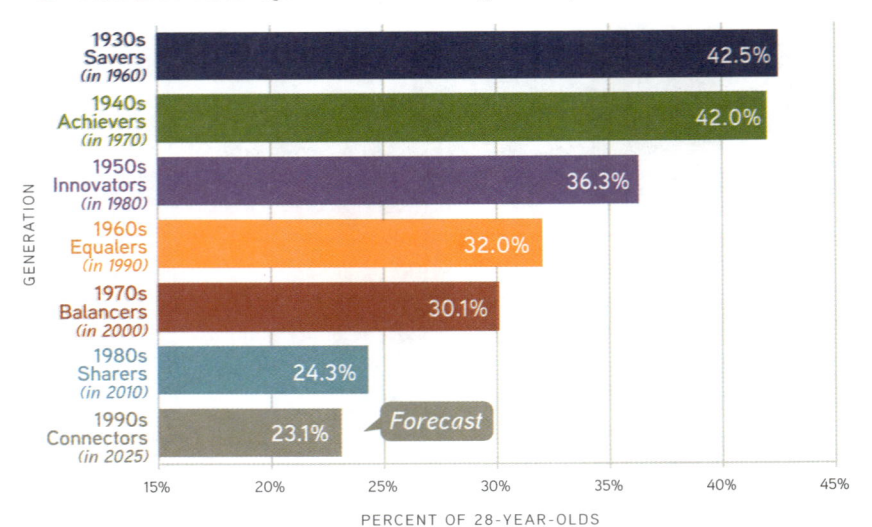

FORECASTING EVEN FEWER MARRIED BY AGE 28

FIGURE 7.9 Percentage of 28-Year-Olds Living with a Spouse/Partner Household Head

Generation	Percent
1930s Savers (in 1960)	42.5%
1940s Achievers (in 1970)	42.0%
1950s Innovators (in 1980)	36.3%
1960s Equalers (in 1990)	32.0%
1970s Balancers (in 2000)	30.1%
1980s Sharers (in 2010)	24.3%
1990s Connectors (in 2025)	23.1% (Forecast)

PERCENT OF 28-YEAR-OLDS

Source: US Census Bureau Decennial Census (1950–2000), American Community Survey (2010–2013) via IPUMS-USA, forecast by JBREC

Living with parents spiked in the 2000s, exacerbated by the Great Recession at the end of the decade. Almost 24% of 28-year-olds lived with their parents in 2010, compared to just 17% in 2000. For many of the reasons articulated throughout the book—student debt, multiple generations living together, less social stigma, etc.—

we believe the percentage of young adults living with their parents will continue to rise. We forecast that 26.5% of 28-year-old Connectors will live with their parents in 2025, a record percentage. This continued trend to live with parents will drag on household formations. If the trend ends or reverses, even more households will form than we forecast. Tremendous upside potential for household formations exists.

THE 1990s CONNECTORS WILL INCREASINGLY LIVE WITH THEIR PARENTS OR OTHER RELATIVES LATER IN LIFE.

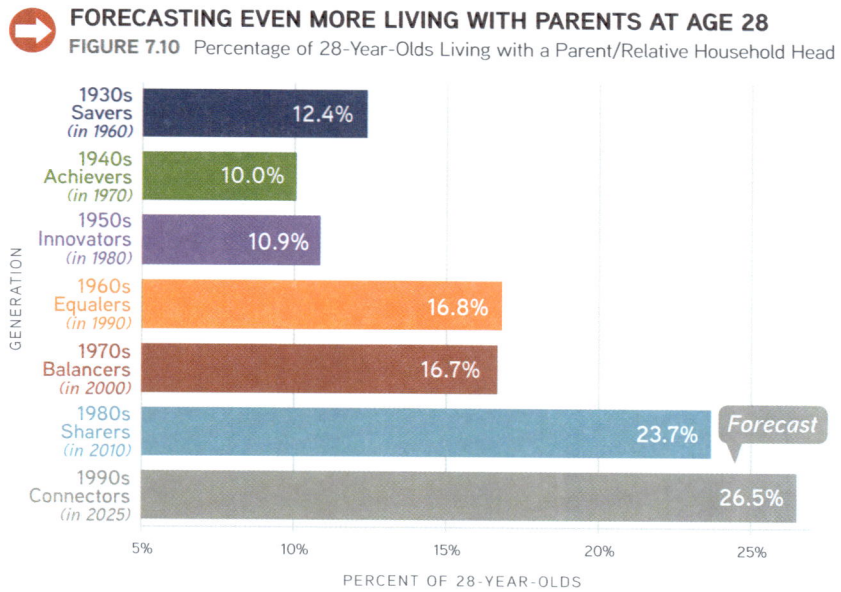

FORECASTING EVEN MORE LIVING WITH PARENTS AT AGE 28

FIGURE 7.10 Percentage of 28-Year-Olds Living with a Parent/Relative Household Head

Generation	Percent
1930s Savers (in 1960)	12.4%
1940s Achievers (in 1970)	10.0%
1950s Innovators (in 1980)	10.9%
1960s Equalers (in 1990)	16.8%
1970s Balancers (in 2000)	16.7%
1980s Sharers (in 2010)	23.7%
1990s Connectors (in 2025)	26.5% (Forecast)

Source: US Census Bureau Decennial Census (1950–2000), American Community Survey (2010–2013) via IPUMS-USA, forecast by JBREC

We also expect that 10.5% of 1990s Connectors will live with a roommate who is considered the head of household—almost 12 times the percentage of 1940s Achievers at the same age. This percentage includes those who live as a boarder or nanny in someone else's house. While this looks like a huge increase from the 7.7%

rate in 2010, note that the percentage has already grown to 9.3% by 2013. Again, if fewer than 10.5% live in a house headed by their roommate, more households than we forecast will form.

1990s CONNECTORS LIVE WITH ROOMMATES MORE THAN ANY GENERATION BEFORE THEM.

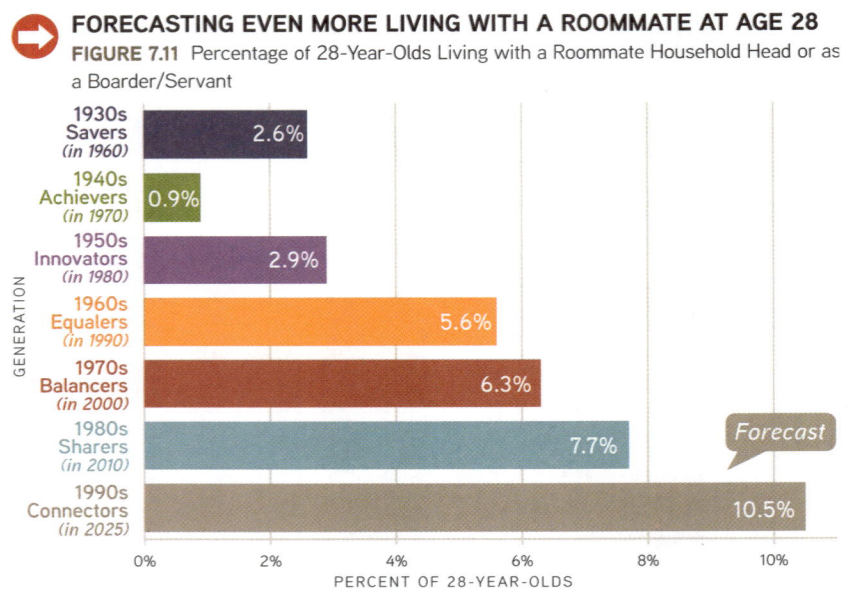

FORECASTING EVEN MORE LIVING WITH A ROOMMATE AT AGE 28

FIGURE 7.11 Percentage of 28-Year-Olds Living with a Roommate Household Head or as a Boarder/Servant

Generation	Percent
1930s Savers (in 1960)	2.6%
1940s Achievers (in 1970)	0.9%
1950s Innovators (in 1980)	2.9%
1960s Equalers (in 1990)	5.6%
1970s Balancers (in 2000)	6.3%
1980s Sharers (in 2010)	7.7%
1990s Connectors (in 2025)	10.5% (Forecast)

Source: US Census Bureau Decennial Census (1950–2000), American Community Survey (2010–2013) via IPUMS-USA, forecast by JBREC

Putting this all together, we expect 1990s Connectors to form 14 million more households and the 1980s Sharers to form 4.3 million more households. We included the forecasts for the Sharers and the other groups in appendix 2.

7: FINALLY LEAVING THE NEST

THE 1990s CONNECTORS WILL CREATE 14 MILLION HOUSEHOLDS FROM 2016 THROUGH 2025.

HUGE BELATED HOUSEHOLD GROWTH AHEAD
FIGURE 7.12 Net Household Formation by Those Born in 1990s, 2005–2025

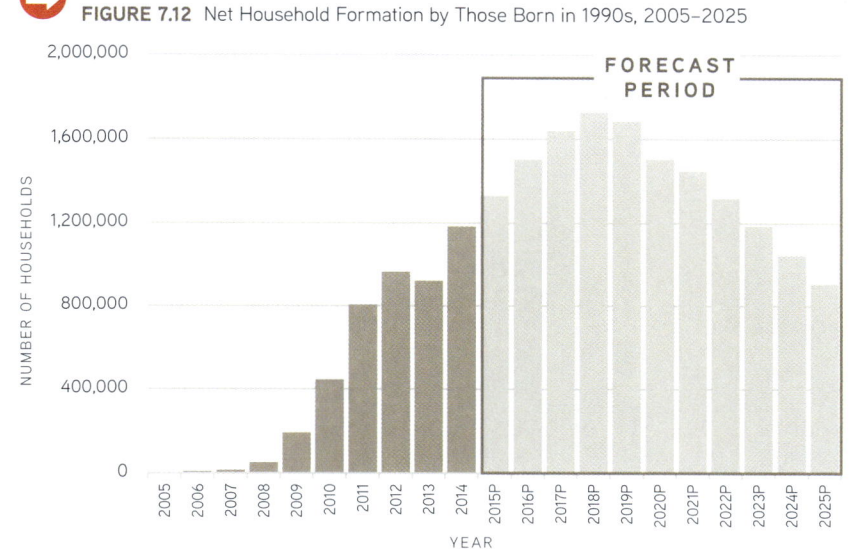

Source: John Burns Real Estate Consulting, LLC based on US Census Bureau data

This forecast hits home for single mom Lisa Jackson. Will her 28- and 25-year-old daughters be living with Mom in 2025? Will they be married? Living with a roommate? Only time will tell.

1980s SHARERS SHOULD FORM 4.3 MILLION MORE HOUSEHOLDS OVER 10 YEARS.

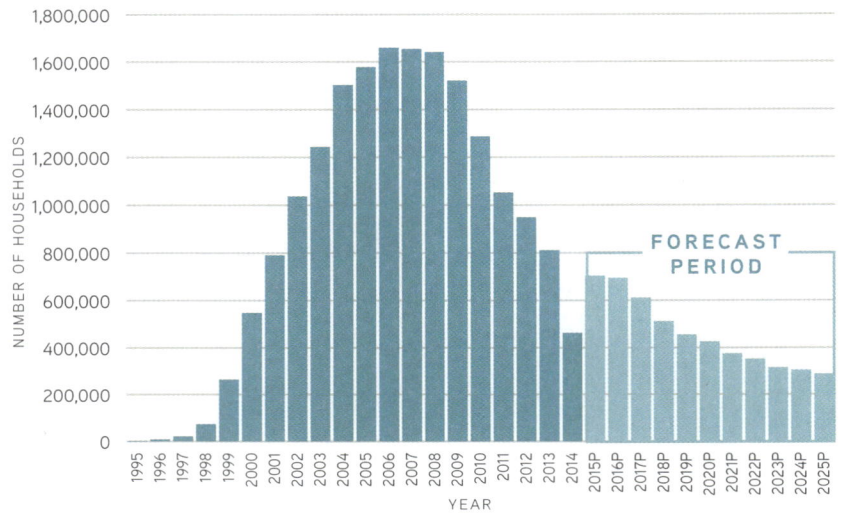

➡ SHARERS WILL FORM 4.3 MILLION MORE HOUSEHOLDS
FIGURE 7.13 Net Household Formation by Those Born in the 1980s

Source: John Burns Real Estate Consulting, LLC based on US Census Bureau data

The 1980s Sharers should lead a minor resurgence in living with spouses or partners since the Great Recession delayed their marriages. The percentage of them who live with a parent or a relative should also decrease, as more of them get out of the house.

We forecast 5.9 million additional households to come from the 44 million 2000s Globals by 2025, who will be aged 16–25 at the time. We assume they will form households slightly earlier than the 1990s Connectors did due to a better economy. Compared to prior generations, however, their households will form quite late in life. In 2025, they will just be getting started.

All forecasts come with assumptions. Most large businesses forecast one, three, or five years into the future. While all of those businesses assume some sort of macroeconomic outlook that they cannot control, very few actually write down their assumptions. Our macroeconomic assumptions, which we will revise and update as we get new information, follows:

- **Healthy economy.** Over the next ten years, we assume 2% average annual GDP growth and less than 1% employment growth annually—both slightly below their long-term averages. The lack of labor and the high level of government indebtedness will slow the rate of job growth.

- **High immigration.** We assume no major changes in immigration policy, allowing a net inflow of 1.2 million to 1.3 million immigrants each year, similar to recent history and per current Census Bureau estimates. Twelve to thirteen million immigrants over the next decade would result in approximately 4.5 million households this decade (and more in future decades). A full 36% of forecasted household growth should come from people not living in America in 2015.

- **Substantial entitlements.** We anticipate no significant changes to Medicare, Social Security, and other retirement benefits before 2025, although the risk will certainly rise each year. A reduction in benefits could shift behavior dramatically, requiring people to work longer and to live on less in retirement.

- **Continued social shifts.** We foresee continued rising college-education costs and associated delays in household formation, marriage, and children, consistent with recent historic trends. We expect younger generations to save more than their parents and to borrow less.

- **Life-extending technology.** Technology will continue to allow women to have children later, allowing their early careers to prosper. Technology will also continue to help people live longer, propping up the number of households while challenging retiree budgets.

- **Favorable mortgage policy and terms.** We assume fixed 30-year mortgage rates that started at just under 4% in 2015 will stay low for years and then rise to 6% by 2025. This will challenge housing affordability and hurt homeownership. We also envision a loosening in mortgage documentation requirements, particularly for the self-employed and retired.

- **Home prices and rents.** We assume home prices and rents will increase slightly faster than incomes each year. Home prices shouldn't grow much faster than incomes, but mortgage payments will grow faster as interest rates rise. Increased regulation and supply constraints around the country will continue to limit supply, applying upward pressure on prices and rents, particularly along the coasts. Housing affordability will get even worse.

The unknown or untested concerns us the most. We cannot predict with any level of certainty the eventual outcome of what some call the *debt supercycle*. For decades, governments, businesses, and consumers worldwide financed their spending with debt, to the point that most realize that governments cannot repay

> **WE CANNOT PREDICT WITH ANY LEVEL OF CERTAINTY THE EVENTUAL OUTCOME OF WHAT SOME CALL THE DEBT SUPERCYCLE.**

their debts. We assume governments will continue to refinance their debts at maturity. Read Reinhart and Rogoff's *This Time is Different* or Mauldin and Tepper's *Endgame* if you want more information. We conclude from their work that economic and possibly political collapse will likely result, but nobody can predict the decade that will occur.

OUR BULLISH 12.5 MILLION HOUSEHOLD-FORMATION FORECAST ASSUMES LOW HEADSHIP RATES IN COMPARISON TO HISTORY.

BY 2025, NEARLY EVERY AGE GROUP WILL HAVE LOWER HEADSHIP THAN IN 2010
FIGURE 7.14 Headship Rates by Age

Age	Decennial Census Average Since 1960	1980	2010	Assumed 2025
28	44.8%	49.1%	42.3%	38.2%
38	51.5%	54.3%	50.9%	48.8%
48	54.7%	55.4%	54.7%	55.4%
58	57.1%	57.4%	57.2%	55.4%
68	62.1%	63.6%	59.9%	59.3%
78	64.5%	66.5%	63.7%	59.1%
85+	49.2%	49.6%	60.7%	56.6%

Source: John Burns Real Estate Consulting, LLC based on US Census Bureau data

In conclusion, young adults will continue to leave home later than ever. The 1990s Connectors will add 14.0 million of the 25.8 million new households from 2016 through 2025. In 2025, we expect the Connectors born in 1997 to see the following at their ten-year high school reunion:

- 38% heading a household, slightly more than the 1980s Sharers at their ten-year reunion but still among the lowest in 60 years
- 26% living with a parent or other family member, the highest ever
- 23% living with their spouse/partner head of household, the lowest ever
- 11% living with a roommate/other, near the highest ever
- 2% institutionalized

PART THREE

LIFESTYLE SHIFTS

8: RENTING IN THE SHARING ECONOMY

The new sharing economy, which includes more opportunities to rent or borrow than ever before, will change many industries. This chapter will focus on the largest rent-versus-buy decision that people make: housing.

The recent Great Recession and massive foreclosure crisis left many scars that will take a long time to heal. Possibly the biggest scar resulted in an enormous 5% plunge in homeownership. Despite strong population growth, six-plus years of economic recovery, and the lowest mortgage rates in history since the Great Recession ended, 1.9 million fewer households own a home in 2015 than in 2006.

Going forward, we believe rental-household growth will outstrip owned-household growth, resulting in less than 61% homeownership in 2025—the lowest homeownership rate since the mid-1950s.

HOMEOWNERSHIP SHOULD REACH 60.8% IN 2025—THE LOWEST SINCE THE 1950s.

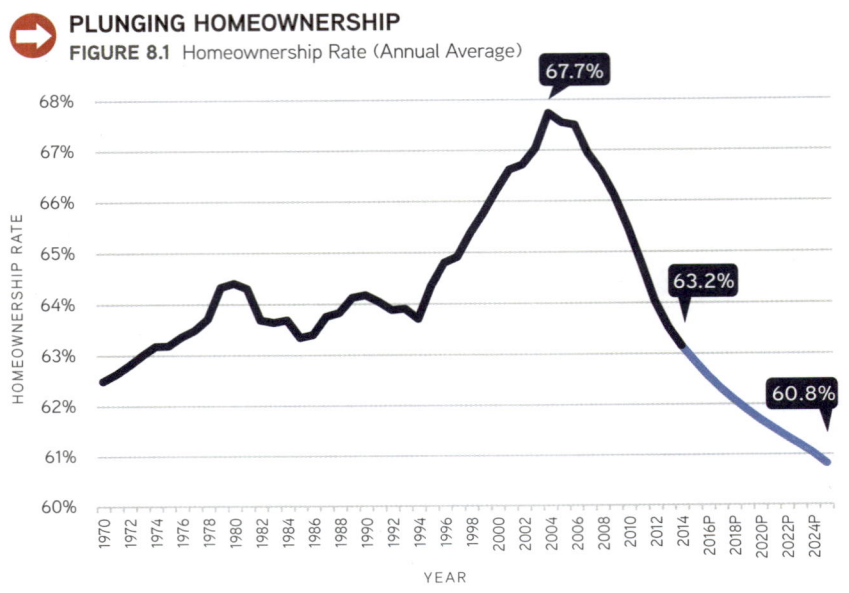

PLUNGING HOMEOWNERSHIP
FIGURE 8.1 Homeownership Rate (Annual Average)

Source: John Burns Real Estate Consulting, LLC based on US Census Bureau data

For the second decade in a row, rental home demand will exceed owned home demand. We should add approximately 5.2 million homeowners and 7.3 million renters from 2015 through 2025. Homebuilders, landlords, and everyone who sells products and services that go into the home will welcome this demand.

The death of so many people born in the 1950s and earlier will exacerbate the percentage of households that rent. More than half (52%) of today's 75 million homeowners were born before 1960, meaning they are at least 55 years of age in 2015. The homeownership rate will fall as almost 11 million homeowners born before 1960 die off or become renters in the next ten years.

Homeownership will also fall because younger generations own far fewer homes than their parents at the same age. Only 55% of today's 38-year-old 1970s Balancers own homes, compared to 65% of the 1960s Equalers and 71% of the 1940s Achievers at the same age. Barring some sort of significant government intervention, the beleaguered Balancers will not catch up to prior generations. The Balancers' low homeownership rates will create huge problems when they retire, when they will struggle to pay rent and be unable to tap into home equity.

39 MILLION OF THE 75 MILLION HOMEOWNERS (52%) WERE BORN BEFORE 1960, MEANING THEY ARE AT LEAST 55 YEARS OLD.

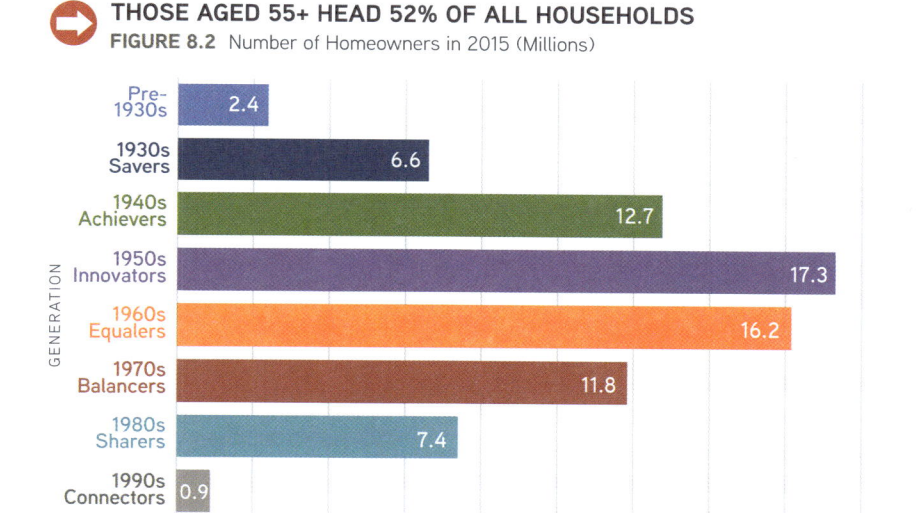

➡ THOSE AGED 55+ HEAD 52% OF ALL HOUSEHOLDS
FIGURE 8.2 Number of Homeowners in 2015 (Millions)

Generation	Number of Homeowners (Millions)
Pre-1930s	2.4
1930s Savers	6.6
1940s Achievers	12.7
1950s Innovators	17.3
1960s Equalers	16.2
1970s Balancers	11.8
1980s Sharers	7.4
1990s Connectors	0.9

Source: John Burns Real Estate Consulting, LLC based on US Census Bureau

Home buying has huge economic implications. Home purchases benefit many businesses, from all of the firms involved in the transaction to every business that sells a product or service that goes into a home. The loss of 2.1 million homeowners from 2007 to 2014 played a huge role in the slow economic growth during that period.

AMERICA LOST 2.1 MILLION HOMEOWNERS FROM 2007 TO 2014.

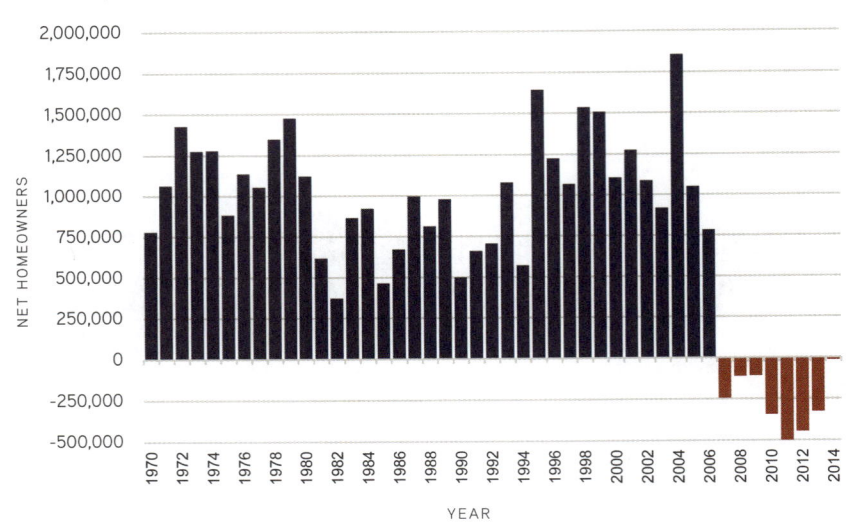

➤ 7 YEARS OF DECLINING HOMEOWNERS
FIGURE 8.3 Annual Homeowner Growth

Source: John Burns Real Estate Consulting, LLC based on US Census Bureau data

America will add 15.8 million total new homeowners born after 1960 to offset the 10.6 million who will pass away, resulting in 5.2 million more homeowners. Because renters will occupy many of those formerly owned 10.6 million homes, new home demand will remain strong, and America will need far more than 5.2 million new homes built to satisfy demand.

Homebuilders should focus on the 15.8 million first-time homebuyers rather than the paltry 5.2 million net new homeowners, as well as the demand among current homeowners to buy something new. America needs far more homes designed for retirees. Many older, affluent homeowners will move to a new home with great technology and first-floor bedrooms designed with them in mind.

WE FORECAST 5.2 MILLION MORE HOMEOWNERS BY 2025.

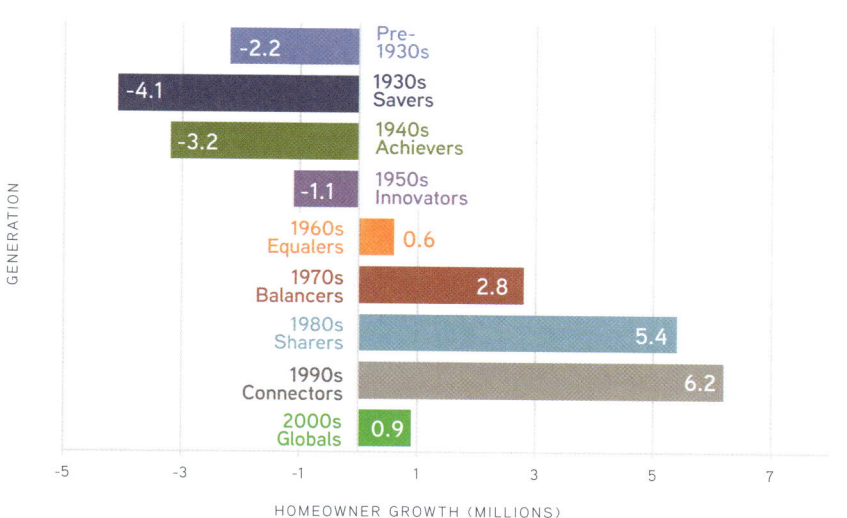

FORECASTING 5.2 MILLION MORE HOMEOWNERS BY 2025
FIGURE 8.4 Homeowner Growth by Generation (Millions), 2016–2025

Generation	Homeowner Growth (Millions)
Pre-1930s	-2.2
1930s Savers	-4.1
1940s Achievers	-3.2
1950s Innovators	-1.1
1960s Equalers	0.6
1970s Balancers	2.8
1980s Sharers	5.4
1990s Connectors	6.2
2000s Globals	0.9

Source: John Burns Real Estate Consulting, LLC

The 15.8 million first-time homeowners will primarily purchase affordable homes and will consist of 0.9 million Globals, 6.2 million Connectors, 5.4 million Sharers, 2.8 million more Balancers, and 0.6 million Equalers.

After decades of government laws designed to make homeownership easier to attain, the 2010 Dodd-Frank Act and its subsequent implementation made it more difficult to own a home. Policy makers want to avoid a repeat of the Great Recession, which resulted in millions of foreclosures and huge losses to banks and bondholders, partially due to millions of risky and fraudulent loans. The new policies require more documentation to prove income and the ability to repay the loan.

Government policy will impact housing decisions for millions. Three major shifts occurred since the 2010 Dodd-Frank Act, giving much more power to the president, causing many to question the future of government's agencies devoted to promoting homeownership, and removing the tax incentive to become a homeowner.

THREE GOVERNMENT POLICY SHIFTS

1. **The New Power of the President.** The President of the United States controls homeownership more than ever, as three presidential appointees now control the majority of the mortgage business:

    - Government created the Federal Housing Finance Agency (FHFA) in 2008 to oversee Fannie Mae and Freddie Mac. Fannie Mae and Freddie Mac play a major role in providing mortgages to homeowners by purchasing mortgages from lenders so they can make more mortgages. Government put these two behemoth publicly traded companies into government conservatorship in 2008. They continue to operate under government control in 2016. The president appoints the conservator.

    - The Federal Housing Administration (FHA) provides mortgage insurance to lower-credit and low-down-payment homebuyers. The president appoints the Housing and Urban Development (HUD) secretary, who oversees FHA.

    - The president also appoints the leader of the newly formed Consumer Finance Protection Bureau (CFPB), which regulates mortgage underwriting.

In other words, the policies of future presidents will make a huge difference in homeownership because the president will be able to appoint those who set mortgage policy.

2. **Continued Debate over Government's Role in the Mortgage Market.** While most politicians seem to want homeownership to grow, they debate the level of mortgage and mortgage-insurance risk the banks and the federal government should take. Numerous elected officials have called for the elimination of Fannie Mae, Freddie Mac, and the CFPB, and for a more conservative FHA. Fannie Mae and Freddie Mac effectively facilitate mortgage securitization, lowering mortgage rates and reducing lender risk at the same time, while taking on the risk for the federal government. The CFPB wants to protect consumers from risky debt, requiring extensive documentation to get a mortgage and reportedly holding back homeownership. FHA insures mortgages to the riskiest borrowers and charges a mortgage insurance premium to cover projected losses. Policy changes by any of these groups determine whether millions can qualify for a mortgage and become homeowners. Pay close attention to policy changes.

3. **Fewer Tax Incentives to Own.** Multiple surveys cite an overwhelming desire among renters to become homeowners. However, a high percentage of renters remains risk-averse to homeownership, aware of the scars that come with foreclosure. Today's prospective homeowners want to own but will likely take less risk than their parents. The flexibility of renting appeals to those who have little savings and lack job security. Additionally, most prospective home buyers no longer see a tax advantage to owning, since the interest and property taxes on the median-priced $200,000 home no longer exceed the standard tax deduction for

a couple. The annual April 15 "kick in the pants" to save taxes by purchasing a home no longer exists for today's young renters, since mortgage interest and property tax deductions fall nearly $2,500 short of the standard deduction for most potential home buyers.

TODAY, HOMEOWNERS' MORTGAGE INTEREST AND PROPERTY-TAX DEDUCTIONS FALL NEARLY $2,500 SHORT OF THE STANDARD DEDUCTION, A REVERSAL OF TREND FROM PRIOR DECADES.

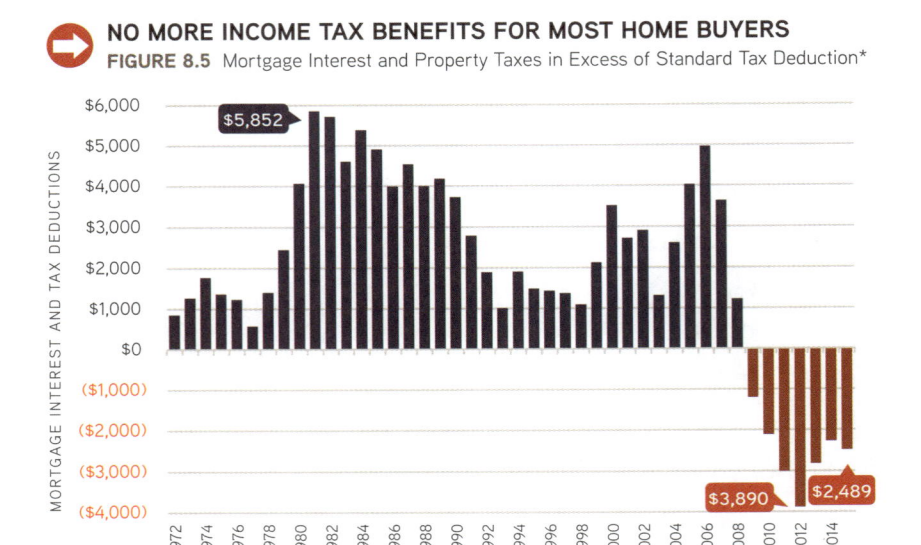

NO MORE INCOME TAX BENEFITS FOR MOST HOME BUYERS

FIGURE 8.5 Mortgage Interest and Property Taxes in Excess of Standard Tax Deduction*

Sources: John Burns Real Estate Consulting, LLC calculations of data from S&P/Case-Shiller National Home Price Index, FHFA, NAR, Freddie Mac, Tax Policy Center
*Assumes a married couple with a mortgage equal to 80% of median home price, and a 1.5% property tax rate.

The United States contains some 121 million households. A 1% change in the homeownership rate means a movement of roughly 1.2 million homeowners. Imagine what will happen if homeownership falls 15%—back to the levels that existed pre-World War II. Before you discount that notion as preposterous, know that today's 38-year-olds have a 15% lower homeownership rate than their parents did at the same age—15%! The Great Recession accounts for much of the decline, but societal shifts also play a role.

A 1% CHANGE IN THE HOMEOWNERSHIP RATE EQUATES TO 1.2 MILLION OWNED HOUSEHOLDS.

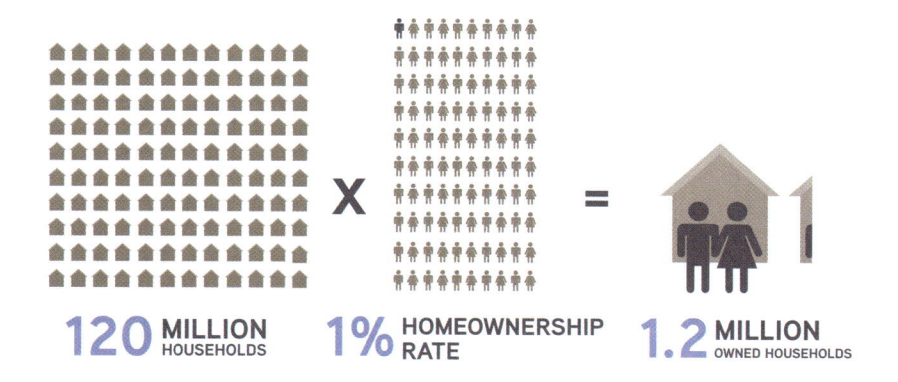

HOMEOWNERSHIP RATE SENSITIVITY
FIGURE 8.6 Homeowner Impact of Change in Homeownership Rate

120 MILLION HOUSEHOLDS X **1% HOMEOWNERSHIP RATE** = **1.2 MILLION OWNED HOUSEHOLDS**

Source: John Burns Real Estate Consulting, LLC

Today's 63% homeownership rate may seem high because the calculation excludes people who live with Mom and Dad. Only households count in the denominator. For example, in 2013, 4.2 million 38-year-old Balancers had formed 2.1 million households—1.2 million owned. These 1.2 million owned homes represent a 55% homeownership rate among the 2.1 million households and 4.2 million people.

AT AGE 38, 50% OF 1970s BALANCERS HEAD A HOUSEHOLD, AND 55% OF THOSE OWN THEIR HOME.

➡ 38-YEAR-OLDS IN 2013 HEADED 2.1 MILLION HOUSEHOLDS, OWNING 1.2 MILLION OF THEM

FIGURE 8.7 Headship and Homeownership for 38-Year-Olds, 2013

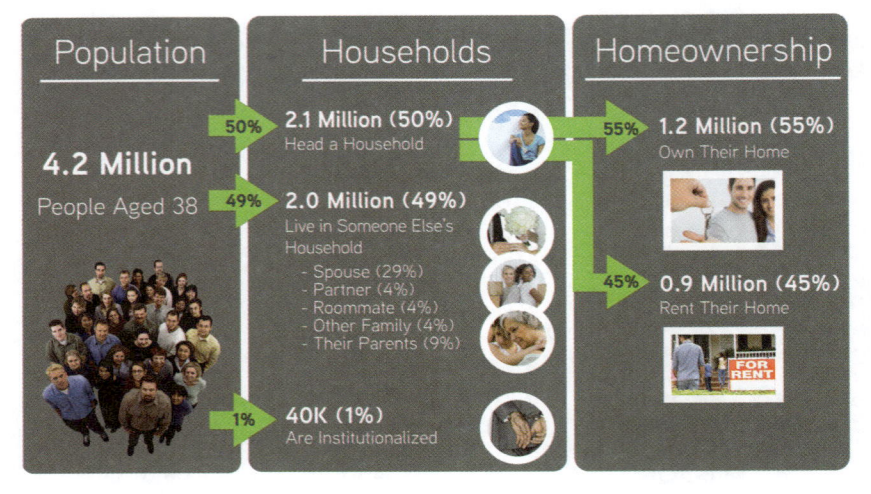

Population	Households	Homeownership
4.2 Million People Aged 38	50% → 2.1 Million (50%) Head a Household	55% → 1.2 Million (55%) Own Their Home
	49% → 2.0 Million (49%) Live in Someone Else's Household - Spouse (29%) - Partner (4%) - Roommate (4%) - Other Family (4%) - Their Parents (9%)	45% → 0.9 Million (45%) Rent Their Home
	1% → 40K (1%) Are Institutionalized	

Source: John Burns Real Estate Consulting, LLC

Homeownership, enabled by mortgages, has played a huge role in building wealth. More than 85% of 1970s Balancer and 1980s Sharer homeowners make mortgage payments. Contrast that with the fact that less than 25% of 1930s Saver and fewer than half of 1940s Achiever homeowners have mortgages. Most homeowners pay off their mortgage over time, creating a nice nest egg for retirement that plays a critical role in funding expenses later in life.

Homeownership also creates more neighborhood stability. Renters move more than twice as often as homeowners. Homeownership has resulted in a disciplined savings plan for millions of retirees, helping people retire, and we wonder how future retirees will have enough savings if they don't buy a home and pay down the mortgage over time. Over the long term, a low homeownership rate will likely result in a more impoverished retirement for future generations.

HOMEOWNERSHIP AND HOME EQUITY RISE WITH AGE.

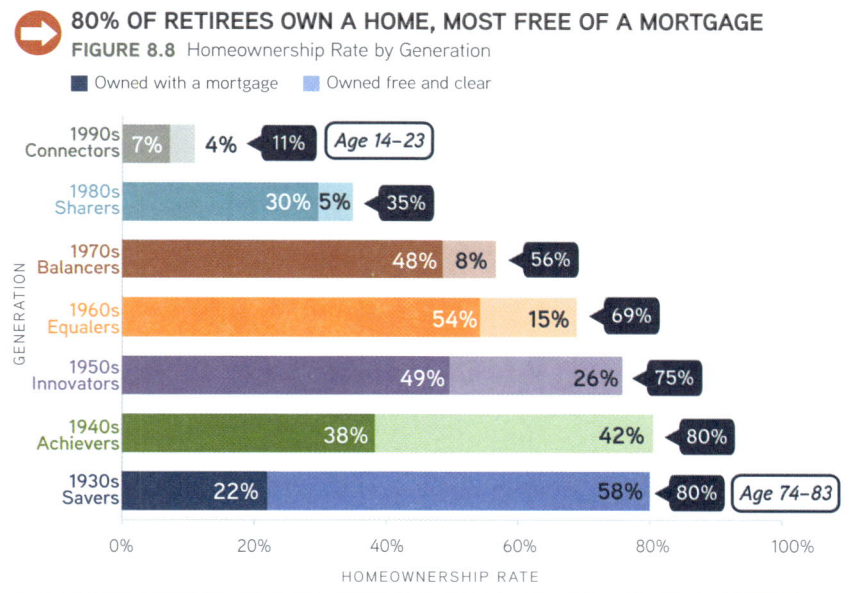

80% OF RETIREES OWN A HOME, MOST FREE OF A MORTGAGE

FIGURE 8.8 Homeownership Rate by Generation

■ Owned with a mortgage ■ Owned free and clear

Generation	Owned with a mortgage	Owned free and clear	Total	Age
1990s Connectors	7%	4%	11%	Age 14–23
1980s Sharers	30%	5%	35%	
1970s Balancers	48%	8%	56%	
1960s Equalers	54%	15%	69%	
1950s Innovators	49%	26%	75%	
1940s Achievers	38%	42%	80%	
1930s Savers	22%	58%	80%	Age 74–83

HOMEOWNERSHIP RATE

Source: John Burns Real Estate Consulting, LLC calculations of US Census Bureau 2013 American Community Survey 1-Year Estimates via IPUMS-USA

Thirty years of falling mortgage rates boosted home prices and homeownership. The lower the interest rate, the bigger the mortgages that buyers can afford. With low rates, homebuyers spend more on homes because they can, putting upward pressure on prices.

FALLING MORTGAGE RATES HAVE BOOSTED HOME PRICES AND HOMEOWNERSHIP.

LOWEST MORTGAGE RATES IN MODERN HISTORY
FIGURE 8.9 Mortgage Rates

Source: Bankrate.com, Freddie Mac, FFIEC

STUDENT DEBT HAS BECOME THE MOST-CITED REASON WHY PEOPLE DON'T OWN HOMES.

Student debt has become the most-cited reason why people don't own homes. Around 56% of those 33 or younger list student loans as the primary reason they can't save enough for a down payment. For the older group aged 34–48, credit-card debt rates as a bigger impediment.[33]

We conclude that rental housing should thrive for some time, including single-family home rentals, which surged after the housing

---

33 National Association of Realtors®, *Home Buyer and Seller Generational Trends*, March 2014, http://www.realtor.org/sites/default/files/reports/2014/2014-home-buyer-and-seller-generational-trends-report-full.pdf.

crash. Approximately 11.6% of all households now rent a single-family home, up from only 9.0% ten years ago. Many professional companies now develop and operate communities of single-family rentals—a level of professional landlord service once rare for this housing option—and house leases now dominate in some markets. Single-family homes constitute 50% of the rental stock in Riverside-San Bernardino, CA, 45% in Phoenix, and 41% in Las Vegas. The rise in single-family rentals perfectly coincides with the rise in 1980s Sharers into their typical homeownership years. Therefore, we believe a larger percentage than ever before will opt to raise their family in a professionally managed, detached rental home.

MORE THAN 1 IN 9 HOUSEHOLDS NOW RENT A SINGLE-FAMILY HOME.

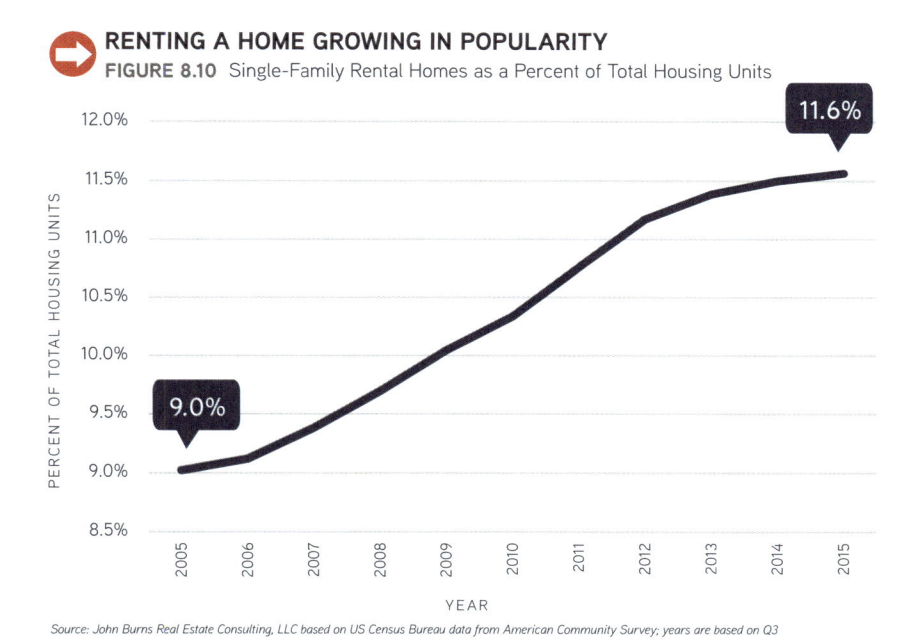

RENTING A HOME GROWING IN POPULARITY
FIGURE 8.10 Single-Family Rental Homes as a Percent of Total Housing Units

Source: John Burns Real Estate Consulting, LLC based on US Census Bureau data from American Community Survey; years are based on Q3

1950s Innovator Steve Burch rents his current single-family home in Las Vegas—his third rental after a lifetime of buying houses. Jobs influenced some of his recent rental decisions. Unsure how long he'd work in Virginia or Atlanta, renting made sense in those places. But the housing crash played a role, too. When he moved back to Michigan for his job, he bought a beautiful home with a California design and more than 10,000 square feet of space on a 37-acre farm. He dug deep for the investment, but why not? All his life he'd made money buying and selling the homes he lived in.

"While I was in Michigan, the downturn occurred and the [housing] crash came," Burch said. "I had made money on every home I owned from the time I first started buying houses in Detroit when I was a kid. I gave it all back, essentially. If it weren't for [my employer] giving me some assistance on the loss when I sold the house, I would have been wiped out, just devastated, so I think that burned me a lot."

The crash did wipe out plenty of others. In 2016, many of the Great Recession's delinquent homeowners still linger. They live in homes they still own but haven't paid the mortgage in years. They will no longer count as homeowners when their foreclosures complete. Burch, like many who suffered in the housing crash, intends to buy again. He likes Las Vegas but prefers Phoenix, Arizona, so he debates his next move. Whenever that occurs, he will become one of many contributing to the rebound in homeownership. Meanwhile, he will continue to rent.

The Great Recession likewise influenced home buying for Kyle Zierer, the 29-year-old consultant, though less directly. Confronting a tough economy and high rents when he graduated college in 2009, Zierer moved back in with his parents for years to save money.

This trend has become common for those born after 1980, who exhibit many traits and preferences that tamp down home buying. Nearly 20% of 1980s Sharers live below the poverty line, the highest percentage of any generation since the young adults of the 1930s. Sharers face great challenges in starting careers. Young people marry later or not at all, cohabitate at a growing rate, delay childbirth, and, increasingly, parent alone—all of which discourages home buying. They move fewer times and tend to shun long commutes, a preference that encourages urban living and renting, since buying in big cities takes big bucks.

> **NEARLY 20% OF 1980s SHARERS LIVE BELOW THE POVERTY LINE, THE HIGHEST PERCENTAGE OF ANY GENERATION SINCE THE YOUNG ADULTS OF THE 1930s.**

In early 2016, Zierer had amassed enough for a down payment and was preparing to move out, but like many ready to contribute to the imminent explosion in household formations and a gradual rise in homeownership, he decided to rent before buying.

"It's getting to that point where I should move out—I'm close to 30—and I do have enough saved to buy something, but the market scares me a little right now. Prices have gone up so much . . . if I move out, I'll rent for a couple of years first."

Facing a horrendous economy as they entered the workforce and watching their parents navigate the housing crash affected the mind-set of many 1980s Sharers like Zierer. In 2015, seven years after the Great Recession, the most qualified renters—those in the most expensive apartments—still delayed purchasing homes.

Despite the lowest mortgage rates ever, fewer than 15% of renters who moved in 2015 did so in order to buy a home, compared to a historical average of 17%. Opportunities to rent—and increasingly to rent houses—are plentiful. Craigslist and other new online services have also made it much easier for landlords and tenants to get together, including tenants who want to rent just a room in a house.

RENTERS REMAIN IN PLACE, DESPITE HISTORICALLY LOW MORTGAGE RATES AND RISING RENTS.

➡ **RENTERS STAYING AS RENTERS**
FIGURE 8.11 Percentage of Apartment Move-Outs to Purchase a Home
As reported by publicly-traded REITs; Historical Average = 17%

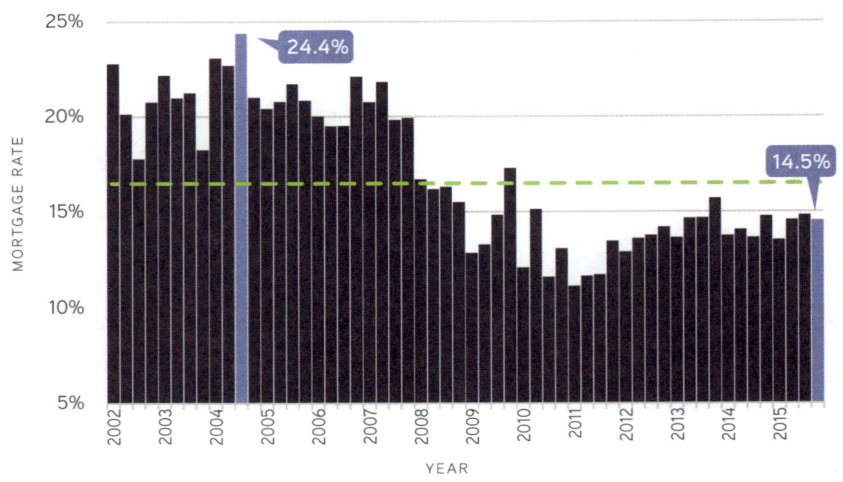

Source: John Burns Real Estate Consulting, LLC calculations of publicly traded REIT quarterly filings

Renting, even for long stretches, no longer looks like the necessary evil or poor alternative it once did, although, as for Zierer, buying a home remains a goal for most young people. According to a 2013 Fannie Mae survey, around 90% of renters who would prefer to own intend to own someday.[34] Other recent surveys report that 74% of people aged 18 to 34 plan to buy a home in the next five years,[35] and 72% list buying as part of their "personal American dream."[36]

[34] Fannie Mae, "Fannie Mae National Housing Survey: Renters: Satisfied, but Reaching for Homeownership," June 6, 2013, http://www.fanniemae.com/resources/file/research/housingsurvey/pdf/nhsq32012presentation.pdf.
[35] "Majority of Millennials Plan to Purchase a Home in Next Five Years: BMO Harris Bank Study," BMO, July 18, 2014, https://newsroom.bmoharris.com/press-releases/majority-of-millennials-plan-to-purchase-a-home-in-1124663.
[36] "Trulia Survey: 'Renter Nation' Just a Myth as 93 Percent of Millennial Renters Plan to Buy a Home," Trulia, December 12, 2012, http://info.trulia.com/trulia-american-dream-survey-winter-2012.

Like many goals held by the 1980s Sharers and 1990s Connectors, though—buying a car, getting married, having kids, moving out of their parents' place—the desire to own a home doesn't come with a burning sense of urgency.

For some, their excellent educations will soon translate into higher incomes that will help them purchase homes. Many will also receive down-payment assistance from their parents and grandparents, including inheritances. New government programs to boost homeownership appear likely as well. Putting it all together, a lower percentage will achieve homeownership than prior generations.

As Kyle Zierer demonstrates, the younger generations exhibit caution regarding buying homes postrecession. They want a savings cushion in the bank before borrowing. Owning seems less socially important in a sharing economy. Also, the tax benefits disappeared for most now that the standard deduction exceeds mortgage interest and property taxes. As a result, the homeownership rate for younger people will continue to drag down the overall rate.

We forecast future homeownership by comparing each generation's homeownership levels today to prior generations and applying our best estimate. We know how each generation compares to prior generations at the same age today and how homeownership typically trends as people age, allowing us to make a reasonable estimate. As you read some of our forecast charts, you may wonder "how can they predict such a decline in homeownership?" We cheated a bit. Much of that decline has already happened by 2015. Our 2025 forecast for those under age 55 is as follows:

BIG SHIFTS AHEAD

> 1990s Connectors at 28 in 2025 (born 1997): They will achieve 27% homeownership, compared to 38.1% for the 28-year-old Sharers in 2010, and 47.5% for 1950s Innovators at the same age in 1980.

WE EXPECT 27% OF 1990s CONNECTOR HOUSEHOLDS TO OWN IN 2025, AND 73% TO RENT.

HOMEOWNERSHIP FOR THE CONNECTORS WILL BE VERY LOW

FIGURE 8.12 Homeownership Rate among 28-Year-Old Householders

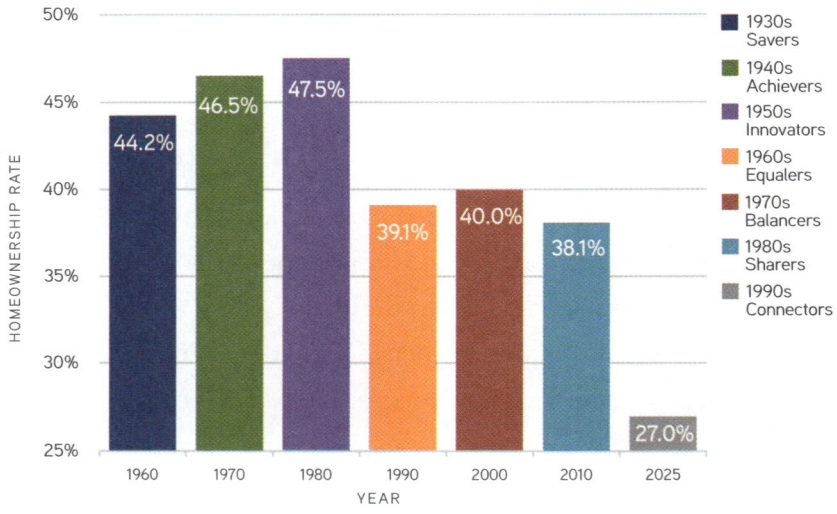

Year	Cohort	Homeownership Rate
1960	1930s Savers	44.2%
1970	1940s Achievers	46.5%
1980	1950s Innovators	47.5%
1990	1960s Equalers	39.1%
2000	1970s Balancers	40.0%
2010	1980s Sharers	38.1%
2025	1990s Connectors	27.0%

Source: John Burns Real Estate Consulting, LLC based on US Census Bureau data and extensive analysis of each age cohort.

8: RENTING IN THE SHARING ECONOMY

> 1980s Sharers at 38 in 2025 (born 1987): They will achieve 52% homeownership, compared to 60% for the 38-year-old Balancers in 2010 and 71% for 1940s Achievers at the same age in 1980.

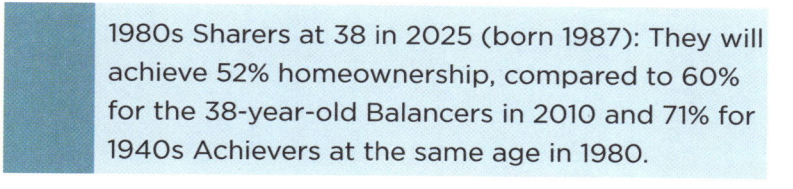

WE EXPECT 52% OF 1980s SHARER HOUSEHOLDS TO OWN IN 2025, AND 48% TO RENT.

➡ FORECASTING HISTORICALLY LOW HOMEOWNERSHIP FOR 38-YEAR-OLDS

FIGURE 8.13 Homeownership Rate among 38-Year-Old Householders

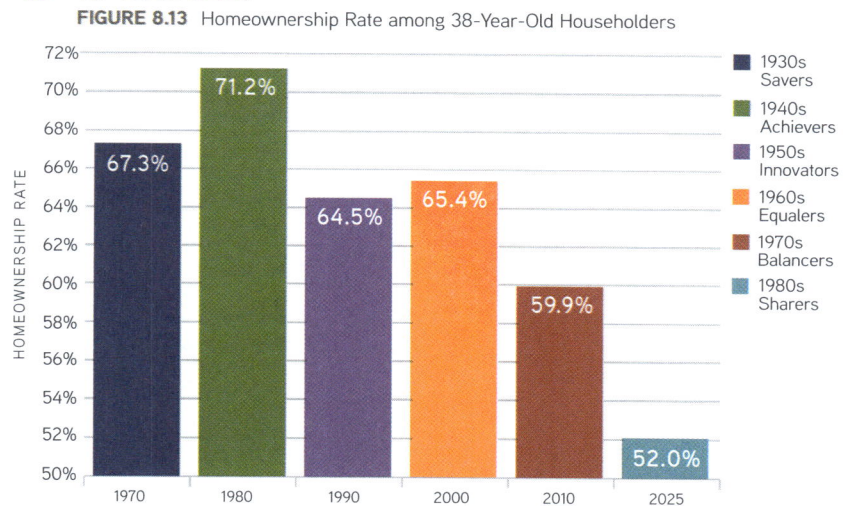

Year	Cohort	Homeownership Rate
1970	1930s Savers	67.3%
1980	1940s Achievers	71.2%
1990	1950s Innovators	64.5%
2000	1960s Equalers	65.4%
2010	1970s Balancers	59.9%
2025	1980s Sharers	52.0%

Source: John Burns Real Estate Consulting, LLC based on US Census Bureau data and extensive analysis of each age cohort.

> 1970s Balancers at 48 in 2025 (born 1977): They will achieve 63% homeownership in 2025, compared to 68% for 48-year-olds today and 78% for Savers at that age in 1980. Our 63% homeownership forecast is low by historical standards, but a bold call given the low home-ownership today.

WE EXPECT 63% OF 1970s BALANCER HOUSEHOLDS TO OWN IN 2025, AND 37% TO RENT.

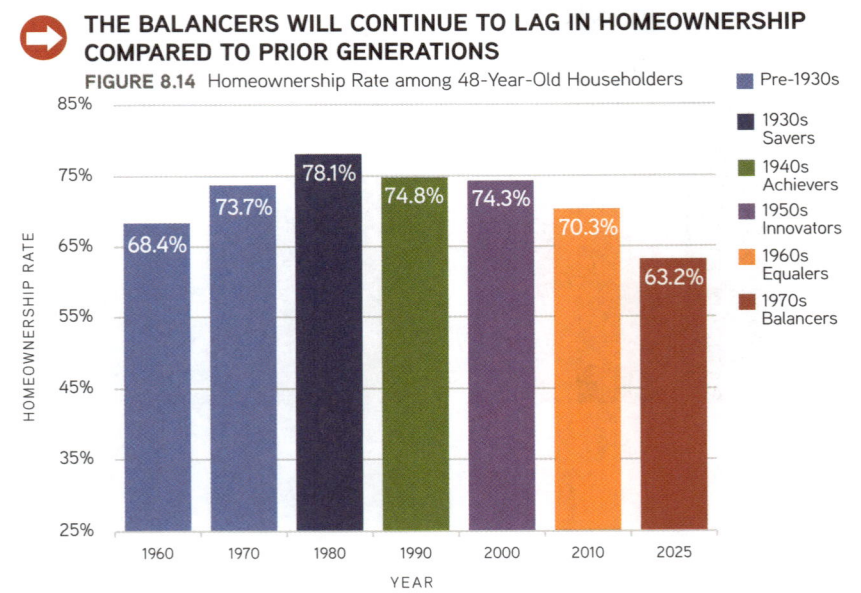

THE BALANCERS WILL CONTINUE TO LAG IN HOMEOWNERSHIP COMPARED TO PRIOR GENERATIONS

FIGURE 8.14 Homeownership Rate among 48-Year-Old Householders

Year	Rate	Cohort
1960	68.4%	Pre-1930s
1970	73.7%	1930s Savers
1980	78.1%	1940s Achievers
1990	74.8%	1950s Innovators
2000	74.3%	1960s Equalers
2010	70.3%	
2025	63.2%	1970s Balancers

Source: John Burns Real Estate Consulting, LLC based on US Census Bureau data and extensive analysis of each age cohort.

Older homeowners will increasingly start renting too. Some will prefer the flexibility that renting offers, especially when moving near their children and grandchildren or trying urban living for a while. The lower home-maintenance lifestyle will also draw homeowners to a rental lifestyle. For others, a lack of sufficient savings for their elongated retirement will cause them to cash out on their current home by selling, renting, or obtaining a reverse mortgage.

All of this housing demand will result in the need to construct 13.7 million homes from 2016 to 2025. If homebuilders and apartment developers could profitably build lower-cost homes and apartments, we would project even more construction. However, rising construction costs in almost every market in the country, coupled with lower-than-usual consumer demand to drive to outlying areas where land costs less, will prevent a stronger construction industry. The aforementioned immigration reversal from Mexico also wiped out much of the trained construction labor needed to build houses.

> **ALL OF THIS HOUSING DEMAND WILL RESULT IN THE NEED TO CONSTRUCT 13.7 MILLION HOMES FROM 2016 TO 2025.**

Construction will remain low partially because homebuilders and apartment developers overbuilt the housing market by 4.8 million homes in the 2000s. That decade, contractors built 15.8 million homes while only 11.0 million additional households formed. In 2015, 1.3 million excess vacant homes remain, varying heavily by market. The surplus homes include:

- single-family rental vacancies: 670,000 above norm

- homes listed for sale: 210,000 above norm (many of them former foreclosures)

- homes in foreclosure/other: 640,000 above norm

- apartment vacancies: 200,000 *below* norm (the main reason rents are rapidly rising)

We excluded 680,000 excess second-home vacancies from our total.

OVER THE LONG TERM, CONSTRUCTION OUTPACES HOUSEHOLD GROWTH, DUE PRIMARILY TO TEARDOWNS AND SECOND HOMES.

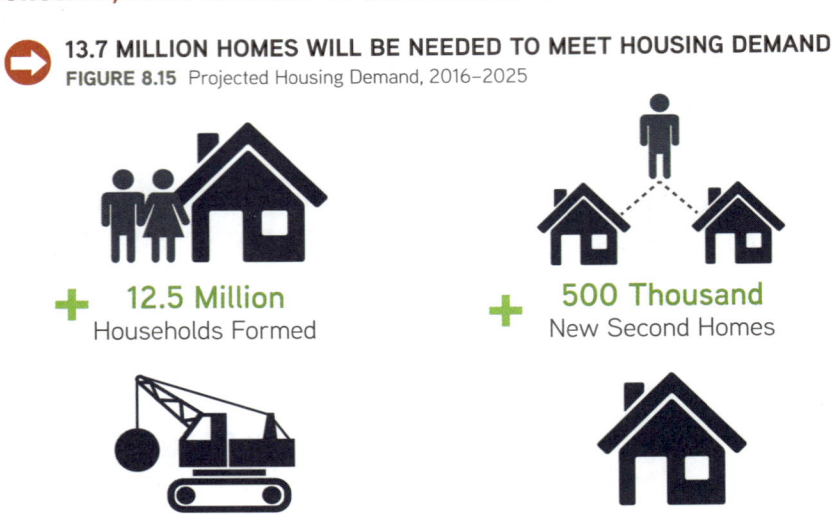

13.7 MILLION HOMES WILL BE NEEDED TO MEET HOUSING DEMAND
FIGURE 8.15 Projected Housing Demand, 2016–2025

+ **12.5 Million** Households Formed

+ **500 Thousand** New Second Homes

+ **2.0 Million** Teardowns

− **1.3 Million** Excess Vacant Homes

Source: John Burns Real Estate Consulting, LLC

Constructing 1.37 million new homes per year over an entire decade to satisfy demand will please the construction industry, which only built 1.1 million homes in 2015. Builders will construct an average of 850,000 single-family homes and 520,000 multifamily homes, including apartments and condos, each year. Renters will occupy an increasing share of all homes.

Examining the demographics behind the recovery reveals unique opportunities. Demand for nonfamily housing will surge, since the resale stock already provides sufficient homes designed to service the 29% of households with kids. Fifty years ago, 48% of households included kids. Only 28% of households will have children in 2025.

In summary, housing demand should steadily rise, resulting in approximately 12.5 million more households in 2025 than in

2015. By 2025, Americans will own 5.2 million more homes and rent 7.3 million more apartments and homes. Over the decade, builders will construct 4.6 million multifamily units, 8.3 million single-family homes, and 800,000 manufactured homes—13.7 million homes in total.

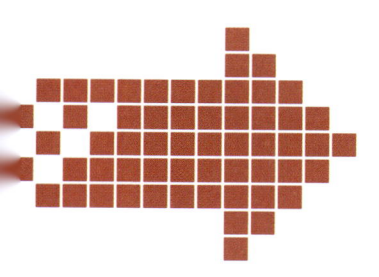

9: HEADING SOUTH IN DROVES

Growth will continue to tilt heavily south, toward the affordable, sunshine states of the Sunbelt. Florida, Texas, the Southeast, and the Southwest grew from just 32% of households in 1970 to 42% of all households today. We forecast that 62% of household growth will occur in these four regions over the next decade.

THE WARM, AFFORDABLE, PRO-GROWTH SOUTH WILL ATTRACT 62% OF THE HOUSEHOLD GROWTH.

62% OF GROWTH IN THE SOUTH
FIGURE 9.1 Estimated Share of Household Growth, 2016–2025

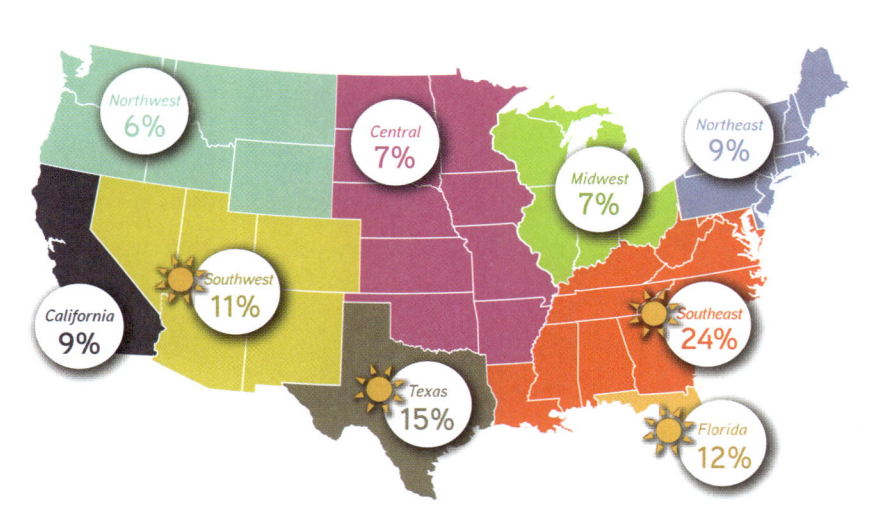

- Northwest 6%
- Central 7%
- Midwest 7%
- Northeast 9%
- California 9%
- Southwest 11%
- Southeast 24%
- Texas 15%
- Florida 12%

Source: John Burns Real Estate Consulting, LLC

209

The South will grow fastest for three primary reasons:

- **Employment.** Employers will continue to flock to the pro-growth states light on taxes and regulations and aggressive on business recruitment and incentives.

- **Affordability.** Affordable housing and low income and property taxes will continue to pull residents from more expensive regions. Young families in expensive housing markets like New York and California will continue to move south. Retirees on fixed incomes leave locations in the Northeast and Midwest, which charge high property and income taxes, for affordable living in warm climates.

- **Retiree Proximity to Kids.** The coming generation of retirees wants to live near their grandkids, and their children will find better employment opportunities in the South. Many 1950s Innovators will live close to employment centers so they can continue working. The same 1950s Innovators who couldn't get out of the house fast enough after finishing school are the ones connected to their kids and grandkids and want to live near or with them later in life.

Given the massive population growth in sizeable Texas cities such as Dallas, Fort Worth, Houston, Austin, and San Antonio—as well as in smaller cities like Frisco and San Marcos—the fact that Texas tops our forecast of regional growth rates won't shock many. The rapid rates of population growth that we'll see in Texas, Florida, and the Southwest during the next decade, however—in the range of 22% to 24%—might surprise some. These areas will likely grow more than twice as fast as the US overall.

TEXAS WILL GROW FASTER THAN ANY OTHER STATE.

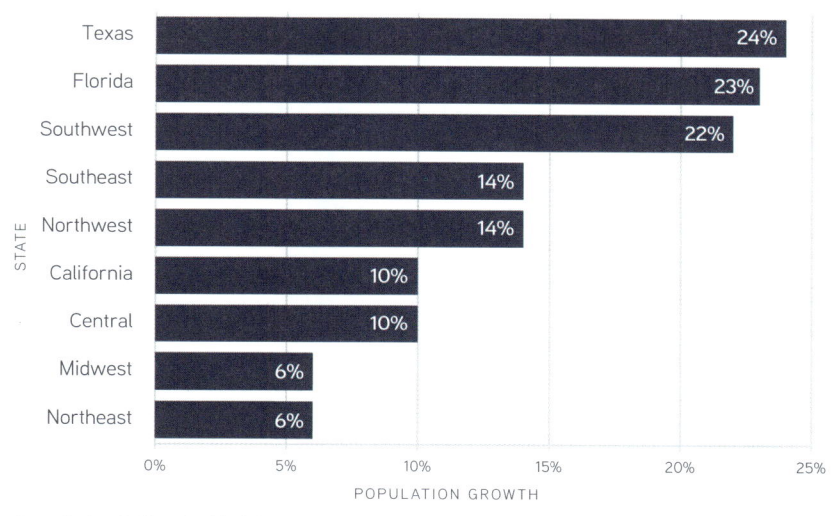

PROJECTED POPULATION GROWTH BY REGION
FIGURE 9.2 Projected Population Growth by Region, 2016–2025

State	Population Growth
Texas	24%
Florida	23%
Southwest	22%
Southeast	14%
Northwest	14%
California	10%
Central	10%
Midwest	6%
Northeast	6%

Source: John Burns Real Estate Consulting, LLC calculations of US Census Bureau data

Note that we forecast positive population growth even in the Midwest and Northeast. Trends in births, life expectancy, and immigration make net declines in regional population rare, creating growth almost everywhere.

1950s Innovator Steve Burch represents the migration patterns well. Born and raised in Michigan, he worked for a large corporation in Michigan for years. However, career opportunities often presented themselves in the South, where he relocated many times over the years. His employer eventually relocated their headquarters to Atlanta, and Steve went with them before making the move to Las Vegas. Rarely do companies or individuals relocate to the Midwest or Northeast other than to Chicago or New York City.

Construction activity provides a good illustration of the changes underway. In 1960, 56% of all housing construction took place in just three regions: 19% in California, 20% in the Northeast, and 17% in the Midwest. By 2014, those three regions' piece of the construction pie had been halved. In 2014, they comprised only 27% of the nation's total. Construction has declined steadily in these areas since the late 1980s too. Since 1960, California has lost 11% of the country's market share of growth, while the Northeast and Midwest each lost 8 to 9%.

CONSTRUCTION HAS SHIFTED SOUTH. CALIFORNIA, THE MIDWEST, AND NORTHEAST FELL FROM 56% OF CONSTRUCTION IN 1960 TO 28% TODAY.

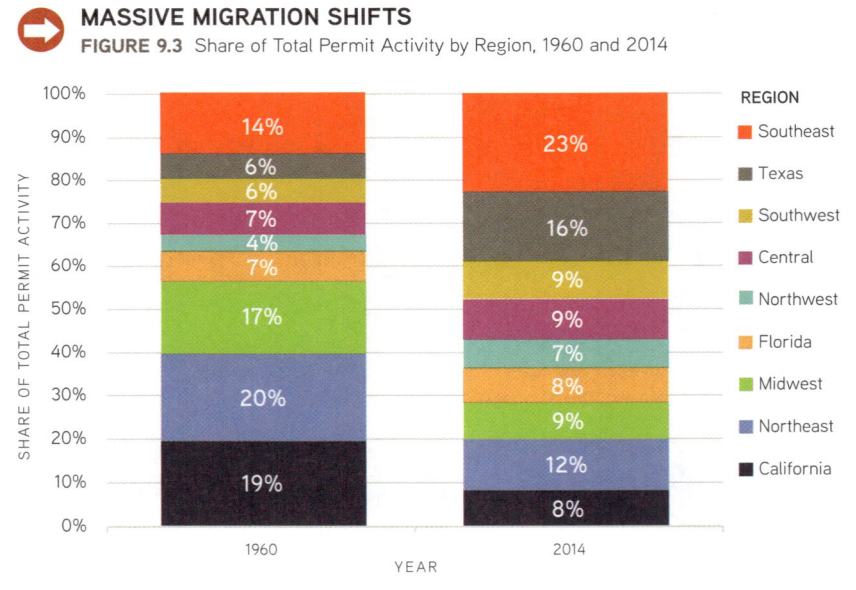

MASSIVE MIGRATION SHIFTS
FIGURE 9.3 Share of Total Permit Activity by Region, 1960 and 2014

Region	1960	2014
Southeast	14%	23%
Texas	6%	16%
Southwest	6%	9%
Central	7%	9%
Northwest	4%	7%
Florida	7%	8%
Midwest	17%	9%
Northeast	20%	12%
California	19%	8%

Source: John Burns Real Estate Consulting, LLC calculations of US Census Bureau Building Permits Survey data

Decades of steady growth have transformed cities and towns throughout the South, particularly in Georgia, Texas, North Carolina, and Florida, and especially near major airports.

The Southeast now accounts for a whopping 23% of all residential construction. This region continues to attract major companies, including car plants, factories, and production facilities at a time when experts have all but pronounced American manufacturing dead. Warm weather, affordable housing, and low taxation adds to the appeal. The Southeast issued fewer than 1.3 million construction permits for single-family homes in the 1960s. In the 2000s, the Southeast issued more than twice as many—3+ million.

Atlanta's Hartsfield-Jackson International Airport has become the busiest in the world, serving more than 101 million passengers in 2015.[37] *Forbes* ranked Atlanta fifth in the nation on its list of "Best Places for Business and Careers."[38] Painful traffic jams attest to the explosive growth of this once-sleepy town.

Texas has grown even more quickly. In recent years, Texas has dominated lists of America's fastest-growing cities. Contractors built new freeways all over Texas in the last few decades, turning rural ranch land into thriving cities. New residents and businesses have transformed the Houston, Dallas, Austin, and San Antonio metro areas. A 2012 study by *The New York Times* found that Texas spent around $19 billion per year—more than any other state—in business incentives, creating a massive number of jobs.[39] Over the last 25 years, the rate of job growth in Texas has doubled the national average. Fifty-four companies on the *Fortune* 500 list make their headquarters in Texas, second only to 55 in New York.[40] Austin, once portrayed as an edgy

---

37 Hartsfield-Jackson Atlanta International Airport, "Monthly Airport Traffic Report," December 2015, http://www.atlanta-airport.com/docs/Traffic/201512.pdf.
38 Kurt Badenhausen, "The 2015 Best Places for Business And Careers," *Forbes*, July 29, 2015, http://www.forbes.com/best-places-for-business/.
39 Louise Story, "As Companies Seek Tax Deals, Governments Pay High Price," *The New York Times*, December 1, 2012, http://www.nytimes.com/2012/12/02/us/how-local-taxpayers-bankroll-corporations.html.
40 Maria Halkias, "Texas is No. 2 for Fortune 500 Companies, Topping California," *The Dallas Morning News*, June 8, 2015, http://www.dallasnews.com.

bohemian college town, has always treasured its quirks. Recently, an influx of tech companies such as Dell and Apple, the growth of SXSW, and rapid development have molded Austin into a tech leader.

Houston has benefited from the Hurricane Katrina out-migration from New Orleans, the oil fracking boom, expanded trade through the ports, and huge growth in healthcare companies headquartered in Texas. A growing international airport attracts permanent residents from all over the world, and trade increased after the passage of the North American Free Trade Agreement (NAFTA) in 1992. San Antonio similarly benefited from Katrina and NAFTA. Meanwhile, Dallas has become one of the fastest-growing economies in the country, attracting a diverse group of employers looking for convenient air travel, a pro-growth environment, and no state income taxes.

Like many transplants to the South, Lisa Marquis Jackson moved to Dallas because of employment. Her husband at the time, who worked in telecommunications, moved the family from Chicago to the Dallas suburb of Flower Mound to advance his career.

"It was a really new developing suburban area, so it didn't have a lot of the retail. The few restaurants were all chains," Jackson said. "As we lived there over the twelve years, though, it was clearly becoming more and more established and more things were coming in. About the time we left is when it really hit its peak, and it's a great place now. There's great retail and lots of things to do." The Jackson family witnessed firsthand the emergence of a thriving suburb, a shift we will cover in the next chapter.

Warm weather did not factor much into Jackson's decision, though she doesn't exactly yearn for Chicago winters. Economic

---

com/business/headlines/20150605-texas-is-no.-2-for-fortune-500-companies-topping-california.ece.

opportunity brought her young family, like so many others, to rapidly growing Dallas-Fort Worth. She only planned on staying a few years, but energy and growth permeated the air. Jackson quickly learned that Dallas offered great opportunities for kids, as well as careers.

"It's a great place to raise a family—there are just a lot of young people," Jackson said. "It's a place where you could move into a new community, and everybody moving in at the same time were open to new friendships. The kids are young, so it's very easy to find a social dynamic with all of that."

Florida skews older and has always welcomed strangers. Many Central Americans come to America through Miami. Disney and other tourist attractions create tens of thousands of jobs to serve millions of tourists each year in Orlando. Tampa has become a very affordable place to live, and retirees in search of warm weather, no state income taxes, beautiful golf courses, and great medical care dominate population growth in the rest of Florida.

Changes in technology, one of the 4 Big Influencers, drive migration patterns. The rise of automated manufacturing drove the population from the South to the North in the late 1800s. The rise of air conditioning and refrigeration technology helped reverse the migration in the mid-1900s. The decline of manufacturing in the Northeast and especially in the Midwest also contributed to southern migration. Many of the industrial jobs that fortified these northern regions disappeared or moved overseas, which sent residents to areas with stronger job growth.

CHANGES IN TECHNOLOGY, ONE OF THE 4 BIG INFLUENCERS, DRIVE MIGRATION PATTERNS.

Recent technologies, many of which reside in a smartphone, create huge employment opportunities, especially in the San

Francisco Bay Area. Many of the smartest young programmers and robotics experts from all over the world moved to the area, causing rents and home prices to skyrocket. California also has plenty of sunshine, plus endless beaches, mountains, world-famous vineyards, and world-class schools. Why move from the state once considered America's paradise to Texas? In some ways, California has become a victim of its own success. Housing costs are high, which keeps home-ownership low—just 56% in 2010, when all other regions achieved a homeownership rate of at least 62%. Comparatively high taxes in the Golden State compound its retention challenges. The Northeast, California, and parts of the Midwest bear a particularly high tax burden in relation to incomes.[41] Texas and states in the Southeast promote a more consumer-friendly tax environment.

Californians seeking a change of venue look north. Technology has driven growth in Seattle and Portland, with companies such as Amazon and Microsoft creating high-paying jobs and spurring development. A November 2014 article on GeekWire estimated that Amazon's planned office space would employ 7% of the city of Seattle.[42]

Clearly, far more young people are fleeing to the Northwest than vice versa. In early 2016, we calculated that a U-Haul truck from San Francisco to Portland cost seven times the price to take the same truck back. Technology has also

IN EARLY 2016, WE CALCULATED THAT A U-HAUL TRUCK FROM SAN FRANCISCO TO PORTLAND COST SEVEN TIMES THE PRICE TO TAKE THE SAME TRUCK BACK.

---

41   The Tax Foundation, "State-Local Tax Burden Rankings FY 2012," January 20, 2016, http://taxfoundation.org/article/state-local-tax-burden-rankings-fy-201.2

42   Jeff Reifman, "'Amageddon': How Amazon's culture is taking a toll on Seattle's future," *GeekWire*, November 19, 2014, http://www.geekwire.com/2014/commentary-amageddon-seattles-increasingly-obvious-future/.

driven Southern growth, especially in Raleigh and Austin. Technology jobs drive growth in Denver, where the Denver Tech Center nurtured major players such as AT&T Broadband and United Cablevision.

What do all these regional shifts mean for future patterns of household growth? We'll conclude this chapter with some revealing numbers. The total number of US households increased 27% from 1990 to 2010, with several regions experiencing higher growth:

REGION	GROWTH, 1990–2010
Southwest	67%
Texas	47%
Florida	45%
Northwest	39%
Southeast	33%

NATIONALLY, HOUSEHOLDS GREW 27% FROM 1990 TO 2010. FIVE REGIONS OUTPACED THAT GROWTH—THE SOUTHWEST IN PARTICULAR.

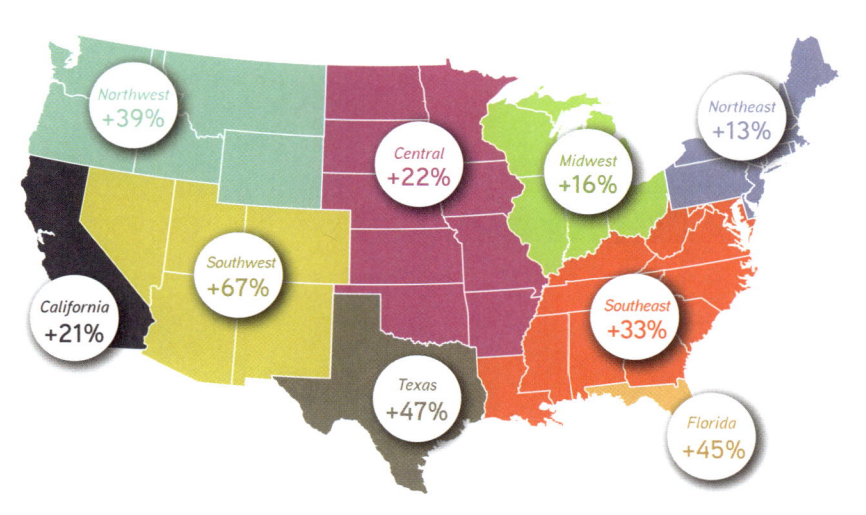

PAST GROWTH
FIGURE 9.4 Estimated Share of Household Growth, 1990–2010

- Northwest +39%
- Northeast +13%
- Central +22%
- Midwest +16%
- Southwest +67%
- California +21%
- Southeast +33%
- Texas +47%
- Florida +45%

Source: John Burns Real Estate Consulting, LLC calculations of US Census Bureau, Decennial Census 1990 and 2010

Compare their growth with that of regions trailing the 27% national average:

Central	22%
California	21%
Midwest	16%
Northeast	13%

These four slower-growing regions generally tax their residents heavily and discourage growth. The Northeast and Midwest continue to lose a massive share of the population to the South.

THE SOUTH GROWS WHILE THE NORTH SLOWS.

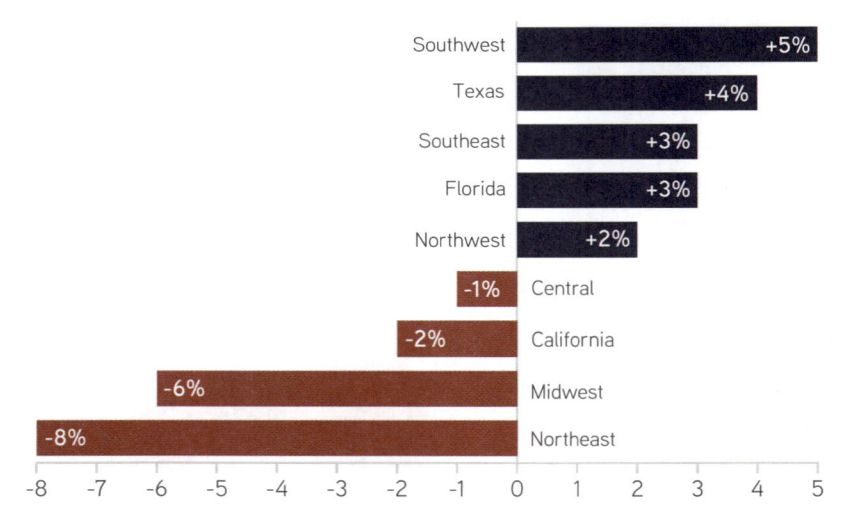

THE SOUTH IS GAINING SHARE FROM THE NORTH AND CALIFORNIA
FIGURE 9.5 1990–2010 Share of Household Growth Less 2010 Share of All Households

Southwest	+5%
Texas	+4%
Southeast	+3%
Florida	+3%
Northwest	+2%
Central	-1%
California	-2%
Midwest	-6%
Northeast	-8%

Source: John Burns Real Estate Consulting, LLC calculations of US Census Bureau, Decennial Census 1990 and 2010

The Northeast and Midwest continue to rapidly lose their share of US households.

In conclusion, we expect the South to capture 7.8 million of the 12.5 million additional households. The large Southeast region will grow by 3.0 million households. Pro-growth Texas will grow by 1.9 million households. Retirees will continue to flock to Florida, which will add 1.5 million households. The pro-growth Southwest will also grow by 1.4 million households.

THE SOUTH WILL CAPTURE 7.8 MILLION OF THE 12.5 MILLION HOUSEHOLDS ADDED.

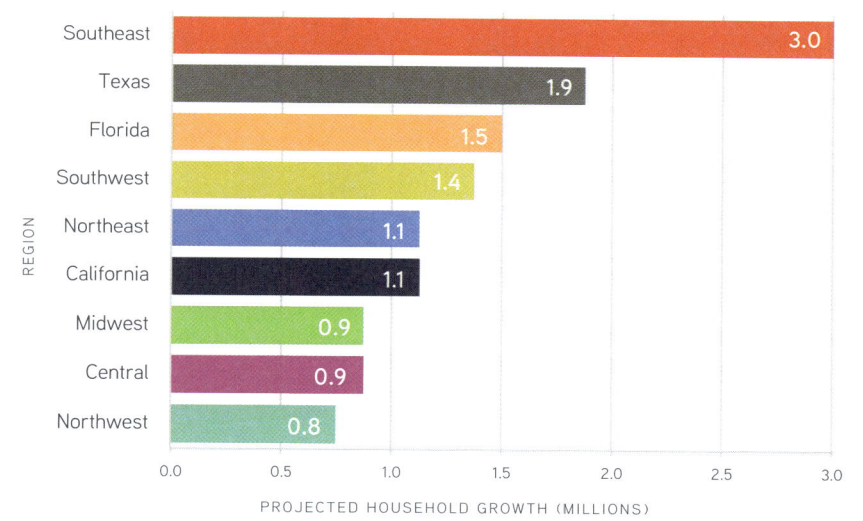

SOUTH TO DOMINATE FUTURE GROWTH
FIGURE 9.6 Projected Household Growth by Region (Millions), 2016–2025

Region	Projected Household Growth (Millions)
Southeast	3.0
Texas	1.9
Florida	1.5
Southwest	1.4
Northeast	1.1
California	1.1
Midwest	0.9
Central	0.9
Northwest	0.8

Source: John Burns Real Estate Consulting, LLC

We also suggest paying attention to new technologies, economic cycles in specific industries, and new government policies that can impact the forecast dramatically. Our analysis helps decision makers calculate the growth in demand for their products and services but not the supply their competitors will add. The most successful businesses will focus on the areas of greatest demand and supply imbalance, not simply where demand will grow the fastest. In other words, don't ignore the slow-growing Northeast and Midwest.

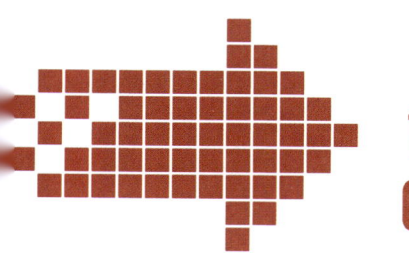

10: A NEW SURBAN™ WAY OF LIFE

Urban areas more than doubled their share of household growth recently—from 8% of growth in the 2000s to 21% of growth in the first half of this decade. Urban areas haven't captured that percentage of growth since the Roaring 1920s.

URBAN CAPTURED 21% OF HOUSEHOLD GROWTH IN THE FIRST HALF OF THE 2010s—DOUBLE ITS USUAL CAPTURE RATE.

URBAN CAPTURED 21% OF RECENT HOUSEHOLD GROWTH
FIGURE 10.1 Urban Share of Household Growth

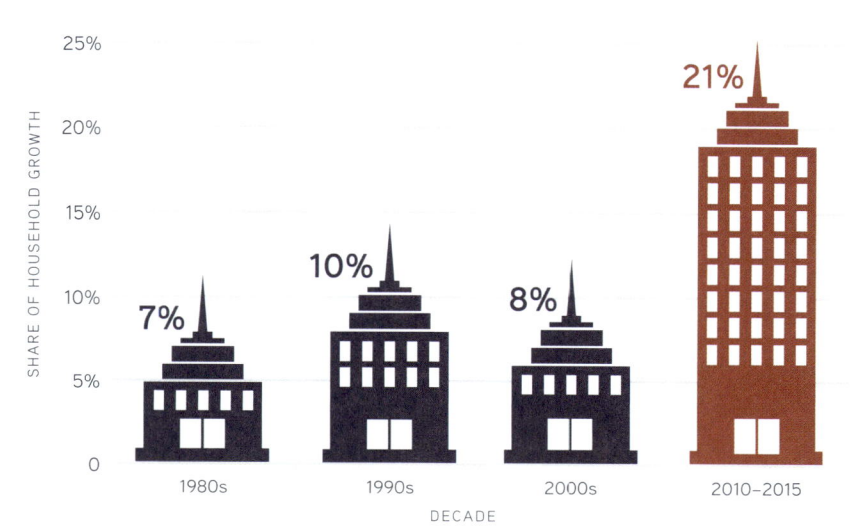

Decade	Share
1980s	7%
1990s	10%
2000s	8%
2010–2015	21%

Source: John Burns Real Estate Consulting, LLC based on US Census Bureau data

221

To analyze urban, suburban, and rural growth, we developed and analyzed two categories of urban (downtown and neighborhood), four categories of suburban (big, booming, small principal, and small), and three categories of rural (exurb/commuter, micropolitan, and rustic). These nine categories, defined more specifically in appendix 1, bring far more clarity to the discussion.

Based on our definitions, 15% of households live urban:

- 8.1% in urban downtowns
- 7.0% in the surrounding urban neighborhoods

64% live suburban:

- 7.7% in big suburban cities
- 10.3% in small principal cities
- 1.6% in booming suburbs
- 44.7% in small suburban cities

21% live rurally:

- 5.3% in exurbs
- 8.9% in micropolitan areas
- 6.3% in rustic areas

10: A NEW SURBAN™ WAY OF LIFE

15% PERCENT OF AMERICANS LIVE URBAN, 21% LIVE RURALLY, AND 64% LIVE SUBURBAN.

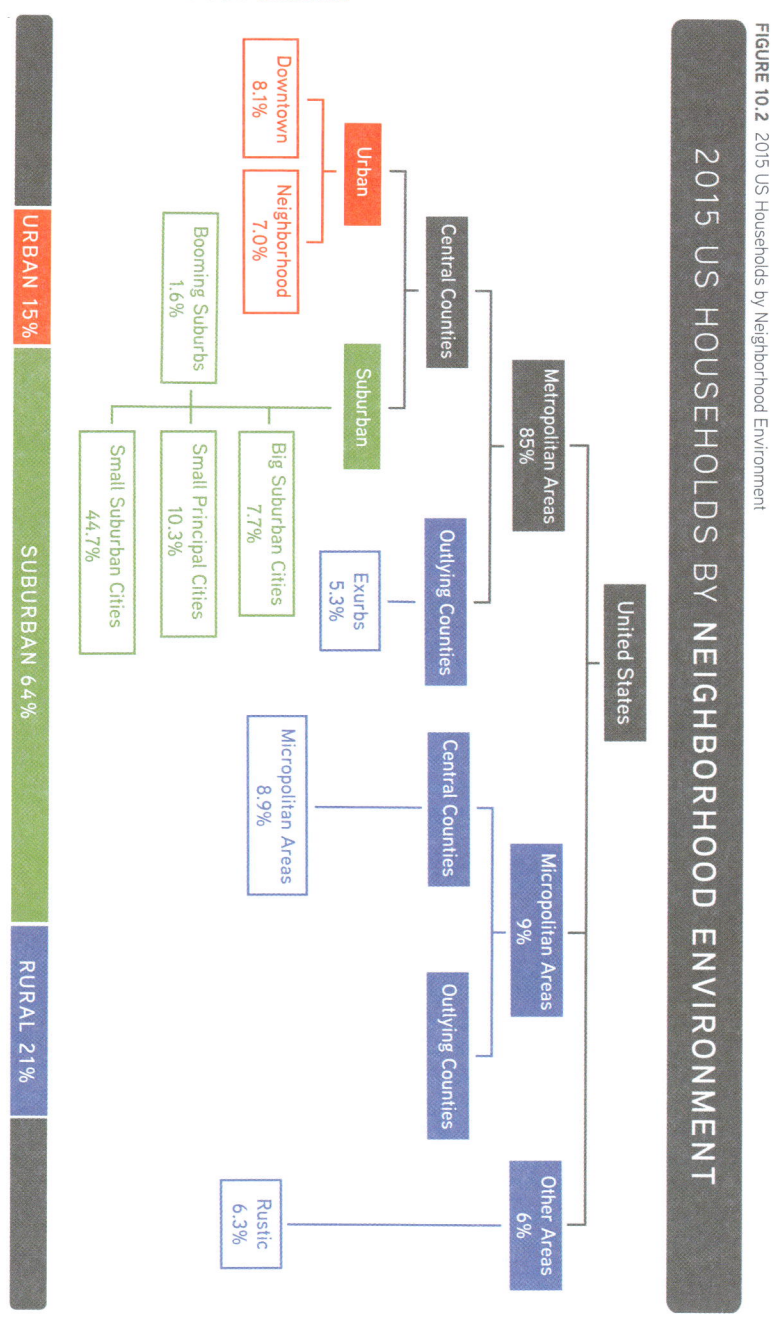

FIGURE 10.2 2015 US Households by Neighborhood Environment

2015 US HOUSEHOLDS BY NEIGHBORHOOD ENVIRONMENT

United States

- Metropolitan Areas 85%
  - Central Counties
    - Urban
      - Downtown 8.1%
      - Neighborhood 7.0%
    - Suburban
      - Booming Suburbs 1.6%
      - Big Suburban Cities 7.7%
      - Small Principal Cities 10.3%
      - Small Suburban Cities 44.7%
  - Outlying Counties
    - Exurbs 5.3%
- Micropolitan Areas 9%
  - Central Counties
    - Micropolitan Areas 8.9%
  - Outlying Counties
- Other Areas 6%
  - Rustic 6.3%

URBAN 15%
SUBURBAN 64%
RURAL 21%

223

The number of US households grew 10.7% in the 2000s, led by the booming suburbs, exurbs, small suburban cities, and small principal suburbs. Downtowns and rustic areas barely grew, while the exurbs and three of the four suburban categories grew the fastest. Big cities grew less, whether big suburban or urban, and rural growth lagged as well. Every neighborhood category grew.

9 CATEGORIES OF URBAN/SUBURBAN/RURAL BRING CLARITY TO WHERE PEOPLE LIVE.

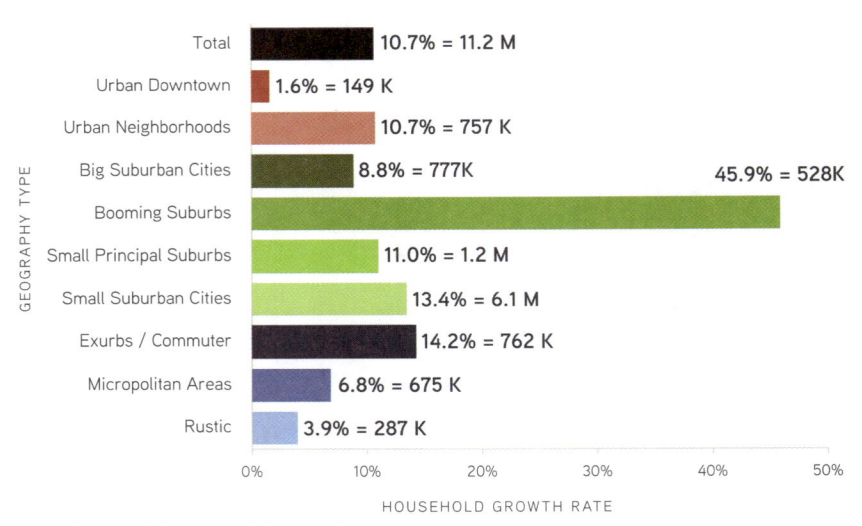

NINE CATEGORIES OF NEIGHBORHOOD
FIGURE 10.3 Household Growth Rate by Geography Type (2000–2010)

Geography Type	Household Growth Rate
Total	10.7% = 11.2 M
Urban Downtown	1.6% = 149 K
Urban Neighborhoods	10.7% = 757 K
Big Suburban Cities	8.8% = 777K
Booming Suburbs	45.9% = 528K
Small Principal Suburbs	11.0% = 1.2 M
Small Suburban Cities	13.4% = 6.1 M
Exurbs / Commuter	14.2% = 762 K
Micropolitan Areas	6.8% = 675 K
Rustic	3.9% = 287 K

Source: John Burns Real Estate Consulting, LLC based on US Census Bureau data

A number of factors contribute to recent urban growth. Fifteen million more people in the traditional urban-living years (aged in early 20s and early 60s) certainly explains a lot of the shift. Cities devoting billions of dollars to clean up their downtowns also drove some of the urban growth.

Those 15 million people, however, will age into their 30s and early 70s this decade, shifting demand to areas with better schools and great healthcare.

THE "URBAN LIFESTYLE" POPULATION AGES, 20–29 AND 55–64, GREW BY 15 MILLION PEOPLE IN THE LAST DECADE.

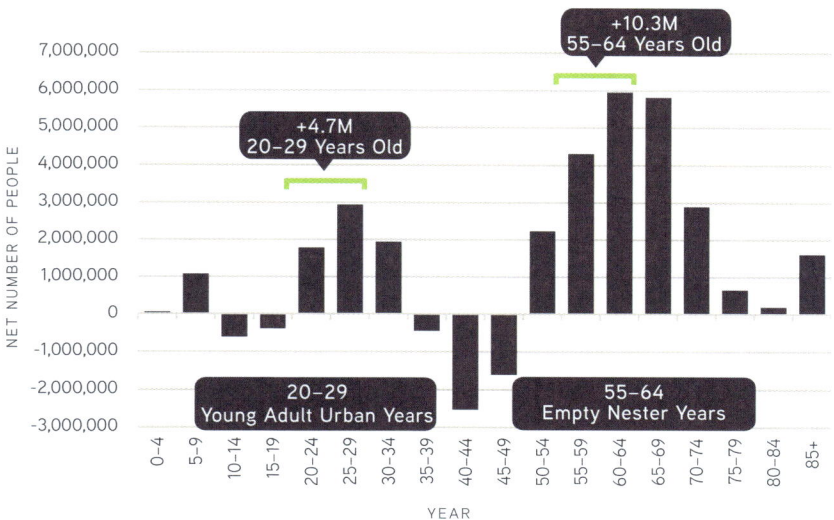

POPULATION GROWTH HAS BEEN SKEWED TO URBAN
FIGURE 10.4 Change in Population by Age, 2005–2015

+10.3M 55–64 Years Old

+4.7M 20–29 Years Old

20–29 Young Adult Urban Years

55–64 Empty Nester Years

Source: John Burns Real Estate Consulting, LLC calculations of US Census Bureau Population Estimates and 2014 National Projections

Seemingly everywhere we go we see the wave of future growth, a blend of suburban and urban. We call it surban™ living. Urban areas abound with vibrant restaurants, public transportation, and plenty to do. But urban rents and home prices cut deeply into resident incomes. Urban schools tend to rank low, and crime tends to rank high. For all of these reasons, families tend to move to the suburbs.

Mature suburban areas took note of urban revitalization. City leaders redeveloped their downtowns or zoned an area for a vibrant mix of retail, housing, and sometimes jobs. Urban planners call these areas "mixed use," but surban™ better describes the mix of urban and suburban living. We trademarked the term, but everyone has the permission to use the word surban without the trademark. We just want credit for coining the phrase.

EXAMPLES OF SURBAN™ AREAS INCLUDE:

- Reston Town Center in the Washington, DC, suburb of Reston, Virginia
- Downtown Naperville, Illinois, in the suburbs of Chicago
- Old Town Pasadena, California, in the suburbs of Los Angeles
- A-Town in Anaheim, California, in a neighborhood around the Angels Major League Baseball park
- Legacy Town Center in Plano, Texas, in the suburbs of Dallas
- Santana Row in San Jose, California, on a former run-down mall site
- CityCentre in Houston, Texas, on a former run-down mall site
- Downtown Tempe, Arizona, in the suburbs of Phoenix
- Larkspur, California, north of San Francisco, with new housing sandwiched between a top-notch high school and a rejuvenated old downtown
- Geneva, Illinois, in the suburbs of Chicago

Determining the location of future growth becomes especially important when big shifts occur. Consider how the suburbs' rising percentage of household growth affected housing, retail, roads, and all manners of economic development after World War II. From 1900 to 1910, 40% of people lived suburban. Encouraged by the GI Bill, the growth of the automobile industry, and highway-transportation improvements, suburbs captured nearly 90% of growth during the 1950s, dramatically altering the American landscape—literally, socially, and economically.

Replicating the success of early models such as Levittown, New York, planned communities cropped up on the outskirts of urban centers throughout the United States in the 1950s through the 1990s. In cities like Chicago, much larger rings of suburbs surrounded the urban core. Those suburbs gained the lion's share of new households, housing, retail, and local tax revenue. Cities such as Detroit, Los Angeles, and Philadelphia saw suburban growth many layers deep, with the burgeoning communities that offered the most affordable prices moving farther and farther from city centers over the years. The catchall "Chicagoland" label now links a string of suburbs stretching from northwest Indiana to southeast Wisconsin. The Dallas "Metroplex" includes close to 7 million people in thirteen counties.

Many of these suburban cities created decades ago that are now largely built-out continue to reinvigorate themselves with vibrant surban™ downtowns comprised of new retail and residential developments. Even Irvine, California, a relatively new city largely created as a Los Angeles suburb, now has far more jobs than homes and has created a vibrant surban™ living environment around the Irvine Spectrum retail area.

The 4 Big influencers drove the recent urban and surban™ renaissance. For example:

- **Government**. Local governments have reinvested heavily in cleaning up their downtowns. They have also invested less in the highway infrastructure needed to create more suburbs.

- **Economy**. The economy contracted heavily after 2008. Job growth shifted back toward the urban job core, like it usually does in recessions.

- **Technology**. Smartphone location and payment technologies have enabled urban and suburban dwellers to use Uber to live car-free. Interestingly, technology has also made living rural easier due to online access for telecommuters and shopping, yet rural living has not become more popular. The technology now exists for a rural resurgence, but we cannot find any trends that rural living will become more popular.

- **Societal Shifts**. The shift to start families later in life has rendered living urban viable for longer. Also, social media has helped place a higher premium on experiencing fun activities than purchasing things, and urban areas offer far more to do. Urban activities appeal to the millions who post their activities on Facebook, Instagram, Twitter, or send Snapchat photos to their friends.

Consumers who can afford them love surban™ developments. High construction costs force high home prices and rents, though less expensive than the best urban downtowns in the country. In surban™ areas, housing affordability, home size, privacy, and kid friendliness feel more urban than suburban, while school quality, public transportation, and proximity to employment feel more suburban.

10: A NEW SURBAN™ WAY OF LIFE

FIGURE 10.5 The Surban™ Lifestyle

THE SURBAN™ LIFESTYLE

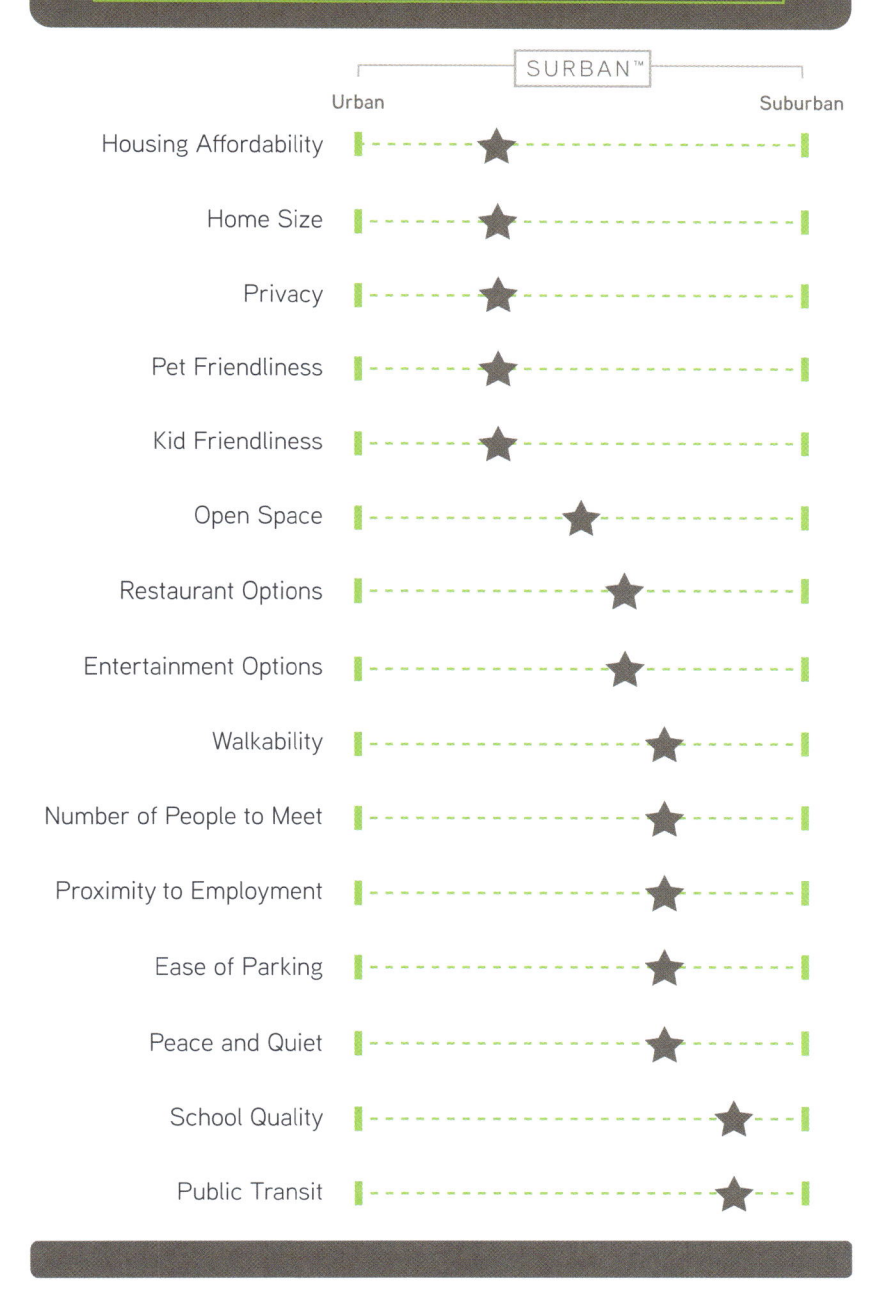

SURBAN™
Urban — Suburban

Housing Affordability	Urban-leaning
Home Size	Urban-leaning
Privacy	Urban-leaning
Pet Friendliness	Urban-leaning
Kid Friendliness	Urban-leaning
Open Space	Middle
Restaurant Options	Middle
Entertainment Options	Middle
Walkability	Suburban-leaning
Number of People to Meet	Suburban-leaning
Proximity to Employment	Suburban-leaning
Ease of Parking	Suburban-leaning
Peace and Quiet	Suburban-leaning
School Quality	Suburban
Public Transit	Suburban

229

Suburbs of all kinds will dominate the coming wave of household creation. The 1980s Sharers and 1990s Connectors will start families. As they shop for houses, schools, and communities where they want to raise their families, most people will turn to the 'burbs. Housing costs and school quality drive the location decision for most young families.

The urban renaissance leads some to believe that the suburbs have struggled. The data supports the opposite. Both urban and suburban areas continue to capture more of the growth, at the expense of rural. Suburban growth exceeds urban growth by more than three times.

Since the 1980s, cities have spent billions of dollars, often selling bonds and using creative tax-increment financing, to encourage redevelopment, reduce crime, and create central entertainment districts. San Diego turned a site of urban decay around Fifth Avenue into an active area of shops, restaurants, and nightlife. Washington, DC, did the same thing with the Penn Quarter, as did Miami with its Design District, and New York with the newly chic sections of Brooklyn and Queens. In 2016, Houston continued to develop Discovery Green, and Phoenix continued to spruce up its downtown, both hoping to mirror such efforts. Residents—including some empty nesters selling suburban homes—now pay top dollar to live in these once-shabby downtown neighborhoods. Many of these former homeowners now rent.

Uber and Lyft have completely transformed life for Connectors and Savers, giving them the freedom to get wherever they want, whenever they want, without needing to own a car. Only around 78% of 1990s Connectors held drivers' licenses in their early 20s, the lowest percentage in decades. In 2025, we believe only 67% of 20–24-year-olds will own drivers licenses. Ride-sharing services will continue to grow in popularity.

YOUNG ADULTS DRIVE MUCH LESS THAN THEIR PARENTS DID.

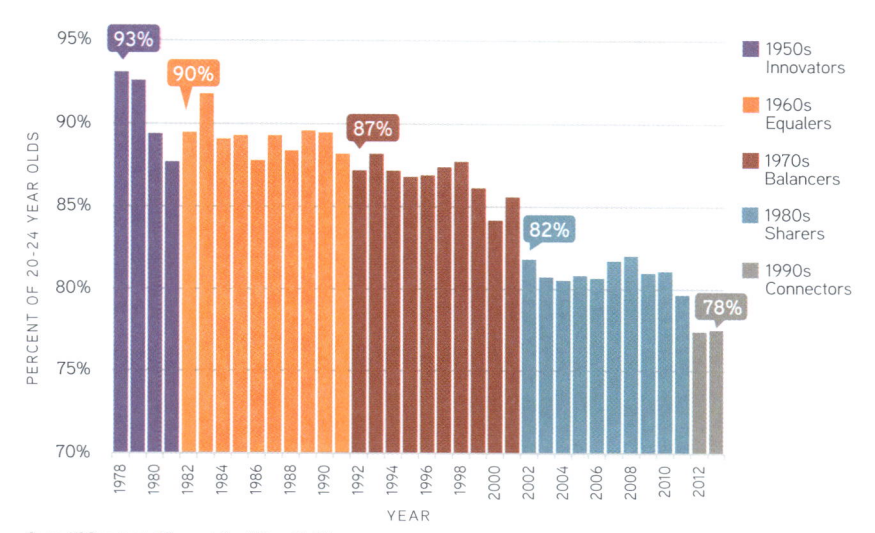

BAD NEWS FOR THE AUTO INDUSTRY
FIGURE 10.6 Percent of 20–24 Year-Olds with a Driver's License

Source: US Department of Transportation, Highway Statistics

Complementing the rising number of young urban renters, the return of some of the jobs lost to the suburbs over many decades also helped cities. Employers used to shift to suburbia to bring work closer to the places people lived, but that trend has reversed. Many employers have now moved work back to urban areas where much of the young talent now resides.

Seattle provides a primary example of jobs shifting urban. With Amazon leading the way, developers are building enough high-rise office towers to eventually employ 50,000 people, the first of whom moved in late 2015. Even Weyerhaeuser, the behemoth forest-products conglomerate, sold its long-time suburban headquarters to relocate downtown, primarily to recruit talent unwilling to live in the suburbs.

We believe this renaissance of jobs moving urban will slow down. Urban can only grow so fast. Land constraints and high rents limit growth in developed cities, even when you consider transportation savings. Also, the twenty-somethings living urban will eventually start families and need suburban schools. While the most affluent can afford private school, and some good charter schools have improved urban education, most families cannot afford urban living. Surban™ areas solve these problems, providing more affordable quasi-urban living.

> **WE BELIEVE THIS RENAISSANCE OF JOBS MOVING URBAN WILL SLOW DOWN.**

Urban areas also appeal to the affluent empty nesters. A low-maintenance condominium or apartment within walking distance of many entertainment options will appeal to those who can afford it. Lance Ramella and his wife, who lived in the Chicago suburb of Oswego until 2014, considered shifting their household to urban as the couple became empty nesters, but they only entertained that option for "about ten minutes," said Ramella, a 53-year-old executive.

"We have empty-nester friends like us who moved from Oswego to the thirty-eighth floor of a building by Soldier Field in downtown Chicago," Ramella said. "They pay $300 a month for one-car parking and had to sell their other car. It's pretty expensive in some ways."

The Ramellas liked certain elements of urban life—the fine restaurants, cultural options, and walkable neighborhoods—but not the high prices and space limitations. Their 3,000-square-foot home in Oswego included a pond out back and sat on half an acre, a whole lot of lawn to mow. They wanted to downsize once their daughters, now in their mid-20s, moved out. They also wanted to keep their cars and enough space for their children to visit in comfort.

Ramella and his wife settled on a townhouse in the western Chicago suburb of Geneva, a community that fits our definition of surban™. To hear Ramella tell it, the Geneva townhouse offers the best of all worlds. "The new house is 2,300 square feet, a little more than we wanted, but there are four bedrooms, so it is fine having our daughters come back home," Ramella said, explaining that his children, both 1990s Connectors, moved back in with the folks after college for one to two years. "There was plenty of space. The youngest just moved out of the house in August, so we're relatively new empty nesters."

The Ramellas managed to keep a two-car garage and extra bedrooms but gave up significant maintenance, since a homeowners association takes care of snow, grass, and routine care at the new place. Equally important, Ramella said, in Geneva, he and his wife gained many of the benefits of urban living without the attendant costs and hassles.

Downtown Geneva, a five-minute walk from the Ramellas' townhouse, contains more than 150 independent shops and nearly 90 restaurants and cafes. The quieter Third Street shopping strip hosts specialty stores and posh boutiques. State Street, the bigger commercial hub, includes many restaurants and quaint pubs. The town has preserved many of its historic buildings, including some stunning Victorian mansions. Few complain about a lack of charm in Geneva, a place as far removed from the bland bedroom communities the name "suburb" once signified, but with much less noise and congestion than a big city.

"We wanted a walkable European lifestyle, so we walk to the butcher, the baker, the restaurants," Ramella said. "My wife and I sat down one day and counted, and there are 32 sit-down restaurants walkable from our house. It's very lively on the weekends, with horse-drawn carriages, the restaurants packed, and sidewalk cafes everywhere. But we also can bike on a long trail on the Fox River right here."

THE NATION SHOULD SEE HOUSEHOLD GROWTH OF AROUND 10% FROM 2015 TO 2025, AND THE BULK OF IT WILL OCCUR IN THE SUBURBS.

The nation should see household growth of around 10% from 2015 to 2025, and the bulk of it will occur in the suburbs. Overall, the suburbs will grow at a rate of 12.7%. Most of our suburban neighborhood types—big suburban cities, small principal suburbs, and small suburban cities—will grow at rates in the 11% to 13% range, similar to each other and the national average. The booming suburbs, which we expect to grow 20% in the next decade, provide a notable exception.

Urban areas—the combination of urban downtowns and urban neighborhoods—will grow more slowly, at a rate of 10.4%, partly because of a lack of developable land. Property there tends to be pricey and in short supply. Rural areas contain lots of available property and low prices but little employment and few amenities. They will grow at a rate of only 3.2% and lose household share, capturing just 6% of the growth. Today's households just resist commuting and living rural.

What factors might result in a higher growth rate for rural areas in the long term? Could the rapid rise of telecommuting, for instance, encourage more young workers to take advantage of the affordable rural option when they decide to buy homes? Kyle Zierer, the 1980s Sharer, would prefer to live close to nature and outdoor activities but planned to shop for housing in nearby suburbs because he dreaded the notion of a long commute. As workers like Zierer advance in their careers, how might they take advantage of telecommuting? Could they boost the rural areas' share of growth?

Similarly, we assumed that the late-blooming '80s and '90s generations will lean more toward cities than their parents, even as they started families. A large wave of Innovators and Equalers deciding to sell their suburban homes and return to cities should also shift demand.

Putting it all together, we expect the suburbs, including surban™ areas, to capture 79% of household growth over the next 10 years and urban growth to capture 15%. Rural growth will suffer, capturing only 6% of growth. Surban™ areas will continue to emerge throughout the US, appealing to the surge in nonfamily households, as well as the shift to avoid commuting and enjoy nearby entertainment.

Rural areas, which generally include plenty of available land with long commutes to employment centers, will lose some of their share of the total. Our conclusion will disappoint land speculators who invested in future paths of growth. Rural cities will also struggle financially as their tax base will continue to grow only slowly.

BOTH URBAN AND SUBURBAN LOCALES WILL CAPTURE A HIGH SHARE OF GROWTH.

FORECASTING HIGH URBAN AND SUBURBAN GROWTH
FIGURE 10.7 Share of Household Growth by Decade

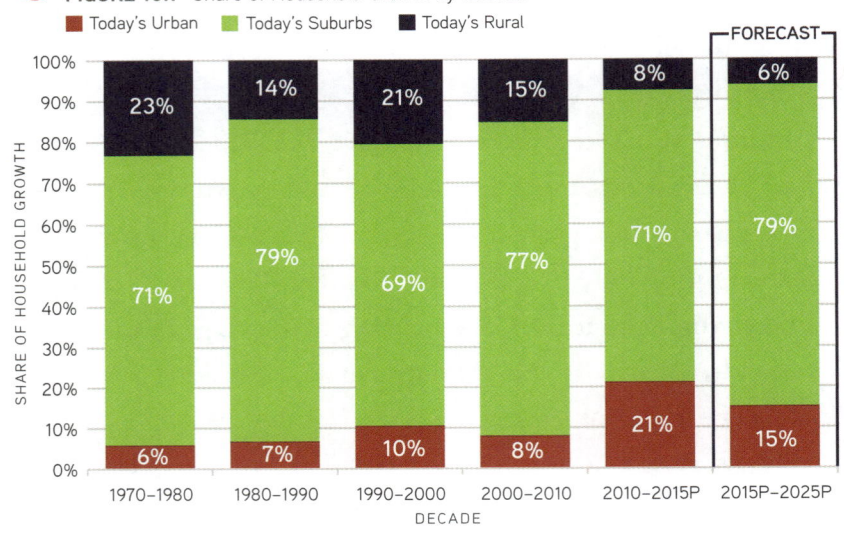

■ Today's Urban   ■ Today's Suburbs   ■ Today's Rural

Decade	Today's Urban	Today's Suburbs	Today's Rural
1970–1980	6%	71%	23%
1980–1990	7%	79%	14%
1990–2000	10%	69%	21%
2000–2010	8%	77%	15%
2010–2015P	21%	71%	8%
2015P–2025P (FORECAST)	15%	79%	6%

Source: John Burns Real Estate Consulting, LLC based on US Census Bureau data

APPENDIX 1: NEIGHBORHOOD CLASSIFICATIONS

Classifying areas as urban, suburban, and rural posed a daunting task. We subdivided the broad groupings of urban, suburban, and rural into nine finer categories. These categories are more useful, using definitions and methodologies from the Office of Management and Budget (OMB), the Census Bureau, and an urban measure pioneered by demographer Wendell Cox of Demographia. The following represents a quick overview of our methodology, which some will find overly detailed, whereas others will appreciate the much-needed clarity of definition. (Those who want to dig even deeper will find more information and charts on www.bigshiftsahead.com).

Our starting point was the OMB geographical definitions:

- **Metropolitan Statistical Areas** (MSAs) include an urban core of 50,000 or more people.

- **Micropolitan Statistical Areas** include an urban core of 10,000 to 50,000 people.

- **Other Areas** are the remainder of the country.

Around 85% of the population lives in the nation's 401 MSAs. The country's 536 micropolitan areas contain another 9% of households, while 6% live in other areas. In the metropolitan and micropolitan areas, we classified the counties closest to or containing the core areas as "central" counties. We classified the commuter counties as "outlying." We consider outlying counties as "rural."

The OMB names MSAs and micropolitan areas for their principal city or cities, and may have anywhere from 1 to 29 counties, such as in the Atlanta MSA. For example, the Census Bureau named the Phoenix-Mesa-Scottsdale MSA after three proximate, closely linked cities. To qualify as a principal city, a town essentially must be large and gain workers during the workday.

The following diagram illustrates our conclusions and methodology.

APPENDIX 1: NEIGHBORHOOD CLASSIFICATIONS

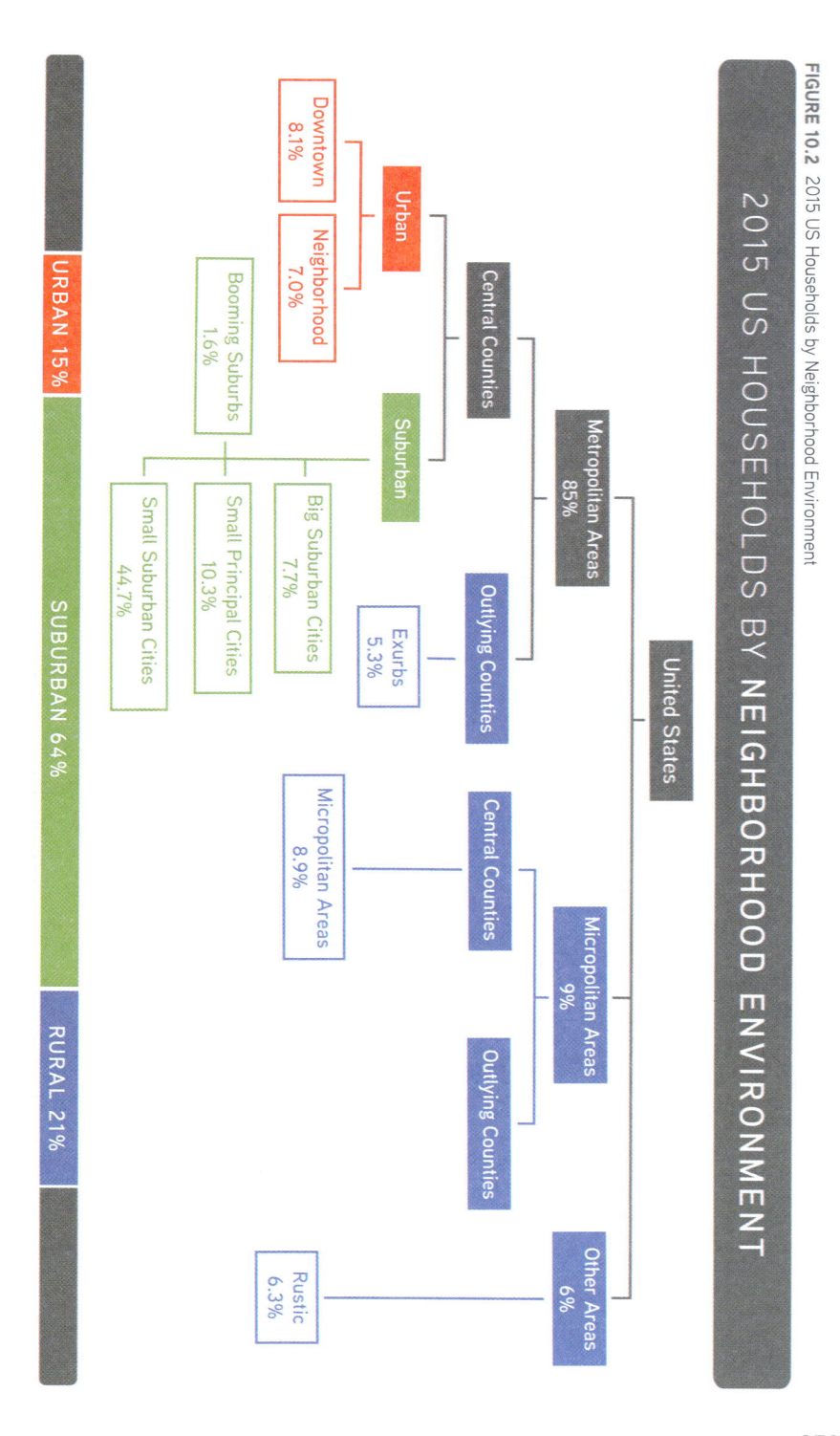

FIGURE 10.2 2015 US Households by Neighborhood Environment

2015 US HOUSEHOLDS BY NEIGHBORHOOD ENVIRONMENT

United States
- Metropolitan Areas 85%
  - Central Counties
    - Urban
      - Downtown 8.1%
      - Neighborhood 7.0%
    - Suburban
      - Booming Suburbs 1.6%
      - Big Suburban Cities 7.7%
      - Small Principal Cities 10.3%
      - Small Suburban Cities 44.7%
  - Outlying Counties
    - Exurbs 5.3%
- Micropolitan Areas 9%
  - Central Counties
    - Micropolitan Areas 8.9%
  - Outlying Counties
- Other Areas 6%
  - Rustic 6.3%

URBAN 15%
SUBURBAN 64%
RURAL 21%

239

Urban living, according to our classification, can only take place in a big city that:

- is a principal city in an MSA of at least 400,000 households and
- has at least 100,000 households within the city limits.

Fifty-four cities met these criteria, and we narrowed the list to 50 by eliminating four that felt more suburban than urban (Mesa, AZ; Virginia Beach, VA; Aurora, CO; and St. Paul, MN). Some MSAs contain multiple urban cities, such as Los Angeles and Long Beach, grouped in a single MSA.

The 50 urban cities, all of which contain a downtown area as well as neighborhoods, are: New York, NY; Los Angeles, CA; Chicago, IL; Houston, TX; Philadelphia, PA; Phoenix, AZ; San Diego, CA; San Antonio, TX; Dallas, TX; San Francisco, CA; Indianapolis, IN; Columbus, OH; Austin, TX; Jacksonville, FL; San Jose, CA; Charlotte, NC; Seattle, WA; Detroit, MI; Washington, DC; Denver, CO; Fort Worth, TX; Boston, MA; Memphis, TN; Baltimore, MD; Nashville, TN; Portland, OR; Louisville, KY; Oklahoma City, OK; Milwaukee, WI; Las Vegas, NV; Kansas City, MO; Atlanta, GA; Sacramento, CA; Cleveland, OH; Minneapolis, MN; Long Beach, CA; Raleigh, NC; Miami, FL; Oakland, CA; New Orleans, LA; St. Louis, MO; Pittsburgh, PA; Tampa, FL; Cincinnati, OH; Arlington, TX; Buffalo, NY; St. Petersburg, FL; Orlando, FL; Henderson, NV; Scottsdale, AZ.

Our urban/suburban historical trends do not account for shifting classifications over time. Sixty years ago, we would classify some areas differently. Formerly rural places such as Loudoun County, VA, and Pinal County, AZ, eventually joined MSAs, and exurbs like Irvine, CA, became popular suburbs.

Urban areas contain job centers with dense housing, walkable neighborhoods, and at least some high-rises. As a reality check that we picked the right cities, all MLB, NFL, NBA, and NHL sports teams are located in these fifty big cities, except for the three franchises in Anaheim, Newark, Salt Lake (three cities that we classify as big suburban cities but are part of large metropolitan areas), and Green Bay.

We divided these 50 cities into two categories using a methodology similar to one developed by demographer Wendell Cox:

- **Urban downtowns** include zip codes that designate areas commonly called "downtown." At least half of their homes must predate 1946 and include at least 7,500 people per square mile, roughly 20% of who walk, bike, or use public transit to get to work. Some 8.1% of US households live in urban downtowns, which grew only 1.6% last decade.

- **Urban neighborhoods** are all other areas within the city limits. Neighborhoods usually appear less dense than downtowns but denser than a city's surrounding suburbs. Some 7.0% of US households live in urban neighborhoods, which grew 10.7% last decade, exactly matching the US household growth rate. While downtown revitalization has received much attention, urban neighborhoods grew faster.

Based on our definitions, 15% of Americans live urban.

Suburban living, according to our classification, takes place in all parts of the MSA's central counties not within urban downtowns or urban neighborhoods. Nearly two-thirds of US households live in the suburbs.

We divided the suburbs into four categories:

1. **Big Suburban Cities**. 112 big suburban cities contain at least 50,000 households and also received the principal city distinction by the Census Bureau. Cities such as Anaheim, CA; Newark, NJ; Birmingham, AL; Richmond, VA; and Salt Lake City, UT, make the list. Many of these communities are large, commutable suburbs outside larger urban areas and with their own job bases. Some 7.7% of households live in big suburban cities, which grew 8.8% last decade—below the US average.

2. **Booming Suburbs**. We identified 32 booming cities not identified as principal cities, with 30,000 to 90,000 households. They grew at least 20% during the last 20 years and are in MSAs with at least 400,000 households. They include cities such as Chandler, AZ; Chesapeake, VA; North Las Vegas, NV; Aurora, IL; and Chula Vista, CA. Booming suburbs had fewer than 2% of households in 2010, but are growing rapidly and host significant home construction. They tend to be family oriented. Nearly 44% of their households include children. Some 1.6% of households live in the 32 booming suburbs, which grew a whopping 45.9% last decade. Growing quickly, they eventually will become big suburban cities.

3. **Small Principal Suburbs**. 520 principal cities do not qualify as big or booming. Suburbs such as Oxnard, CA; Santa Monica, CA; and The Woodlands, TX, are small principal suburbs. These communities emerged from bigger cities to host their own job centers. These towns likely provide jobs for residents of the next suburban category, small suburban cities. Some 10.3% of Americans

live in Small Principal Suburbs, which grew 11.0% last decade.

4. **Small Suburban Cities**. All the suburbs in the MSA's central counties that don't fit into the three categories above comprise this group, by far the largest neighborhood type, with 45% of the country's population. These include middle-America cities such as Sterling Heights, MI; Independence, MO; Pasadena, TX; Garden Grove, CA; Buckeye, AZ; and Hoboken, NJ. They offer some employment, but most residents enjoy short commutes to the large cities nearby. Small suburban cities grew 13.4% last decade, faster than overall US growth.

Based on our definitions, 64% of Americans live suburban.

Rural living tends to include extremely low density, affordable housing, lower incomes, and long distances to employment centers. Families with children dominate, usually in detached single-family houses or in manufactured or mobile homes. Despite the Internet enabling many workers to live wherever they want and allowing rural dwellers to shop online, society has continued to shift away from rural living.

We identified three primary categories of rural living:

1. **Exurbs or Commuter Counties**. This list includes 424 outlying counties that feel rural but fall within MSAs. They lie on the outskirts of the urban core, yet are economically tied to it. These constitute America's long-commute communities, with 25% or more of their workers commuting to or from central counties in the same MSA. Exurbs include Orange County, NY (New York MSA); Lake County, FL (Orlando MSA); and Ottawa County,

MI (Grand Rapids MSA). Some 5.3% of Americans live in the exurbs, which grew 14.2% during the housing boom decade of the 2000s. We believe society has shifted significantly away from commuting.

2. **Micropolitan Areas**. This list includes 641 counties geographically distant from larger cities and centered around their own urban cores of 10,000 to 50,000 people. Micropolitan areas tend to support themselves economically. All but one of these communities' small counties contain fewer than 70,000 households. Examples include Traverse City, MI; Concord, NH; and Key West, FL. Some 8.9% of Americans live in micropolitan areas, which grew only 6.8% last decade.

3. **Rustic Areas**. This group includes 1,335 truly outlying, sparse counties that don't fit any of the definitions above. Rustic areas comprise 53% of the total land area in the US and only 6.3% of households. All but two areas report fewer than 30,000 households. Much of the center of the country is rustic, a designation associated with farming. Examples of rustic areas include Sullivan County, NY; DeKalb County, AL; and Pike County, KY.

Based on our definitions, 21% of Americans live rurally—a percentage in decline.

APPENDIX 2: MORE FORECAST TABLES

These charts provide the historical and forecasted details behind the household formation forecast discussed in chapter 7. We selected the ages 28, 38, 48, 58, 68, and 78 for presentation, figuring that those were the ages of most high school reunions, and thus would be easiest to visualize.

We forecast that the 1990s Connectors will be less likely to head a household at 28 than 1980s Sharers.

FIGURE A.1 Share of 28-Year-Olds Who Head a Household

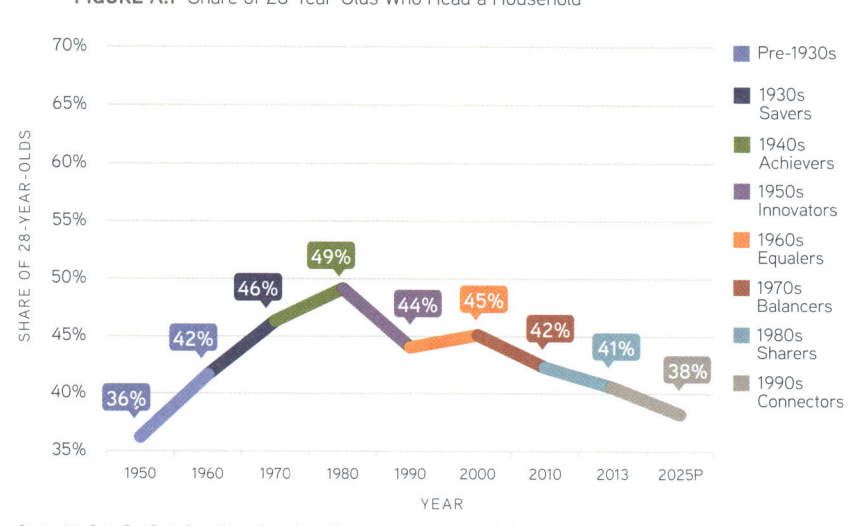

Year	Share	Cohort
1950	36%	Pre-1930s
1960	42%	1930s Savers
1970	46%	1940s Achievers
1980	49%	1950s Innovators
1990	44%	1960s Equalers
2000	45%	1970s Balancers
2010	42%	1980s Sharers
2013	41%	1980s Sharers
2025P	38%	1990s Connectors

Source: John Burns Real Estate Consulting, LLC based on US Census data and extensive analysis of each age cohort; P= Projection

BIG SHIFTS AHEAD

➡ **1980s Sharers heads of household at 38 will fall below the 1970s Balancers.**

FIGURE A.2 Share of 38-Year-Olds Who Head a Household

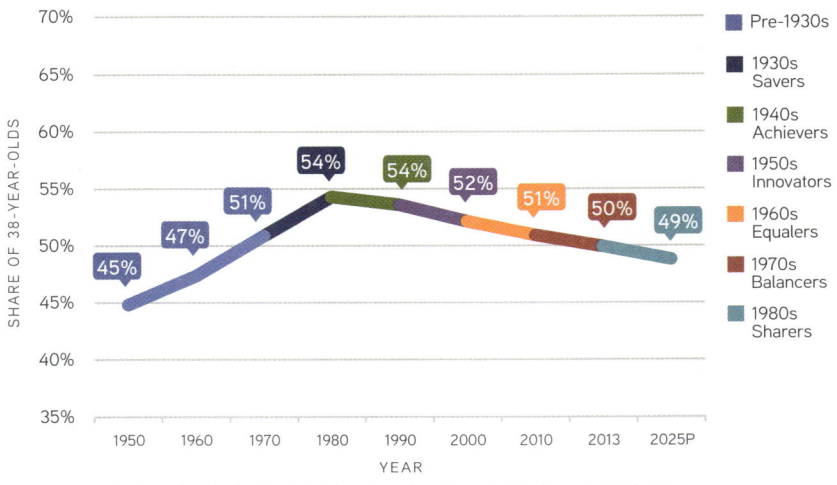

Legend:
- Pre-1930s
- 1930s Savers
- 1940s Achievers
- 1950s Innovators
- 1960s Equalers
- 1970s Balancers
- 1980s Sharers

Data points by year:
- 1950: 45%
- 1960: 47%
- 1970: 51%
- 1980: 54%
- 1990: 54%
- 2000: 52%
- 2010: 51%
- 2013: 50%
- 2025P: 49%

Source: John Burns Real Estate Consulting, LLC based on US Census data and extensive analysis of each age cohort; P= Projection

➡ **1970s Balancers will head households at a greater rate at 48 than the 1960s Equalers, largely due to more single adults.**

FIGURE A.3 Share of 48-Year-Olds Who Head a Household

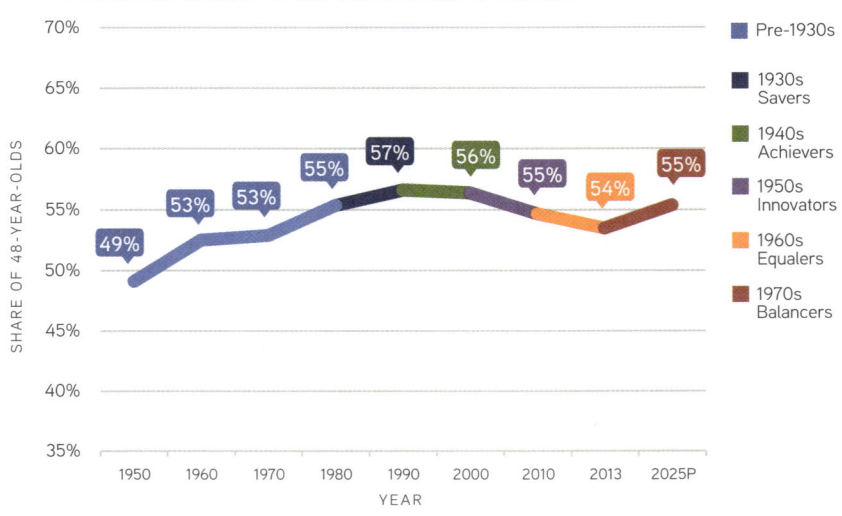

Legend:
- Pre-1930s
- 1930s Savers
- 1940s Achievers
- 1950s Innovators
- 1960s Equalers
- 1970s Balancers

Data points by year:
- 1950: 49%
- 1960: 53%
- 1970: 53%
- 1980: 55%
- 1990: 57%
- 2000: 56%
- 2010: 55%
- 2013: 54%
- 2025P: 55%

Source: John Burns Real Estate Consulting, LLC based on US Census data and extensive analysis of each age cohort; P= Projection

APPENDIX 2: MORE FORECAST TABLES

➡ **1960s Equalers are likely to head a household at a lower rate at 58 than the Innovators and Achievers, as they are more likely to be living with a spouse or multigenerationally.**

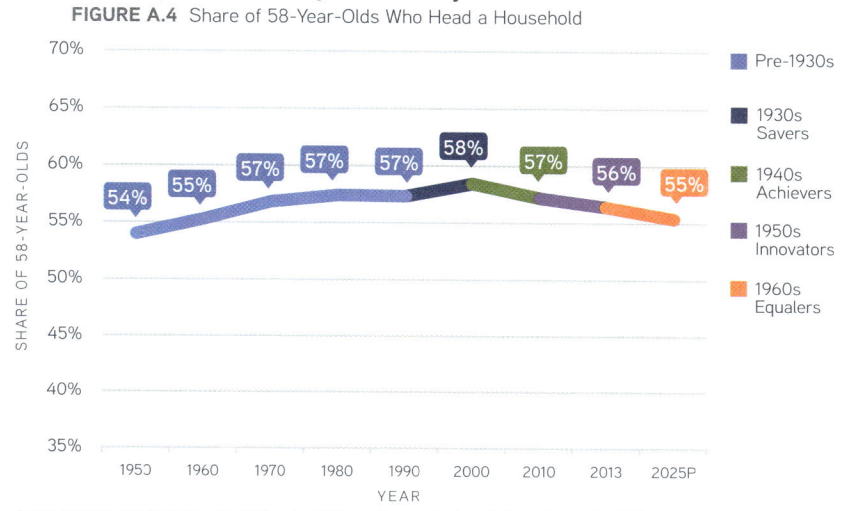

FIGURE A.4 Share of 58-Year-Olds Who Head a Household

Year	Share	Cohort
1950	54%	Pre-1930s
1960	55%	Pre-1930s
1970	57%	Pre-1930s
1980	57%	Pre-1930s
1990	57%	Pre-1930s
2000	58%	1930s Savers
2010	57%	1940s Achievers
2013	56%	1950s Innovators
2025P	55%	1960s Equalers

Source: John Burns Real Estate Consulting, LLC based on US Census data and extensive analysis of each age cohort; P= Projection

➡ **1950s Innovators are slightly less likely to head a household at 68 as 1940s Achievers.**

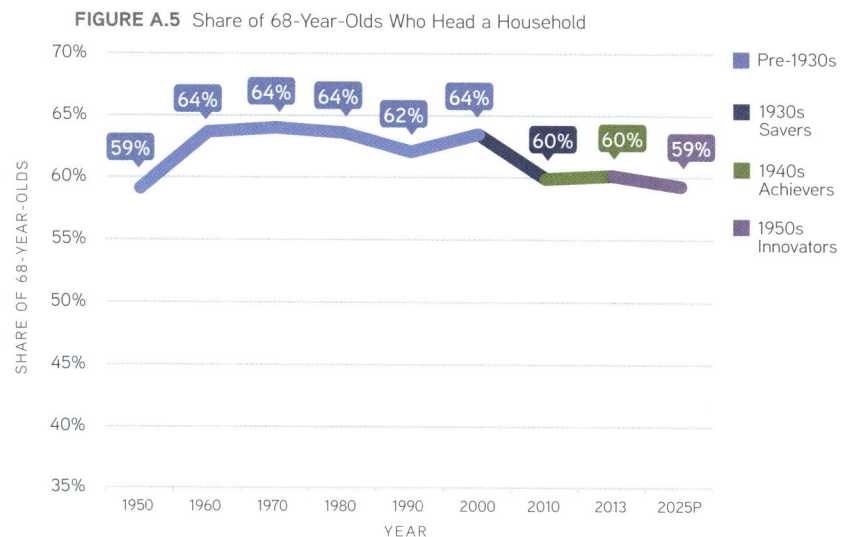

FIGURE A.5 Share of 68-Year-Olds Who Head a Household

Year	Share	Cohort
1950	59%	Pre-1930s
1960	64%	Pre-1930s
1970	64%	Pre-1930s
1980	64%	Pre-1930s
1990	62%	Pre-1930s
2000	64%	Pre-1930s
2010	60%	1930s Savers
2013	60%	1940s Achievers
2025P	59%	1950s Innovators

Source: John Burns Real Estate Consulting, LLC based on US Census data and extensive analysis of each age cohort; P= Projection

BIG SHIFTS AHEAD

➡ **Percentagewise, the 1940s Achievers are much less likely to head a household at 78 than the 1930s Savers, as their spouse is more likely to still be alive.**

FIGURE A.6 Share of 78-Year-Olds Who Head a Household

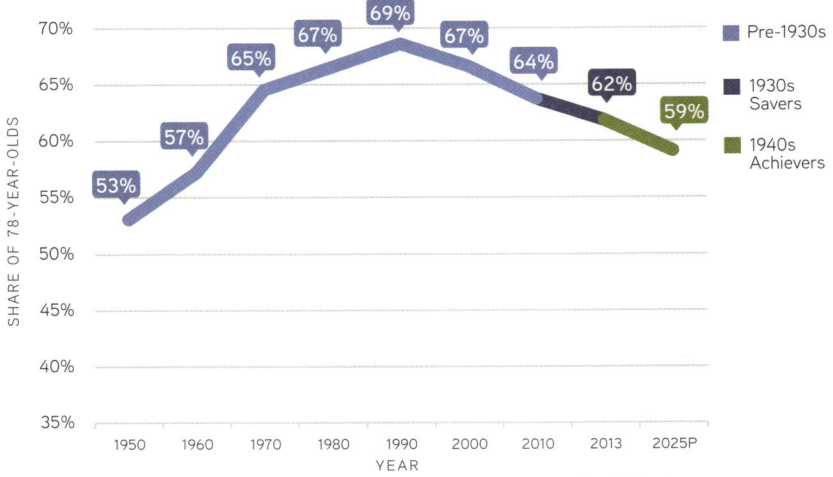

- Pre-1930s
- 1930s Savers
- 1940s Achievers

Year	Share
1950	53%
1960	57%
1970	65%
1980	67%
1990	69%
2000	67%
2010	64%
2013	62%
2025P	59%

Source: John Burns Real Estate Consulting, LLC based on US Census data and extensive analysis of each age cohort; P= Projection

➡ **We expect the 1990s Connectors to continue to delay marriage, which will keep them living with parents or other relatives later. By 28, they will not achieve the headship levels of those born in the 1980s or earlier.**

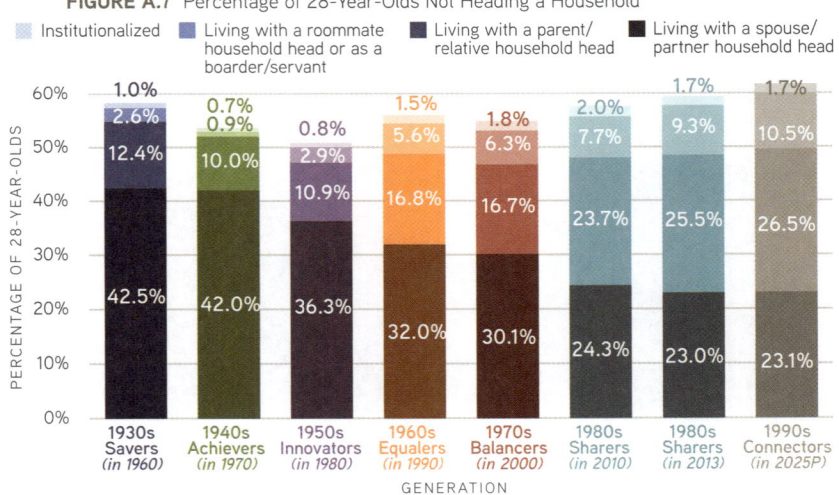

FIGURE A.7 Percentage of 28-Year-Olds Not Heading a Household

Legend:
- Institutionalized
- Living with a roommate household head or as a boarder/servant
- Living with a parent/relative household head
- Living with a spouse/partner household head

Generation	Inst.	Roommate	Parent/Rel.	Spouse/Partner
1930s Savers (in 1960)	1.0%	2.6%	12.4%	42.5%
1940s Achievers (in 1970)	0.7%	0.9%	10.0%	42.0%
1950s Innovators (in 1980)	0.8%	2.9%	10.9%	36.3%
1960s Equalers (in 1990)	1.5%	5.6%	16.8%	32.0%
1970s Balancers (in 2000)	1.8%	6.3%	16.7%	30.1%
1980s Sharers (in 2010)	2.0%	7.7%	23.7%	24.3%
1980s Sharers (in 2013)	1.7%	9.3%	25.5%	23.0%
1990s Connectors (in 2025P)	1.7%	10.5%	26.5%	23.1%

Source: John Burns Real Estate Consulting, LLC based on US Census data and extensive analysis of each age cohort; P= Projection

APPENDIX 2: MORE FORECAST TABLES

➡ **1980s Sharers will lead a minor resurgence in living with their spouse/partner.**

FIGURE A.8 Percentage of 38-Year-Olds Not Heading a Household

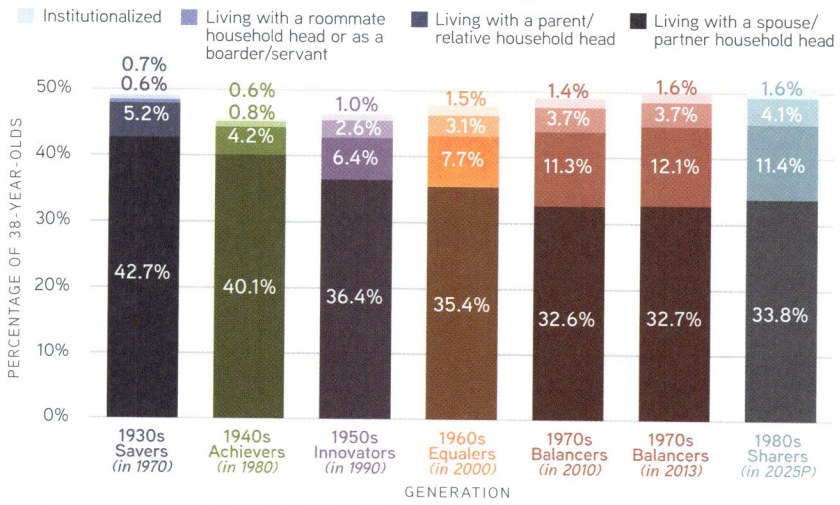

Legend: Institutionalized | Living with a roommate household head or as a boarder/servant | Living with a parent/relative household head | Living with a spouse/partner household head

Generation	Institutionalized	Roommate/Boarder	Parent/Relative	Spouse/Partner
1930s Savers (in 1970)	0.7%	0.6%	5.2%	42.7%
1940s Achievers (in 1980)	—	0.6% / 0.8%	4.2%	40.1%
1950s Innovators (in 1990)	—	1.0% / 2.6%	6.4%	36.4%
1960s Equalers (in 2000)	—	1.5% / 3.1%	7.7%	35.4%
1970s Balancers (in 2010)	—	1.4% / 3.7%	11.3%	32.6%
1970s Balancers (in 2013)	—	1.6% / 3.7%	12.1%	32.7%
1980s Sharers (in 2025P)	—	1.6% / 4.1%	11.4%	33.8%

Source: John Burns Real Estate Consulting, LLC based on US Census data and extensive analysis of each age cohort; P= Projection

➡ **1970s Balancers have a low marital rate today, which we expect to continue.**

FIGURE A.9 Percentage of 48-Year-Olds Not Heading a Household

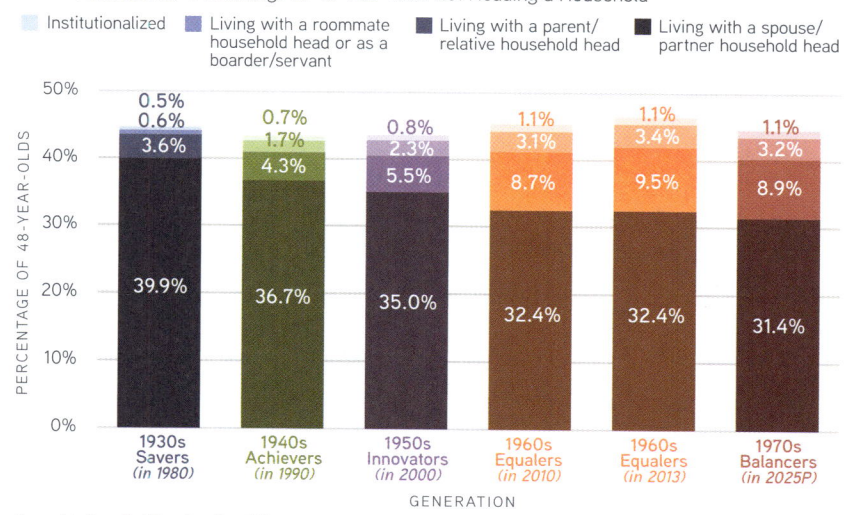

Legend: Institutionalized | Living with a roommate household head or as a boarder/servant | Living with a parent/relative household head | Living with a spouse/partner household head

Generation	Institutionalized	Roommate/Boarder	Parent/Relative	Spouse/Partner
1930s Savers (in 1980)	0.5%	0.6%	3.6%	39.9%
1940s Achievers (in 1990)	—	0.7% / 1.7%	4.3%	36.7%
1950s Innovators (in 2000)	—	0.8% / 2.3%	5.5%	35.0%
1960s Equalers (in 2010)	—	1.1% / 3.1%	8.7%	32.4%
1960s Equalers (in 2013)	—	1.1% / 3.4%	9.5%	32.4%
1970s Balancers (in 2025P)	—	1.1% / 3.2%	8.9%	31.4%

Source: John Burns Real Estate Consulting, LLC based on US Census data and extensive analysis of each age cohort; P= Projection

BIG SHIFTS AHEAD

➡ **1960s Equalers have been divorcing less.**
FIGURE A.10 Percentage of 58-Year-Olds Not Heading a Household

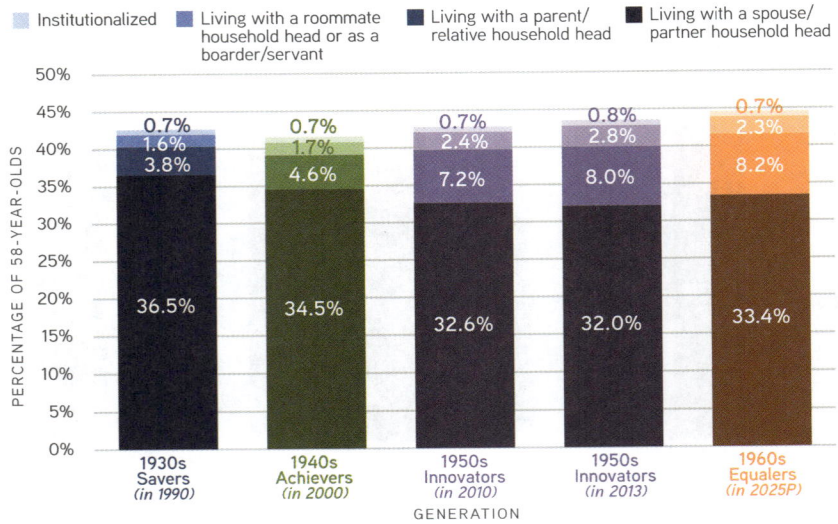

- Institutionalized
- Living with a roommate household head or as a boarder/servant
- Living with a parent/relative household head
- Living with a spouse/partner household head

Generation	Institutionalized	Roommate	Parent/Relative	Spouse/Partner
1930s Savers (in 1990)	0.7%	1.6%	3.8%	36.5%
1940s Achievers (in 2000)	0.7%	1.7%	4.6%	34.5%
1950s Innovators (in 2010)	0.7%	2.4%	7.2%	32.6%
1950s Innovators (in 2013)	0.8%	2.8%	8.0%	32.0%
1960s Equalers (in 2025P)	0.7%	2.3%	8.2%	33.4%

Source: John Burns Real Estate Consulting, LLC based on US Census data and extensive analysis of each age cohort; P= Projection

➡ **The 1950s Innovators are more likely to live multigenerationally, including in a household headed by their son or daughter.**
FIGURE A.11 Percentage of 68-Year-Olds Not Heading a Household

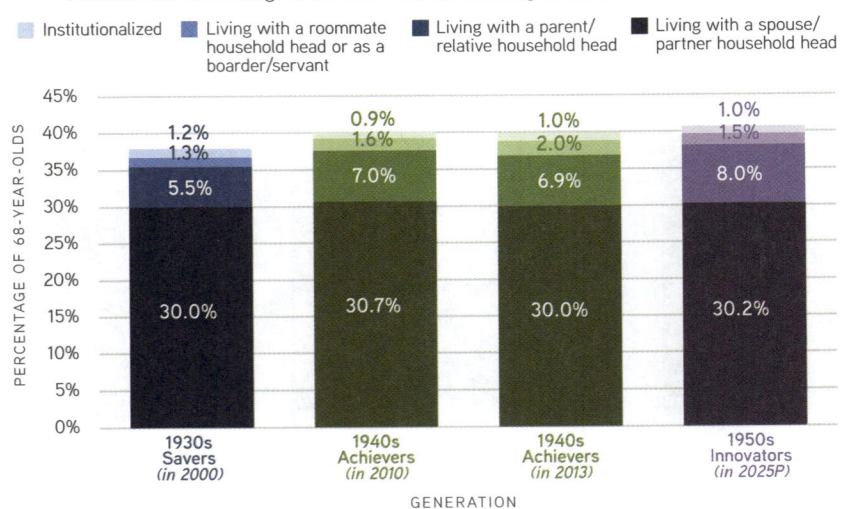

- Institutionalized
- Living with a roommate household head or as a boarder/servant
- Living with a parent/relative household head
- Living with a spouse/partner household head

Generation	Institutionalized	Roommate	Parent/Relative	Spouse/Partner
1930s Savers (in 2000)	1.2%	1.3%	5.5%	30.0%
1940s Achievers (in 2010)	0.9%	1.6%	7.0%	30.7%
1940s Achievers (in 2013)	1.0%	2.0%	6.9%	30.0%
1950s Innovators (in 2025P)	1.0%	1.5%	8.0%	30.2%

Source: John Burns Real Estate Consulting, LLC based on US Census data and extensive analysis of each age cohort; P= Projection

APPENDIX 2: MORE FORECAST TABLES

12.5 million households should form over the next decade.
FIGURE A.12 Net Household Formation, 1961–2025

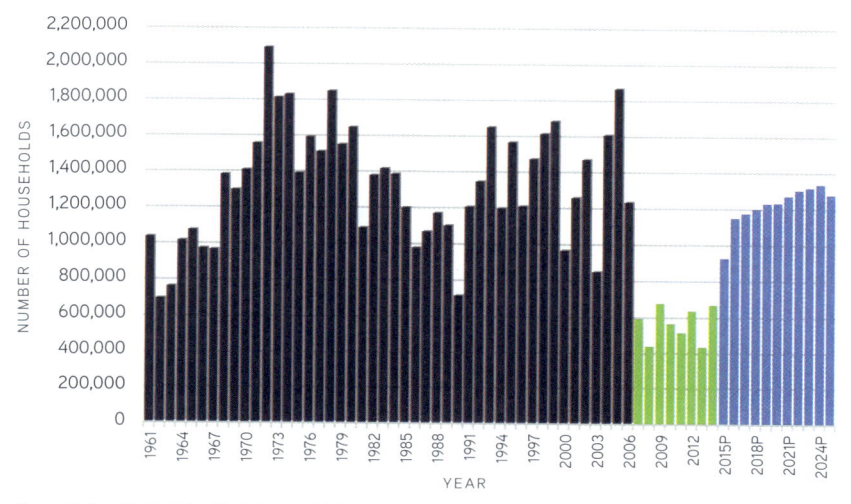

Source: John Burns Real Estate Consulting, LLC based on US Census Bureau data; P= Projection

The 1990s Connectors have formed relatively few households to date. However, they will be the main driver of household formations over the next decade, adding 1.4M +/- households per year.
FIGURE A.13 Net Household Formation by Those Born in 1990s, 2005–2025

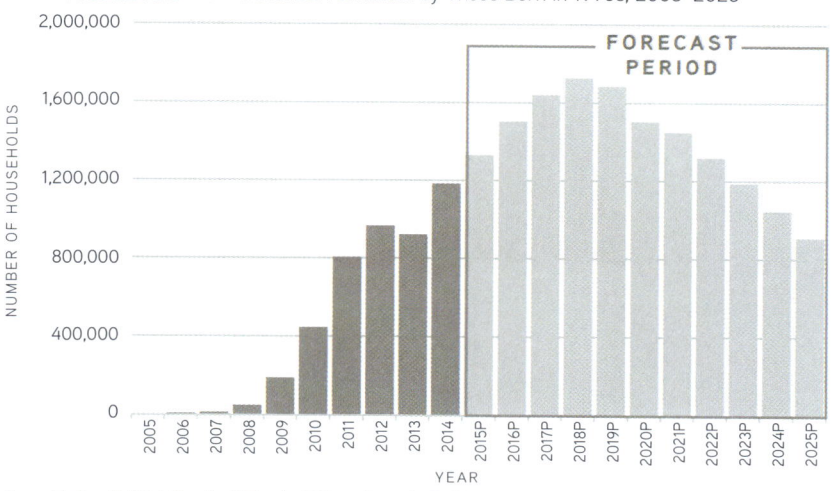

Source: John Burns Real Estate Consulting, LLC based on US Census Bureau data; P= Projection

BIG SHIFTS AHEAD

➡ **The 1980s Sharers continued to form households during the recession, but at a slowed pace. They should add 430K +/- households per year over the next decade.**

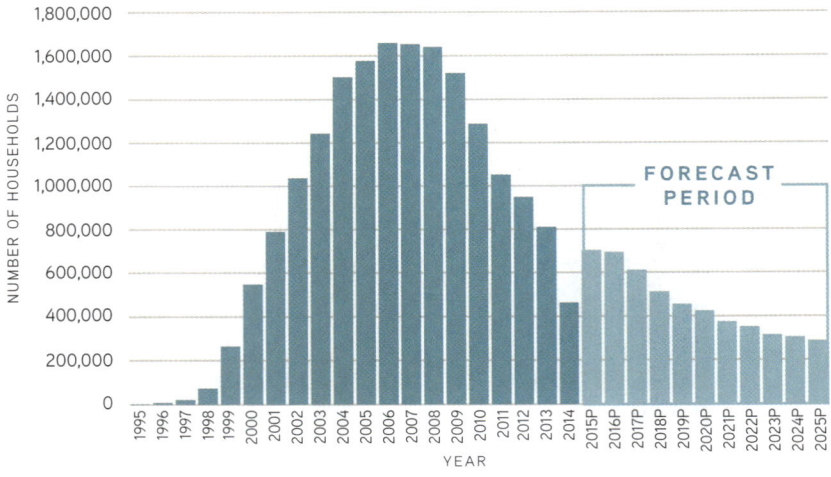

FIGURE A.14 Net Household Formation by Those Born in the 1980s

Source: John Burns Real Estate Consulting, LLC based on US Census Bureau data; P= Projection

➡ **The 1970s Balancers formed few net new households during the recession, and should add 160K +/- households per year over the next decade.**

FIGURE A.15 Net Household Formation by Those Born in 1970s

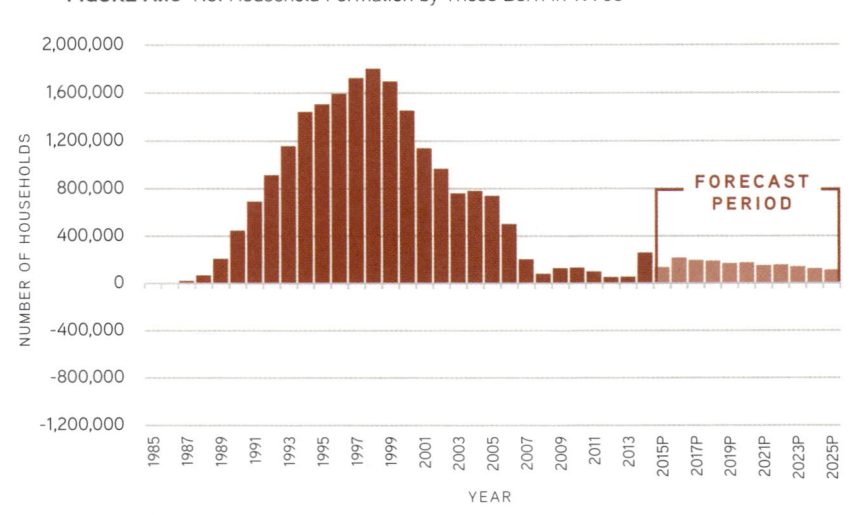

Source: John Burns Real Estate Consulting, LLC based on US Census Bureau data; P= Projection

APPENDIX 2: MORE FORECAST TABLES

➡ **Over the next 10 years, we expect that 55% of net new households will own.**

FIGURE A.16 Net Household Formation

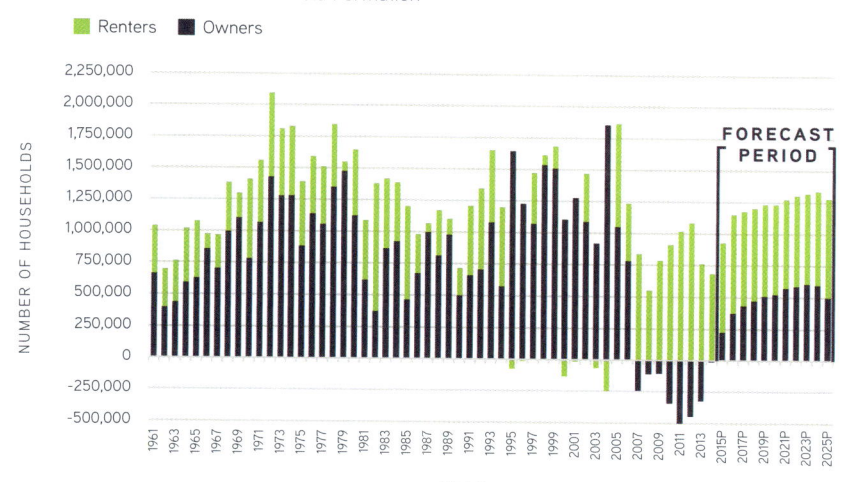

■ Renters ■ Owners

Source: John Burns Real Estate Consulting, LLC based on US Census Bureau data; P= Projection

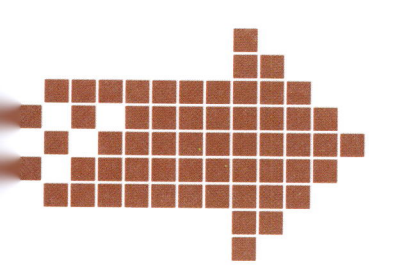

ACKNOWLEDGMENTS

To find great examples of demographic shifts, we looked around our own company. We would like to thank our accounting manager, Cynthia Laguna, and her family for sharing their immigrant success story. Cynthia and our Dallas-based Lisa Marquis Jackson provided great examples of the changing role of women in society. Our Chicago-based consulting leader Lance Ramella's new empty-nester life in suburban Illinois provided a great example many empty nesters will relate to, while many 1950s Innovators will relate to 63-year-old Steve Burch's workaholic motto, "Anything worth doing is worth overdoing." Finally, 1980s Sharers will relate to 29-year-old consultant Kyle Zierer living with his parents and will understand his desire to strike out on his own sometime soon. While the examples in our company all involve highly successful, college-educated people, the shifts identified in this book clearly apply to most of their high school classmates too. The statistics in this book include everyone.

Luckily, we found writer Barry Pearce, who shared our passion for documenting the demographic shifts, and made the book much easier to read. Eland Mann at Advantage provided great insight as we went through the editing process. Thank you as well to Channelle Tatman, who referred us to all three interns who helped with the project—Mikaela Sharp, Liz Rhee, and Danielle Nguyen. All three eventually joined our team full time upon graduation. Richard Mones, our marketing manager, created many of the charts.

Because we devote the bulk of our business day to serving clients, this book took three times as long as planned, with much of the work occurring at night and on weekends. For their boundless patience during that process, John thanks his wife, Anne, and children, Kevin and Kelsey. Thankfully, his home was designed in a way that allows everyone all to work near each other, whether writing books or completing homework. Chris and his wife, Jessica, welcomed both Gracelyn and Finley into this world while research was in full swing, and the family joined him for dinner at our office many Thursday nights in an inspiring show of support.

This work also owes thanks to the many demographers outside our organization whose research educated us. We appreciate their hard work and tremendous attention to detail, notably the invaluable contributions from those who work at the Census Bureau. They gave us the confidence to identify and articulate the many trends explored here. We cited all of our sources so that those interested in specific definitions or more detail can pursue additional research. We include even more information on www.bigshiftsahead.com.

We would also like to thank the reporters we work with who constantly try to uncover the truth behind the many demographic shifts. The pressure they put on us to provide a conclusion forces us to see the forest through the trees more than they know, and their readers and listeners benefit greatly. We benefited most from conversations with Nick Timiraos and Kris Hudson at the *Wall Street Journal*; Diana Olick at CNBC; Prashant Gopal, John Gittelsohn, and Tom Keene at *Bloomberg*; Andrew Khouri at the *Los Angeles Times*; Jeff Collins at *The Orange County Register*; and a plethora of regional reporters who always ask us to apply the trends to their markets.

A few Wall Street sell-side analysts, as well as economists at data and real estate companies conduct great research. In particular, we learned a lot from discussions with John Mauldin at Mauldin Economics, Doug Duncan at Fannie Mae, Stan Humphries at Zillow, Jed Kolko (formerly with Trulia), Ron Johnsey at Axiometrics, and Bill McBride at Calculated Risk. Rick Sharga at Ten-X, Barry Habib at MBS Mortgage, Ed Pinto at American Enterprise Institute, Bruce Norris at The Norris Group, Stephen East at Wells Fargo, Stephen Kim at Evercore ISI, and Nishu Sood at Deutsche Bank all informed us as well. Our conversations with them challenged us to look further into the data to figure out what was actually happening.

We also need to thank Dan Roth, Chip Cutter, Amy Chen, and Marisa Wong at LinkedIn, who gave us the opportunity to share our preliminary findings with hundreds of thousands of people interested in the changing American consumer. To date, this has resulted in more than 370,000 people following us on LinkedIn and hundreds of useful comments giving us confidence in our conclusions or suggesting that we needed to be clearer in our communications.

Speaking of useful comments, good friend and *New York Times* best-selling author Martin Dugard reminded John multiple times to tell a story. Those three simple words challenged us more than you can imagine.

We would also like to thank our many clients who challenge us every day, especially Adrian Foley at Brookfield Residential, who gave some great examples of targeting foreign-born customers in the book. In 2015, executives at almost 400 companies hired our team to help them make good decisions, and thousands more listened to early presentations of our findings. Many asked very difficult and thought-provoking questions and required thoroughly supported answers, which kept us learning and on our toes all the time. The regular feedback we receive from them makes us smarter. In a big way, they contributed to the conclusions in this book. For example, we initially concluded higher construction volumes, but our clients convinced us they could not build that many homes due to land constraints and costs.

Finally, we need to thank the biggest critics of our work—our team members. We built a culture of continuous learning and challenging each other, requiring highly accurate data collection and a rigorous peer-review process on every report. We presented our findings numerous times to the team and changed our presentations to the better because of it. We write this knowing that we will still suffer through one final peer review, but confident that the review will make the book even better. Team members who challenge us all the time, contribute to the data collection, and help us in many ways include: Aaron Stubblefield, Adam Artunian, Alex Martinez, Alex Wilson, Amie Stiener, Andrew Durkee, Annie Radecki, Cynthia Laguna, Dan Fulton, Dana Mitteer, Danielle Leach, David Jarvis, David Kalosis, Dean Wehrli, Don Walker, Eric Freeman, Erik Franks, Isabell Kerins, Jacob Belk, Jeffrey Hallam, Jeff Kottmeier, Jennifer Lantz, Jody Kahn, Kathy Ayuyao, Kathleen Ripley, Kellie Sanchez, Ken Perlman, Kristin Matthews, Kristine Smale, Kyle Zierer, Lance Ramella, Laura Harvey, Lesley Deutch, Lisa Jackson, Maria McNamara, Matthew Condon, Michael Gladwill, Mike Willinger, Mollie Carmichael, Nicole Murray, Pete Reeb, Raina Hemraj, Rick Palacios, Rosemary deButts, Rudy Zavaleta, Sean Fergus, Steve Burch, Steve Dutra, Ted Beam, Tene Hunt, Todd Tomalak, and Will Frank.

ABOUT THE AUTHORS

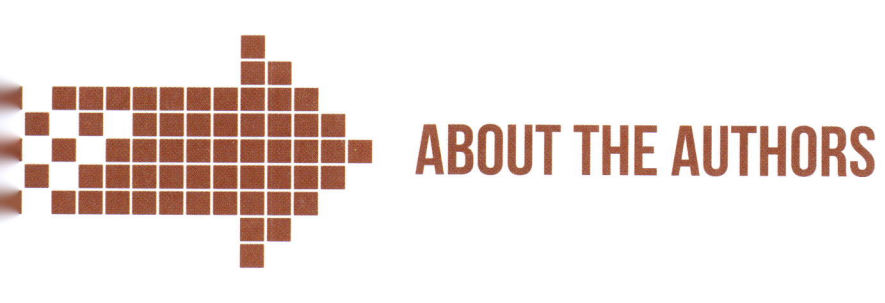

John Burns challenges the John Burns Real Estate Consulting team he founded in 2001 to be better every day, hiring great people and empowering them to provide the best advice possible. He spends much of his time meeting with clients, sharing our research findings, and learning from them. Before founding John Burns Real Estate Consulting in 2001, he worked at a national consulting firm for four years and for ten years at KPMG Peat Marwick—two as an auditor and eight in their consulting practice. Highly regarded as an authority in the housing industry, 370,000+ people follow John's Influencer column on LinkedIn, 30,000+ subscribe to his free e-mail newsletter, and major media has quoted him as many as 60 times in one year. John has a BA in Economics from Stanford University and an MBA from the University of California, Los Angeles. He lives in Irvine, California, with his Equaler wife, Anne, his Connector son, Kevin, and his Global daughter, Kelsey. On a more personal note, John has attended home games for all 30 Major League Baseball teams, seen every Academy Award-winning Best Picture, and regularly runs the hills in Southern California.

Chris Porter plays an important role as chief demographer for John Burns Real Estate Consulting. He helps our clients understand the role demographics plays in shaping the demand for housing in the short and long terms. The research he leads informs many of our firm's forecasts. Before joining John Burns Real Estate Consulting in 2005, Chris accumulated a diverse resume including investment consulting and homebuilding industry journalism. He was a director of electronic media for Reed Business Information and an analyst at Rogerscasey. Chris has a BA in Economics from Princeton University and a MS from Northwestern University's Medill School of Journalism. Chris enjoys public speaking, staying actively involved with Toastmasters for more than seven years. Chris and his Sharer wife Jessica live in Irvine with their two post-Global daughters, Gracelyn and Finley.

Chris Porter and John Burns have worked together for more than 11 years and separated the work based on their strengths. John drove the project, starting in the spring of 2013 with a 21-page outline that surprisingly didn't change much as they reshaped the initial manuscript into its current structure. John wrote most of the generational history, documenting how we got here, with tremendous data collection help from Chris and three interns: Mikaela Sharp, Danielle Nguyen, and Liz Rhee. With an expertise in summarizing complex information into usable summaries, John developed the generational names, the 4–5–6 Rule, and the main conclusions.

Chris led the hard part, digging into numerous databases to clarify the controversies that surround the shifts underway and what they mean for the future, such as where and how people will live. John and Chris worked together on the tough calls, such as household formation rates and future location decisions for people now in college, which Chris authored. For many, the proprietary research Chris championed will be the most valuable part of the book, clarifying issues debated daily in the media and boardrooms. Chris has the highest standards for accuracy and attention to detail, which should give you a high degree of comfort throughout the book.

EXHIBIT LIST

FIGURE

1.1 2015 Population by Year Born, page 8
1.2 The 4-5-6 Rule for Demographic Predictions, page 14
2.1 Generational Clarity, page 20
2.2 2015 US Population by Place of Birth, page 22
2.3 US Births per Year, page 23
2.4 US Homeownership Rates (1900–2015), page 29
2.5 Vehicle Miles of Travel, page 30
2.6 Divorces and Annulments, page 31
2.7 Share of 75+ Year-Old Population Heading a Household, page 32
2.8 Total Consumer Credit Owned and Securitized, page 35
2.9 Number of Children per Woman, page 36
2.10 Female Median Real Income, Women Aged 25–34 (2013 Dollars), page 37
2.11 Real Median Income of People 55 to 64 (1947–2013), page 38
2.12 New Start-Ups as a Percent of All Businesses, page 41
2.13 Real Median Income of People 45 to 54 (1947–2013), page 42
2.14 Net Worth by Generation, page 44
2.15 Family Median Net Worth 45–54 Year Olds, Adjusted for Inflation, 2013, page 48
2.16 Percent of Nonworking Fathers that Stay Home to Take Care of Home/Family, page 50
2.17 Female Labor Force Participation Rate, Ages 20–64, page 53
2.18 Percent of Family Households with 2+ Earners, page 54
2.19 Share of Moms Who Stay at Home Full Time, page 55
2.20 Median Net Worth 35–44 Year-Olds, Adjusted for Inflation, page 57
2.21 Percent of People Aged 18–40 with Student Loan Debt who Delayed These Milestones Because of That Debt, page 60

2.22   Percent of 25–29 Year-Olds Single and without Children, page 61
2.23   Student Loans Outstanding (Trillions), page 62
2.24   Real Median Income, People Aged 25–34 (2013 Dollars), page 63
2.25   Percentage of Obese 12–19 Year-Olds, page 68
2.26   Underemployment Rate of Recent High School Graduates, page 69
3.1   The 4-5-6 Rule for Demographic Predictions, page 73
3.2   Homeownership Rate, Annual Average, page 78
3.3   Legal Immigration by Decade, page 80
3.4   Retirees Receiving Social Security Benefits (Millions), page 81
3.5   Real GDP Growth, page 84
3.6   Average Real GDP Growth per Person during Prime Working Years (25 to 54), page 86
3.7   US Life Expectancy at Birth, page 90
3.8   Share of Households That Moved in the Prior Year, page 91
3.9   Number of Years from an Issue's Trigger Point Until Federal Action Was Taken, page 94
3.10   Women's Median Age at Birth of First Child, page 95
3.11   Percent of People Married by Age and Birth Year, Age 35–39, page 96
4.1   Bachelor's and Master's Degrees Conferred by Females, page 101
4.2   Difference between US Women & Men Aged 25–34 with Bachelor's Degree or Higher, page 104
4.3   Share of Married Couples Where Both Spouses Have a College Degree, page 105
4.4   Full-Time, Year-Round Workers by Median Income and Sex (2013 Dollars), page 108
4.5   Married Households with Wife Earning More Than Husband, page 109
4.6   Labor Force Participation—Rolling 12-Month, Population 20–64, page 110
4.7   Median Age at First Marriage, page 111
4.8   Percent of Total Births per Year to Women 40+, page 112
4.9   Women's Median Age at First Birth, page 113
4.10   Average Number of Hours Spent on Childcare per Week by Fathers, page 116
4.11   Percent of Births to Unmarried Women, page 118
4.12   Single Mothers and Fathers, page 119
4.13   Single-Parent Share of Households with Children (Own Children under 18), page 120

EXHIBIT LIST

5.1 Foreign-Born Population in the United States, 1900–2010, page 122
5.2 Foreign-Born Share of US Population, page 123
5.3 US Population Growth by Birthplace, page 125
5.4 Nominal Economic Growth, 2000 to 2014, page 128
5.5 Net Increase in US Residents Born in Mexico, page 130
5.6 Net Increase in US Residents Born in India, page 132
5.7 Net Increase in US Residents Born in China, page 133
5.8 1990–2010 Share of US Foreign-Born Population Growth, page 135
5.9 Growth of Foreign-Born Population by County, 2000–2010, page 137
5.10 Highest Share of Foreign-Born Population, 2009–2013 (Counties with 50,000+ People), page 138
5.11 Homeownership Rate by Nativity, page 140
5.12 Adults per Household (for Population in Households), page 141
5.13 Percent of 2015 Population That Is Foreign-Born, page 142
6.1 65+ Population by Decade of Birth, page 146
6.2 Percent of 65–69 Year-Olds Working Full Time, page 147
6.3 Labor Force Participation at Age 60–64, page 148
6.4 US Life Expectancy at Birth, page 149
6.5 Share of Households below the Poverty Line (Household Heads Aged 65–69), page 152
6.6 Population Aged 65, page 154
6.7 Growth of US Resident Population Aged 20–64, page 155
7.1 Estimated 2016 Households by Decade Born, page 160
7.2 Household Growth by Decade (Millions), page 161
7.3 Net Change in Households by Decade Born, 2016–2025 (Millions), page 163
7.4 Net Household Formation, 1965–2014, page 165
7.5 Percentage of 28-Year-Olds Living with a Spouse/Partner, page 167
7.6 Percentage of 28-Year-Olds Living with a Parent/Relative/Roommate Household Head, page 168
7.7 Percentage of Population 18+ Heading a Household, and Adults per Household, page 172
7.8 Percentage of 28-Year-Olds Heading a Household, page 173
7.9 Percentage of 28-Year-Olds Living with a Spouse/Partner Household Head, page 174
7.10 Percentage of 28-Year-Olds Living with a Parent/Relative Household Head, page 175

7.11   Percentage of 28-Year-Olds Living with a Roommate Household Head or as a Boarder/Servant, page 176
7.12   Net Household Formation by Those Born in 1990s, 2005–2025, page 177
7.13   Net Household Formation by Those Born in the 1980s, page 178
7.14   Headship Rates by Age, page 181
8.1   Homeownership Rate (Annual Average), page 186
8.2   Number of Homeowners in 2015 (Millions), page 187
8.3   Annual Homeowner Growth, page 188
8.4   Homeowner Growth by Generation (Millions), 2016–2025, page 189
8.5   Mortgage Interest and Property Taxes in Excess of Standard Tax Deduction, page 192
8.6   Homeowner Impact of Change in Homeownership Rate, page 193
8.7   Headship and Homeownership for 38-Year-Olds, 2013, page 194
8.8   Homeownership Rate by Generation, page 195
8.9   Mortgage Rates, page 196
8.10   Single-Family Rental Homes as a Percent of Total Housing Units, page 197
8.11   Percentage of Apartment Move-Outs to Purchase a Home, page 200
8.12   Homeownership Rate among 28-Year-Old Householders, page 202
8.13   Homeownership Rate among 38-Year-Old Householders, page 203
8.14   Homeownership Rate among 48-Year-Old Householders, page 204
8.15   Projected Housing Demand, 2016–2025, page 206
9.1   Estimated Share of Household Growth, 2016–2025, page 209
9.2   Projected Population Growth by Region, 2016–2025, page 211
9.3   Share of Total Permit Activity by Region, 1960 and 2014, page 212
9.4   Estimated Share of Household Growth, 1990–2010, page 217
9.5   1990–2010 Share of Household Growth Less 2010 Share of All Households, page 218
9.6   Projected Household Growth by Region (Millions), 2016–2025, page 219
10.1   Urban Share of Household Growth, page 221
10.2   2015 US Households by Neighborhood Environment, page 223
10.3   Household Growth Rate by Geography Type (2000–2010), page 224
10.4   Change in Population by Age, 2005–2015, page 225
10.5   The Surban™ Lifestyle, page 229
10.6   Percent of 20–24 Year-Olds with a Driver's License, page 231
10.7   Share of Household Growth by Decade, page 236

EXHIBIT LIST

A.1 Share of 28-Year-Olds Who Head a Household, page 245
A.2 Share of 38-Year-Olds Who Head a Household, page 246
A.3 Share of 48-Year-Olds Who Head a Household, page 246
A.4 Share of 58-Year-Olds Who Head a Household, page 247
A.5 Share of 68-Year-Olds Who Head a Household, page 247
A.6 Share of 78-Year-Olds Who Head a Household, page 248
A.7 Percentage of 28-Year-Olds Not Heading a Household, page 248
A.8 Percentage of 38-Year-Olds Not Heading a Household, page 249
A.9 Percentage of 48-Year-Olds Not Heading a Household, page 249
A.10 Percentage of 58-Year-Olds Not Heading a Household, page 250
A.11 Percentage of 68-Year-Olds Not Heading a Household, page 250
A.12 Net Household Formation, 1961–2025, page 251
A.13 Net Household Formation by Those Born in 1990s, 2005–2025, page 251
A.14 Net Household Formation by Those Born in the 1980s, page 252
A.15 Net Household Formation by Those Born in the 1970s, page 252
A.16 Net Household Formation, page 253

**THE FOLLOWING SOURCES WERE USED IN
THE CREATION OF THESE EXHIBITS:**

Bankrate August 2014 Financial Security Index

Bloomberg

Bureau of Justice Statistics

Bureau of Labor Statistics

Bureau of Labor Statistics Consumer Expenditures Survey

Bureau of Labor Statistics, Annual Social and Economic Supplements to the Current Population Survey

Centers for Disease Control and Prevention, National Vital Statistics Report

Department of Health and Human Services, National Center for Health Statistics and CDC

Department of Homeland Security

Fannie Mae National Housing Survey

Federal Housing Administration

Federal Housing Finance Agency

Federal Reserve Bank of New York Consumer Credit Panel/Equifax

Federal Reserve Bank of St. Louis

Federal Reserve Board 2013 Survey of Consumer Finances

Ford 2015 Trends, citing Pew Research and BAV Consulting Global Survey

Freddie Mac (Federal Home Loan Mortgage Corporation)

Guttmacher Institute

Hartsfield-Jackson Atlanta International Airport Operating Statistics

National Association of Realtors®

National Institute of Health Care Management

New York Federal Reserve Consumer Credit Panel/Equifax

Pew Research Center

S&P/Case-Shiller National Home Price Index

Senn High School

Tax Policy Center

Trulia year-end 2012 American Dream Survey

U-Haul.com

US Census Bureau

US Census Bureau December 2014 Population Projections

US Census Bureau Decennial Census, American Community Survey, 2005-2013

EXHIBIT LIST

US Census Bureau, 2014 National Population Projections

US Census Bureau, Characteristics of New Single-Family Houses Completed

US Census Bureau, Current Population Survey, Annual Social and Economic Supplements

US Census Bureau, Decennial Census, 1950-2010

US Census Bureau, Housing Vacancies and Homeownership Survey

US Department of Agriculture

US Department of Education, National Center for Education Statistics

US Department of Homeland Security

US Department of Transportation Bureau of Transportation Statistics

US Department of Transportation, Highway Statistics

US Social Security Administration

Our analysis includes data downloaded from IPUMS, which requests to be cited as:

IPUMS-USA: Steven Ruggles, Katie Genadek, Ronald Goeken, Josiah Grover, and Matthew Sobek. Integrated Public Use Microdata Series: Version 6.0 [Machine-readable database]. Minneapolis: University of Minnesota, 2015.

IPUMS-CPS: Sarah Flood, Miriam King, Steven Ruggles, and J. Robert Warren. Integrated Public Use Microdata Series, Current Population Survey: Version 4.0. [Machine-readable database]. Minneapolis: University of Minnesota, 2015.

INDEX

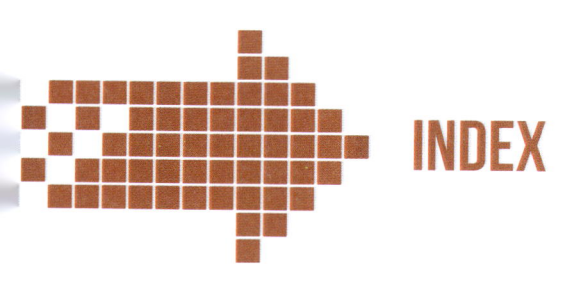

4-5-6 Rule 13, 14, 71, 73

4 Big Influencers 3, 12-13, 71-76, 158, 159, 165, 227-228

5 Main Life Stages 13, 71, 73, 74-75

6 Key Consumer Questions 13-14, 71-72, 73, 83, 86, 93, 97

9/11 13, 15, 17, 52, 53, 62, 74, 110

40+ moms 74, 89, 111-112, 180

A

Abbott 114

Abortion 35, 43, 82, 94

Airbnb 59, 64, 88, 153

Air travel 87-88, 121, 126, 128, 135, 214

Allen, Paul 40

Amazon 92, 216, 231

AOL 27

Apartment rents 82, 87, 169, 180, 198, 216, 225, 228, 232

Apple Computer 40, 89, 111, 214

Armstrong, Neil 40

Assisted-living facilities 31, 153, 162, 164

AT&T Broadband 217

B

Baby Boomers 2, 19, 20, 21, 170

Background checks 13, 91-92

Bieber, Justin 25, 65, 66

Birth control pill 10, 12, 35, 43, 74, 82, 89

Births 21, 23, 34, 35, 36, 39, 42-43, 65, 74, 79, 80, 82, 89, 97

Boeing 87

Borders Books 92

Brin, Sergey 126

Brookfield Residential 128, 139, 140, 142
Brown v. Board of Education 47
Bryant, Kobe 51
Buffett, Warren 25, 26

C

Car buying 60, 201
Castro, Fidel 129
Childcare 10, 11, 15, 49, 55, 95, 116, 119
Childhood obesity 52, 67, 68, 90
Children born out of wedlock 11, 15, 102, 117, 118
Clinton, Bill 33
Cohabitation 96, 97, 117, 173–174, 182, 199
College degrees 1, 3, 11, 15–16, 28, 33, 46–47, 61, 75, 94–95, 97, 101, 103, 104, 105, 120
Construction costs 131, 205, 228
Consumer Finance Protection Bureau (CFPB) 190–191
Consumer spending 12, 69, 75, 76, 88
Couples with degrees 104–105
Craigslist 88, 199
Credit card debt 34, 35, 69

Crime 225, 230
Cruise, Tom 25, 46
Cyrus, Miley 66

D

Deaths 153–154, 162, 164, 186
Debt Supercycle 180
DeGeneres, Ellen 39
Delayed childbirth 12–13, 15, 54, 59, 60, 61, 83, 95, 96, 102, 110, 111, 112, 113, 117, 120, 159, 160, 179, 199, 201
Delayed marriage 13, 30, 59, 60, 61, 74, 83, 95, 102, 110, 111, 117, 120, 159, 160, 178–179, 199, 201
Dell 214
DiCaprio, Leonardo 25, 51
Disposable income 34, 75, 118
Diversity 11, 51, 65–66, 123, 124, 126, 135, 141, 142–143
Divorce 10, 11, 13, 30, 31, 37, 74, 102
Dodd-Frank Act 72, 189–190
Domestic roles 27, 55, 95, 115, 116–117, 120
Don't ask, don't tell 66
DoorDash 153
Downey, Robert, Jr. 46
Driver's license 63, 68, 230, 231

Dual-income households 10, 11, 34, 37, 48, 49, 53, 85, 86, 104, 152

E

eBay 92, 156

Economic growth 83, 84, 85, 127, 128, 154–155, 168, 179

Economy 3, 7, 12–13, 41, 48, 72, 74, 83–86, 103, 159, 165, 199, 219, 228

Egg freezing 74, 89

Employment benefits 114, 117, 153

Employment growth 154–155, 210, 213, 215, 228, 231

Entrepreneurship 10, 41, 64

Entry-level homes 42, 56

Etsy 92

F

Facebook 64, 89, 111, 117, 228

Fannie Mae 28, 43, 76–77, 190–191, 200

Federal Housing Administration (FHA) 28, 76–77, 190–191

Federal Housing Finance Agency (FHFA) 190

Federal Reserve 76–77

FedEx 114

Female breadwinner 15–16, 95, 102, 109

Foreclosures 21, 55–56, 71, 77, 79, 185, 189, 198, 205

Foreign-born 7, 8, 11, 15, 21, 22, 26, 27, 33, 39, 51, 58, 65, 80, 121–143

Foreign-born share 122, 123, 124, 134, 135, 140, 141, 142, 179

Freddie Mac 190–191

G

Garner, Jennifer 25, 51

Gates, Bill 39, 40, 64

Gen X 2, 20, 21

GI Bill 12, 28, 29, 76–77, 227

Gig employment 153, 156

Gomez, Selena 25, 65

Google 126

Government 3, 7, 12–13, 72, 76–83, 142, 153, 190, 201, 228

Government debt 70, 179–180

Government entitlements 31, 32, 158

Great Depression 24, 27, 84, 124, 168

Great Recession 49, 62, 66, 68, 71, 78, 112, 130, 152, 164, 165, 168, 178, 185, 189, 193, 198–199

273

GSE Act 72, 77, 78

H

Headship 31, 32, 40-41, 81, 141, 159-182, 245-250
Health 31, 148, 150, 153, 214
Helicopter parents 43, 59, 68
Highway investments 12, 29, 76, 213, 227-228
Home design 34, 40, 42, 49, 139, 188
Home equity 21, 187
Homeownership 12, 16, 28, 29, 49, 56, 60, 69, 76-78, 82, 140, 150, 162, 185-207
Home price appreciation 87, 180
Household formations 16, 69, 71, 84-85, 159, 161, 163, 164, 172, 175, 199, 251-253
Housing and Urban Development (HUD) 190
Housing market crash 11, 16, 21, 49, 55-56, 198

I

IBM 114
Immigration 1, 3, 15-16, 21, 33, 47, 58, 65-66, 70, 75, 79, 82, 97, 121-143, 154, 179
Immigration Act of 1990, The 126

Immigration and Nationality Act of 1965 79, 125, 129
Immigration Reform and Control Act of 1986, The 126
Income growth 1, 16, 36, 37, 63, 74, 102, 108, 165, 180, 201
Income inequality 34, 75, 104
Incomes 42, 53
Infrastructure 83
Instagram 58, 228
Interest rates 10, 31, 41, 75, 77, 82, 150, 152, 158
Internet 52, 55, 66, 75-76, 88, 90, 91, 92-93, 126
Interracial marriage 71, 93, 94
In vitro fertilization 54, 74, 89, 111, 112

J

Jackson, Michael 52
James, LeBron 58
J.C. Penney 92
Jobs, Steve 25, 39, 40, 64

K

Kennedy, John F. 34
Kickstarter 62
King, Billie Jean 47
King, Martin Luther, Jr. 34, 47
Knowledge workers 13, 103, 155

INDEX

Knowles, Beyoncé 25, 58, 66

L

Labor force participation 28, 102, 110

Labor shortage 44, 131, 145, 154, 155, 158

Lawrence, Jennifer 65

Lehman Brothers 164

LGBT 83, 97

Life expectancy 89–90, 93, 148, 149, 158, 180

Life stage 19, 20, 71

Living with parents 2, 15, 43, 56, 59, 159, 162, 164, 166, 167, 168, 169, 170, 172–173, 174–175, 177, 178, 182, 198–199, 201, 233

Living with roommates 162, 168, 172, 175, 176, 177, 182

Lyft 230

M

Manufacturing 13, 92, 103, 213, 215

Marijuana 82–83

Marriage 96–97, 166, 167, 172, 173, 174, 177, 182

Mauldin, John 181

McCain, John 26

Medicare 31, 75, 80, 89, 179

Microsoft 40, 41, 216

Millennials 2, 19, 20, 21

Mobility 75, 86, 91, 145, 150, 157, 194, 215

Moore, Mary Tyler 25, 26

Mortgage interest deduction 191, 192, 201

Mortgage rates 77, 180, 191, 195, 196, 199

Mortgage underwriting 78, 83, 180, 189, 190

Multigenerational living 50, 97, 150, 158, 164, 174, 210

Musk, Elon 126

N

Netflix 19, 66

Net worth 10, 12, 31, 37, 43, 44, 48, 50, 56, 57, 64, 83, 84–85, 149–150, 152

New home construction 1, 16, 76, 161, 205, 206–207, 211–212

North American Free Trade Agreement (NAFTA) 214

O

Obama, Barack 47, 66

Obama, Malia 65

Obama, Michelle 46

O'Connor, Sandra Day 28, 107–108, 120

Owning 4, 16–17, 83, 86, 253

275

P

Parker, Sarah Jessica 25, 46
Parton, Dolly 25
Pension plans 1, 27, 37, 50
Pent-up demand 160, 164, 170
Personal computers 41, 48, 52
Pinterest 64
Poverty 11, 37, 151–152, 198–199
Productivity 10, 90, 155–156

Q

Quayle, Dan 52

R

Radio Shack 92
Refugee Act of 1980, The 126
Reinhart, Carmen M. 181
Remodeling 10, 31, 150, 153
Renting 4, 16–17, 56, 58, 83, 86, 88, 97, 185–207, 230, 253
Retirees 1, 3, 15, 145–158, 187, 188, 194, 210, 215
Retirement 10, 26, 38, 43, 44, 50, 71, 83, 85, 145–158
Reverse mortgage 153, 205
Ride, Sally 47
Riggs, Bobby 47
Roe v. Wade 82
Rogoff, Kenneth S. 181
Roosevelt, Franklin D. 27

Rural 92, 213, 221–235, 243–244

S

Sallie Mae 40
Same-sex marriage 66, 71, 83, 93, 94, 97
Savings 27, 31, 194, 201, 204–205
Schwarzenegger, Arnold 25, 33
Second homes 49, 206
Senate Bill 1070 82
Sharing economy 11, 13, 24, 58, 62, 88–89, 185, 201
Single-family rental homes 56, 196–197, 205
Single parent 11, 66, 71, 88, 102, 118, 119, 120, 199
Smartphone 12, 41, 58, 70, 92–93, 93, 215, 228
Snapchat 64, 67, 228
Social media 11, 24, 58, 67, 92
Social Security 10, 19, 31, 37, 50, 75, 80–81, 89, 131, 147, 151–152, 153, 179
Societal Shifts 3, 7, 12–13, 21, 24, 74, 93–97, 228
South 3, 12, 17, 64, 135, 209–219
Stay-at-home parents 49, 50, 53, 55, 76, 95, 97, 117
Steinem, Gloria 102

INDEX

Stewart, Martha 33
Student debt 2, 11, 19, 59, 60, 61, 62–63, 69, 94, 160, 169, 174, 196
Suburbs 12, 28, 29, 33, 40, 76, 87, 92, 96, 214, 221–235, 241–243
Supreme Court 28, 47, 97
Surban 4, 17, 38, 92, 225–229, 232, 235
Swift, Taylor 58, 66

T

Tax policies 12, 17, 75, 82, 210, 214–216, 218
Taylor, Elizabeth 26, 30
Technology vii, 1, 7, 11, 12, 13, 27, 39, 54, 74, 126, 156, 158, 180, 214–217, 228
Television 11, 27, 34, 40, 47, 52, 59, 66, 74, 97, 103, 117
Tepper, Jonathan 181
Tesla 126
Title IX 10, 47, 102
Twitter 59, 228

U

Uber 19, 59, 88, 153, 156, 228, 230
U-Haul 216
Underemployment 11, 68, 69, 84
United Cablevision 217
Urban 11, 15, 38, 63, 64, 88, 92, 96, 150, 199, 204, 221–235, 240–244
Urban redevelopment 12, 64, 76, 82, 224, 228, 230
US Census Bureau 141, 179, 237

V

Verizon 114
Video games 11, 52
Visas 122, 132

W

Wage growth 1, 86
Weyerhaeuser 231
WhatsApp 64
Winfrey, Oprah 25, 39
Witherspoon, Reese 51
Women's rights 35, 94
Women working 10, 15, 33, 46–47, 53, 74, 101–120
Working from home 55, 90, 113–115, 117
Working past 65 2, 4, 10, 38, 44, 85, 113, 145, 146, 147, 148, 151, 153
Work-life balance 4, 9, 53, 54–55, 156
Workweek 85, 156
Wozniak, Steve 40

Y

Yelp 59

YouTube 52, 66

Z

Zipcar 59

Zuckerberg, Mark 25, 58, 117

DEAR READER,

Thank you for purchasing *Big Shifts Ahead*. We hope that the facts and ideas in this book bring you great clarity regarding the demographic shifts transforming America.

We posted all of the charts in the book, plus many more that didn't make the cut, online at:

http://www.bigshiftsahead.com/extras

We also intend to update many of the charts as new data becomes available. You can download these charts free by entering the promotional code **JBREC01**. When you download the charts, we will automatically enroll you in our Building Market Intelligence demographic emails. You are free to unsubscribe, but if you enjoyed this book, we think you will be interested in our e-newsletter as well.

Sincerely,

John Burns and Chris Porter
Authors of *Big Shifts Ahead*

Questions? Comments? Contact us at
johnburns@jbrec.com and **chrisporter@jbrec.com**.